Women's work in East and West

Women's work in East and West

The dual burden of employment and family life

Norman Stockman
University of Aberdeen

Norman Bonney
University of Aberdeen

Sheng Xuewen
Chinese Academy of Social Sciences, Beijing

M.E. Sharpe

Armonk, New York
London, England

HD
6196
.S76
1995

First published in 1995 by UCL Press

UCL Press Limited
University College London
Gower Street
London WC1E 6BT

The name of University College London (UCL) is a registered trade mark used
by UCL Press with the consent of the owner.

Library of Congress Cataloging-in-Publication Data

Stockman, Norman, 1944–
Women's work in East and West: the dual burden of employment and family life/
Norman Stockman, Norman Bonney, Sheng Xuewen.
p. cm.
Includes bibliographical references and index.
ISBN 1-56324-708-9. — ISBN 1-56324-709-7 (pbk.)
1. Women—Employment—East Asia.
2. Women—Employment—Great Britain.
3. Women—Employment—United States.
I. Bonney, Norman, 1944– .
II. Sheng, Xuewen, 1956– .
III. Title.
HD6196.S76 1995
331.4—dc20
95-4969
CIP

(c) 10 9 8 7 6 5 4 3 2 1
(p) 10 9 8 7 6 5 4 3 2 1

Front cover:
Peking, China: assembly-line workers at the Beijing Jeep Corporation
(Peter Charlesworth/Panos Pictures)
New York, USA: policewomen (Mark McEvoy/Panos Pictures)
UK: office worker (Malcolm Watson)
Japan: woman and baby (Sean Sprague/Panos Pictures)

Typeset in Palatino.
Printed and bound by
Page Bros (Norwich) Ltd, England.

Contents

List of tables

Preface and acknowledgements

In 1987 the University of Aberdeen in Scotland, following a visit to East Asia by the then university Principal, George McNicol, established postgraduate scholarships for students from the People's Republic of China. That summer, Norman Stockman took with him details of the scheme on his trip to China to pursue his studies of the Chinese language at Beijing Normal University. A chance meeting at BNU with Stanley Rosen, a social scientist from the University of Southern California, helped Stockman to pass the information about the scholarships to a research worker at the Institute of Sociology of the Chinese Academy of Social Sciences (CASS). Eventually two applications for the scholarship reached Aberdeen, one of them from Sheng Xuewen, an established researcher in family sociology at CASS. His research proposal interested members of the Department of Sociology at Aberdeen and Sheng was offered a scholarship, but funding difficulties prevented him coming to Aberdeen until 1990, by which time he had been awarded a K. C. Wong Research Fellowship by the British Academy. Sheng brought with him the results of a recently completed survey on the family and work lives of married women in China and Japan.

In Aberdeen, Stockman was developing a library-based research project on changes in the structure of social inequality in Chinese society, and had particular interests in gender inequality and the division of labour. At the same time, Aberdeen had been one of the six centres chosen to contribute to the Social Change and Economic Life Initiative (SCELI) launched by the Economic and Social Research Council (ESRC). David Oldman and Norman Bonney had been heavily involved in this research, and they and Stockman saw the potential for relating it to the Sino-Japanese material that Sheng described to them. Bonney, as it happens, also had a long-standing interest in Japanese society, having been taught as a postgraduate by Ronald Dore, the doyen of Japanese sociological studies in Britain. David Oldman subsequently left Aberdeen to become a marital psychotherapist, leaving the three present authors to work on this three-way international comparison of women's work and family life, later extended to include the United States, enabling Norman Bonney to continue to develop American research interests begun when he was a graduate student in Chicago in the late 1960s. Of such accidents are books made.

The writing of this study has been an invigorating and illuminating experience, and the first acknowledgements of each of the authors must be to the other two. Sheng Xuewen thanks "the two Normans" for their support and friendship which began at the time of his first visit to Aberdeen in 1990–91. Norman Stockman first encouraged Sheng to apply for the K. C. Wong Fellowship, acted as his K. C. Wong host, and initiated the subsequent application to the British Academy for the Visiting Professorship that enabled a return visit to Aberdeen in 1994 during the final phase of writing the book. Both Normans helped to make both stays in Aberdeen as comfortable and productive as possible. Norman Bonney and Norman Stockman in their turn thank Sheng for starting this whole project, providing the data from the Sino-Japanese survey and doing the bulk of the work of analyzing it in conjunction with SCELI material in his initial research report to the British Academy and K. C. Wong Trust. That report forms the basis for much of the statistical analysis and discussion in this book. The Normans also thank Sheng for many instructive conversations on aspects of Chinese social life, and especially for his tireless organization and unflagging hospitality when each of them visited China, Bonney in 1991 and Stockman in 1992. They also extend those thanks to members of Sheng's family, especially his parents in Beijing and his in-laws in Tianjin, who provided both Normans with invaluable first-hand views of urban Chinese family life as well as some excellent meals. Norman S. thanks Norman B. for his continual encouragement and optimism concerning the outcomes of this research. Norman B. is grateful to Norman S. for his initiative in building the initial contacts in China which made this project possible.

We have all learned much from each other and have come to understand and respect each other's varied points of view. We each recognize that we have all three played a full part in this project, making contributions which while not identical certainly constitute "work of equal value". If his co-authors have allowed Stockman's name to appear first (thus striking a world-historical blow against alphabetic discrimination), it is primarily because he took on many of the co-ordinating, organizational and editorial responsibilities, and was allocated the task of editing the final version of the book. We all take equal responsibility for whatever we have achieved together and for the undoubted deficiencies which remain.

We have debts to many organizations and to individuals who work in them. The British Academy has played an indispensable part in making this project possible. First, as mentioned, the Academy enabled our collaborative work to begin in 1990–91 by awarding Sheng Xuewen a Research Fellowship funded from the K. C. Wong Trust. The K. C. Wong Fellowships provide a unique opportunity for Chinese scholars to work for a period in Britain, and Sheng reiterates his gratitude to the Academy and the Trust for their support. Secondly, Stockman thanks the British Academy, together with the ESRC, for allocating him a quota place on the exchange scheme operated with the Chinese Academy of Social Sciences in 1992. This enabled him to visit CASS and a number of provincial academies of social science to discuss research on women's work and on gender inequalities. Thirdly, Sheng and Stockman are both grateful to the British Academy for their award under the Visiting Professorship programme to enable Sheng to be in Aberdeen during the vital last months of the writing and final revision of the book. Thanks are also due to the staff of the British Academy who administered these awards, most notably Sacha Ward, who gave steady support and cheerfully helped with all our questions and problems.

We are indebted to the Institute of Sociology of the Chinese Academy of Social Sciences, Beijing, and to the Japan Youth Research Institute, Tokyo, for carrying out the surveys and providing the data on which much of this book is based. Particular thanks are due to Tamotsu Sengoku, who led the Japanese side of the research. Sheng Xuewen was a member of the Chinese research team, and we are grateful to his colleagues Ma Youcai, Dai Kejing, Liu Ying and Meng Chen for their support and for permitting us to utilize the data for this further purpose.

Stockman and Bonney are also grateful to the Chinese Academy of Social Sciences for its invitations to pay academic visits to the Institute of Sociology in 1991 and 1992. Stockman profited considerably from his visit under the BA–ESRC–CASS exchange arrangement, and thanks CASS for facilitating this visit. He is also grateful to the Academies of Social Science of Beijing, Tianjin, Shandong, Shanghai and Sichuan for their co-operation in his series of academic visits. Stockman also thanks the All China Women's Federation in Beijing, and the Women's Federation in Shanghai and in Chengdu, for helpful discussions and information.

Norman Bonney acknowledges the support of the Carnegie Trust for the Universities of Scotland in helping to fund his visit to the Institute of Sociology, CASS, Beijing in 1991.

Much of the British data presented in this volume derives from the ESRC-funded Social Change and Economic Life Initiative, co-ordinated nationally by Duncan Gallie of Nuffield College, Oxford, and in Aberdeen by John Sewel. Fellow grant-holders on the Aberdeen team were David Oldman and Peter Sloane. John Love and Eilidh Garrett, who were members of the Aberdeen University team, also contributed in many ways to the preparation of the data for analysis. John Lemon of the University Computing Centre assisted with computing advice on the Sino-Japanese survey.

We are also indebted to our employing institutions. Sheng is grateful to the Family, Marriage and Lifestyle Section of the Institute of Sociology at CASS for freeing him from other duties to allow him to take up the K. C. Wong Fellowship in 1990–91 and the Visiting Professorship in 1994. Bonney and Stockman received the support of the University Research Committee of the University of Aberdeen in the form of a joint award of a University Research Fellowship in 1993–4, which released them from teaching duties for half a year each to concentrate on writing this book. They are also grateful to their colleagues in the Department of Sociology for respecting the terms of the fellowship and for taking on some additional responsibilities without (much) complaint. Sheng also extends his gratitude to the members of the Aberdeen Department of Sociology for their research co-operation in relation to this project and for their hospitality during his two visits to Aberdeen.

Delia Davin and Stephan Feuchtwang supported this project from the outset and made many useful suggestions. Numerous other people have over the years helped us in our understanding of the issues raised in this book or have provided useful information, and among them we would particularly like to mention the following: Vincent Chu, Jim Kemeny, Reinhard Kreckel, Garland Liu, Geoffrey MacCormack, Alison McNaughton, Chikako Usui, Yoshihiro Morita.

Bob Blackburn and Ken Prandy gave us much-appreciated support and encouragement to submit this book for publication in the Cambridge Studies series, following our presentation of a paper to the Cambridge Social Stratification Seminar in 1991. Justin Vaughan, our editor at UCL Press which had recently taken over publication of the Cambridge series, was from the outset enthusiastic about this project and it has been a pleasure to do business with him.

Authors in earlier decades made fulsome acknowledgement of the indispensable aid of an army of female secretaries and typists. It is relevant to the subject of this book that our primary debt in this respect must be to Microsoft, its inventors and workers. This is by no means to belittle the secretarial assistance we have received from Karen Stewart, and we take this opportunity to give her our thanks.

Finally, especial thanks are due to our various household partners, with whom we negotiated household work strategies and divided domestic labour, to which the completion of this book is only one testament.

Chapter 1

Gender, work and industrial society

Introduction: convergence or divergence?

Sociologists have long been interested in the nature of modern industrial society, and have sought to discover the basic trends and tendencies in the transition to industrialism and the course of industrial development. As practitioners of a discipline aiming to discover general patterns in history and society, sociologists have tussled with the problem of whether in all societies there were fundamental similarities to the social process of industrialization, or whether different societies, with different ecological circumstances and different cultural traditions, might find their way to different forms of industrialism. In the 1950s and 1960s, a perspective crystallized out of earlier evolutionary and developmental theories in sociology which argued strongly for the former of these views, and which became known as the "convergence thesis", the thesis that there was a "logic of industrialization" that would drive all societies to manifest essentially the same set of institutions that would be most conducive to the advance of industrial production.

Contrary to many simplified interpretations of this thesis, however, those who are often taken to be the major proponents of the convergence thesis, namely Clark Kerr and his associates (Kerr et al. 1973), were in fact more circumspect. As Kemeny (1993) has shown, they in fact argued that the logic of industrialism was in constant tension with various sources of diversity, and that the outcome of this struggle was unpredictable. As Kerr et al. say in the conclusion to their book (1973: 277):

> Pluralistic industrialism will never reach a final equilibrium.
> The contest between the forces for uniformity and for diversity
> will give it life and movement and change. This is a contest
> which will never reach an ultimate solution.

And in the Postscript to their book, first published in 1971, they
conclude:

> There will not be one single and inevitable result; there will be
> no purity of theory and design; and there will be constant
> movement in specific arrangements. Convergence is towards a
> range of alternatives rather than to a single point (Kerr et al.
> 1973: 297).

This flexibility is admirable, and quite distinct from the rigidity
which sometimes characterizes reports of this sacred text of convergence theory. But it leaves more questions unanswered than it solves,
and in particular it leaves us with no clear view of the limits to diversity, the parameters of the possible range of alternatives that industrialism might allow.

In this book we are particularly concerned with the consequences
of industrialism for that most basic of human differences and social
divisions, gender. What range of alternative institutional arrangements for drawing on the energies of men and women might be possible in industrial societies? Does the logic of industrialism (if there is
such a logic) constrain societies to retain this basic human difference
and incorporate it into their institutions, or does it instead include a
drive towards that form of universalism which might make gender
differences irrelevant in the spheres which most closely touch on the
industrial process? The answers to such questions are not to be found
in any clear form in the basic writings of convergence theorists.

The reason for this is partly to be found in the fact that two quite
different conclusions concerning gender can be drawn from some of
the basic premises of the theory of industrial society. Following an
argument that goes back at least to Max Weber (1978), industrial society theorists claim that industrial society, and industrial capitalism in
particular, necessarily experiences a differentiation of the "household" from the "enterprise", or what is more colloquially known as
the separation of home and work. This occurs partly for technological
reasons, since industrial technology requires location in technically

2

appropriate places which are likely to be at a distance from the homes of either employers or employees, and also requires an investment of capital which increasingly outstrips the means of any single household. But such theorists also stress social reasons for the necessity of this differentiation. Kerr et al. (1973) themselves place the emphasis on the need to shift loyalties away from the extended family to the enterprise and the work group, and the need for a labour recruitment system which places a high priority on ability and competence rather than on family ties. Max Weber himself also emphasizes the different forms of accounting that come into existence with the growth of capitalist enterprise, with the household basing its economic activities on "budgetary management", adjusting expenditure to income, or "living within its means", while the enterprise is oriented towards "profit-making", seeking profit rather than loss, and monitoring its success or failure through "capital accounting" (Weber 1968). Parsons sees this process of the separation of household and enterprise as a typical example of evolutionary change, through which a social system achieves a higher degree of "adaptive capacity" through the increased efficiency or "adaptive upgrading" of each differentiated institution (Parsons 1966).

Weber, of course, also envisaged the structure of the enterprise as approximating to the ideal type of rational bureaucracy, seen as the most efficient way of organizing to pursue specific goals. The principles of rational bureaucracy stand in direct contrast to those underlying interaction in the family-based household. More recently, Niklas Luhmann has provided an abstract characterization of the specific features of "organization". The key difference between organization (which Luhmann sees as a specific level of evolutionary development in complex societies) and social systems such as families (where there is continuous face-to-face interaction) is to be found in the nature of "membership". Membership of organizations is temporary and linked to specific conditions controlled by the organization itself. Impersonal membership rules (such as submission to authority in exchange for wages, characteristic of the capitalist enterprise) make it possible to generalize motives, so that all occupants of a given position have to fulfil specific requirements in order not to be deprived of membership. As Luhmann (1982: 75) puts it: "soldiers march, secretaries type, professors publish, and political leaders govern – whether it happens, in this situation, to please them or not". It is the specific membership rules that establish the features of rational bureaucracy: impersonally defined offices, specific channels of communications, spheres of competence, chains of command, and so on. All these clearly differ from the ideal typical family household, in which membership is defined by particularistic, personal and permanent relations of kinship, and rights and duties are diffuse and laden with affect.

What, then, are the consequences of the differentiation of household and enterprise for the activities and social roles of men and women? There are two possible lines of argument.

First, it is argued that industrialism entails a shift towards the "isolated nuclear family", a kinship system in which lineage relationships become increasingly attenuated and in which each nuclear family is responsible for its own economic welfare (Parsons 1943). This small conjugal unit is functional for industrial capitalism because it allows high labour mobility, both in geographical and occupational terms, and because it is well adapted to fulfil socialization functions in the new mobile society. Parsons then argues that the solidarity of the conjugal family is promoted by gender specialization, with the husband taking the primary occupational and breadwinner role, while the wife takes the primary nurturing and socializing role. In Parsons's later work, this specialization is theorized in terms of a functional division between instrumental and expressive roles (Parsons et al. 1955). Industrial society thus intensifies the age-old identification of women with home and children, and marginalizes their economic activity, which becomes intermittent and secondary.

An alternative argument is, however, also at hand. Industrial society is a society of increasing individuation, with people treated by others in terms of their individual attributes rather than their social linkages. This process has both economic and political aspects. As we have already seen, industrial society is held to be one that requires people to be recruited to economic positions on the basis of their abilities and promoted on the basis of their performance. Thus, achievement categories, such as ability or merit, increasingly displace ascriptive categories, such as kinship categories, race, ethnicity, religion or gender. Politically, industrialism comes increasingly to require a more inclusive concept of societal membership (Parsons 1966), which translates into an idea of individual citizenship, most obviously manifested by a right of universal franchise, irrespective of any particularistic identity, including gender. The implication here is that modern industrial society breaks down all patriarchal structures which tie both women and younger men to the privileges of the patriarch (Mann 1986), and allows women to enter into economic and political life as individuals on equal terms with men.

There is clearly a tension between these two lines of thought, both of which are representative of theorizing on industrial society. They appear to have quite different implications for the lives of men and women, and for the significance of gender in modern industrial societies. As Harris (1983) points out, Parsons himself was fully aware of this tension, concluding that "the feminine role is a conspicuous form of the strains inherent in our social structure" (Parsons 1943: 36). If so, there may be many ways in which the strain could be resolved or not resolved. Not surprisingly then, Kerr, in his later reflections on the convergence thesis, retreats into a hypothesis of indeterminacy. The movement towards convergence in the institutions of industrial societies is likely to be greatest in those parts of societies that most bear the imprint of industrialism, those closest to the organization of work and working life. In contrast, movement towards convergence is likely to be least in those areas "dominated by popular beliefs", of which Kerr's prime example is the role of women in the labour market (Kerr 1983).

This hypothesis of indeterminacy is more open and flexible than a rigid thesis of determinate convergence. But it is not a satisfactory resting place for sociological analysis. It is not sufficient to suggest that the role of women in the labour force might be open to significant variation between different industrial societies as a consequence of the variation of "popular beliefs" between them, while at the same time proposing that the institutional separation of family from economy is a basic structural feature of industrial society, since the latter must have some, even though possibly variable, consequences for the roles of women and men. What is required is a more careful analysis of the possibilities for variation in the form this structural feature may take, and this task is best carried out as an exercise in comparative sociology.

The argument of this book starts from the basic structural transformation of society that accompanied the growth of capitalist industrialization in Western societies. It has been widely recognized that one of the most fundamental social structural features of modern capitalist societies is the institutionalized separation of a private, family sphere and a public sphere of organized social action. As just mentioned, Max Weber was perhaps the first major sociologist to lay weight on this structural division in society, seeing in the separation of the household and the enterprise one of the main structural preconditions for the development of a capitalist economy with rational capital accounting (Weber 1968). In Weber's writings one finds the emphasis laid not so much on the spatial separation of home and workplace, which has become a prominent theme in recent analysis of the historical conditions for gender asymmetry and inequality, but on the difference in the basic social principles underlying action-orientations in each context, and thus on the differences in normative and legal frameworks regulating social action in them.

It is this institutional separation of the private household from the public enterprise that embodies another fundamental distinction in modern capitalist societies, that between productive and reproductive activities. In pre-capitalist forms of social economy, this distinction could not be clearly made. In pre-capitalist and especially pre-industrial societies, with the work necessary to sustain life centred on what Brunner called "the whole house" (*das ganze Haus*) (Brunner 1968), or the more or less extended family household (Segalen 1986), all members of the household were engaged in necessary activities, allocated on principles of dividing labour according to age and sex, following an annual round which changed only gradually from generation to generation, and which could not clearly be differentiated into what later comes to be seen as the distinct spheres of production and reproduction. It is the principles of capitalist accounting and the capitalist labour contract which first make such a distinction possible and even necessary. The employer is only interested in those aspects of the employee's activities which go to produce commodities, which can be sold on the market to realize value in the form of profit for the owner of capital. For this, the employer commits himself to paying a wage, determined by the complex processes of the labour market, which is to serve as the material basis for the life of the employee. How this life is arranged, how the worker is fed, clothed, housed, kept clean and even possibly sane, and into what social relationships the employee enters in order to meet these ends and to reproduce the collective body of workers in the next generation, is of no concern to the employer. They are the private affairs of the workers, to be managed in their own way. Furthermore, using the terms of Luhmann, membership of a productive organization is conditional on the usefulness of the member for the goals of the organization, and thus potentially temporary, whereas reproductive needs are unavoidable and typically met through membership of groups, such as family households, which are intended to be permanent.

As has often been argued in recent years by a great variety of sociologists of different theoretical persuasions (Delphy 1984, Kreckel 1992, Mann 1986, Tilly & Scott 1989, Walby 1990), this socially and historically produced distinction between production and reproduction lies at the heart of gender asymmetries and inequalities in modern capitalist societies. For a number of reasons, not least of which is the age-old association of women with children and the hearth, the reproductive sphere has come to be seen as the preserve of women, while the productive sphere is dominated by men. Even in recent decades, during which women, and especially married women, have markedly increased their involvement in the labour force, they have nonetheless retained, whether through choice or through constraint, primary responsibility for reproductive activities within the family household: cooking, cleaning, shopping, looking after children and other dependants and so on. Sociologists have, on the basis of this common ground, sought to trace relationships between women's primary responsibility for reproduction, on the one hand, and their relatively disadvantaged position within the sphere of employment, on the other. Analyses of processes of gendered segregation in the occupational structure, or of the dual burden of paid work and unpaid housework, and of many other aspects of gender asymmetry and inequality in modern capitalist societies, come back in one way or the other to the basic institutionalized distinction between production and reproduction, and the structural separation of the private and the public, the household and the enterprise.

Nonetheless, comparative analysis reveals considerable diversity in these respects between industrial capitalist societies. As we will show in more detail later, capitalist industrial societies differ in the way in which productive roles and institutions articulate with reproductive ones. Variations are found in such areas as the labour force participation of women and their work histories, the provision the society makes for the care of young children, and whether employing organizations take account of the family circumstances of members. The case of Japan is the most instructive here, since both large corporations and small family enterprises in Japan diverge markedly from the ideal type of rational bureaucratic productive enterprises which we have previously outlined, and which we shall illustrate from the examples of Great Britain and the United States.

In addition, societies that have undergone the major part of their industrialization process under the leadership of a political party that proclaims its goal to be the building of socialism may also vary considerably in the way in which the family and the economy, the realms of the private and the public, or the activities of production and reproduction are articulated. All such societies, following the canonical texts of Marx and especially Engels (Engels 1962 [1884]), have seen the transformation of gender relations as intimately related to the building of socialism. Since the collapse of the Soviet Union and the "really existing socialist societies" of Eastern and central Europe, there has been increasing discussion of the extent to which such claims were justified (Corrin 1992, Funk & Mueller 1993). China, one of the few such countries still governed by a communist party, has recently reinforced its claims to combine the liberation of women with the construction of a socialist society (one with Chinese characteristics), by passing a new consolidated law on the protection of the rights of women. It has, as we shall see, a very high rate of female participation in the paid workforce, a high level of provision of child care facilities, and a relatively high degree of sharing of domestic labour by husband and wife. It also has an organizational form, the work-unit, which departs radically from the specialized bureaucratic productive enterprise characteristic of the West, and also from the large Japanese corporation.

It is through a careful analysis of the social contexts and the patterns of the work, both paid and unpaid, productive and reproductive, of women and men in these four societies, that we hope to further our understanding of the range of variation between industrial societies, and of the possibilities for convergence or continued diversity between them.

Research and sources

Our intention in this book is to compare the experience of women in our chosen four countries who have young children, and who are therefore at precisely that stage of the life course at which, according to conventional views in Western societies, they are least likely to be engaged in paid work. The main sources of primary information on such women are two large-scale surveys in which the authors were, at first separately, involved.

8

The Chinese and Japanese data mainly come from the Sino-Japanese Working Women's Family Life Survey. This was a joint project of the Institute of Sociology of the Chinese Academy of Social Sciences, Beijing, and the Japan Youth Research Institute, Tokyo. These two surveys used a common methodology, involving the administration of a self-completion questionnaire to mothers of children attending child care facilities in the two countries. The sample was restricted to married mothers of children below school age, with the proviso that the mother should also be employed in paid work or, as the Chinese phrase has it, engaged in social labour. The Chinese samples were collected from 12 nurseries attached to women's workplaces, public kindergartens and other child care centres in three major Chinese cities, namely Beijing, Shanghai and Xian. There were a total of 2072 respondents. The Japanese samples were taken from ten public and ten private nursery schools and kindergartens in the whole country, including the four largest cities, four regional cities and twelve smaller communities. The total sample numbered 1865 respondents. Both surveys were undertaken and finished in the summer of 1987. A Chinese-language report on this comparative research project was published in 1992 (Ma et al. 1992), and it is one of the most authoritative sociological research projects on the problem of women and employment in China after the economic reforms. Besides this survey, data from other national surveys in the two countries also were used for some purposes of the analysis, for instance the 1987 China 1 Percent Population Sample Survey (State Statistical Bureau 1988).

The British data are taken from the Social Change and Economic Life Initiative (SCELI) of the UK Economic and Social Research Council. This major survey involved interviews with 1000 respondents in each of six medium size British urban labour market areas (Aberdeen, Kirkcaldy, Coventry, Rochdale, Swindon and Northampton) in 1986 and 1987. The interviewing was conducted in the homes of randomly selected respondents by Public Attitude Surveys of High Wycombe with funds granted by the ESRC. In order to gain a reasonable degree of comparability with the Sino-Japanese survey, the data reported in this book mainly derive from a sub-sample of respondents who were female, married, employed and who had children of pre-school or primary school age. This sub-sample comprises 466 such women interviewed in the first wave in 1986 and 246 interviewed in the second wave in 1987. For interested readers, a fuller account of the methodology of the SCELI research is provided by Gallie (1988).

These two surveys were not planned with comparison between them in mind. There are many topics on which the Sino-Japanese survey reveals fascinating information but on which SCELI is relatively silent. In order to fill the gaps which thus appear, we have drawn on other published survey material on British women (as we have done to provide our comparative data on the United States). The major survey on which we have drawn is the Women and Employment Survey carried out by Jean Martin of the Office of Population Censuses and Surveys and Ceridwen Roberts of the Department of Employment in 1980 (Martin & Roberts 1984). This survey was based on a representative sample of women of working age (age 16–59) in Great Britain, irrespective of whether or not they were employed; 5588 respondents were selected randomly and step by step from a sample of general population in England, Wales and Scotland. Other British data such as the Labour Force Surveys (OPCS 1992) have also been used when necessary.

The American situation is the best documented of the four countries, and for our analysis we have drawn primarily on published official government and non-governmental collections of statistics (e.g. US Bureau of the Census 1991, Mishel & Bernstein 1993), the reports of major national surveys (such as Goldscheider & Waite 1991, Shelton 1992), the General Social Survey (Davis & Smith 1991) and numerous journal articles reporting survey findings.

The primary data sources on which this book is based are therefore predominantly large-scale sample surveys. Other researchers have used other methods to study family life and family relationships. Methodology textbooks give us a catalogue of advantages and disadvantages of different research methods, and it is quite understandable if some readers feel doubtful about the usefulness of the standardized survey in the study of intimate and problematic aspects of people's lives. However much truth there might be in Thoreau's dictum that "the mass of men [sic] lead lives of quiet desperation" (and however applicable it might be to women too), that truth is unlikely to be revealed, some may argue, by the impersonality of the survey method, but rather through persistent and intimate questioning and discussion (Sennett & Cobb 1977, Rubin 1976, Hochschild 1990, Brannen & Moss 1991). Such studies may well have problems of reliability and representativeness but they do, some believe, penetrate further into the life-worlds of people in their families. There has also arisen a considerable literature that calls into question the appropriateness of conventional sociological methodologies (which are supposed to have grown up during a period of male domination of the discipline and of the exclusion of gender issues from its core concerns) to the study of women's lives, and that searches for a distinctively "feminist methodology" (for a representative selection, see Harding 1987), although the survey method has not been without its feminist defenders and practitioners (Marsh 1982, Dex 1987, 1988).

Whatever the merits of these arguments (and we acknowledge that there is room for much debate concerning them), there is the added problem for our purposes in this book that there is a lack of available studies of this kind on family life in China and Japan. In the case of China especially, this has to be seen in terms of the historical experience of sociology as a discipline. After a very rapid growth of sociology in the period between the two world wars, sociology in the early 1950s came under suspicion as a bourgeois, counter-revolutionary subject, and was effectively banned until the late 1970s, when the "fall of the Gang of Four" allowed a change in the climate of scholarly research and teaching, and university sociology departments and research institutes in the academies opened their doors once again. While sociology in other societies was developing its research techniques, unfolding conceptual and theoretical frameworks, and building up a wide-ranging stock of knowledge of social behaviour and social processes in diverse institutional settings, in China there is just a quarter-century of emptiness. Chinese sociologists were unable to practise their discipline and new sociologists were not trained. Thus, sociological research into the lives of women, as into any other sociological topic, is much less developed in the case of China than in either Japan or the West.

Western sociological research on Chinese society was, however, also hampered by political circumstances. It was almost impossible for Western researchers to gain access to the People's Republic of China (PRC) to conduct research. Research on Chinese women, as on other topics, was dependent either on documentary sources or on the interviewing of émigrés. In a few cases, official study visits to China were possible, but were made under the restricted conditions laid down by the Chinese authorities. Thus, even such path-breaking studies as those by Delia Davin (1976) and Elisabeth Croll (1978) were dependent primarily on documentary sources. On the other hand, the two studies by William Parish and Martin King Whyte (Parish & Whyte 1978, Whyte & Parish 1984), which provide much fascinating information concerning women's social existence, relied on interviews with Chinese migrants to Hong Kong rather than on first-hand research within the PRC. The two feminist studies by Kay Ann Johnson (1983) and Judith Stacey (1983) were also based mainly on published documents and Chinese reports.

Since the opening up of China after the death of Mao and the fall of the Gang of Four, the situation has improved markedly. It is much more possible for Western researchers to visit China to conduct research. Elisabeth Croll (1983) was able to carry out interviews with some women in 1980 to supplement the documentary sources available to her. However, the conditions for empirical research are still not favourable. Two important books on Chinese women illustrate this. The social anthropologist Margery Wolf visited China in 1980 and conducted research into the changes in women's lives in both rural and urban areas in China. Her book (Wolf 1987) provides many interesting observations but, as she herself acknowledges, her samples of women were small and their representativeness was uncertain. Her interviews were also closely monitored by party officials. Honig & Hershatter (1988), rather than attempting detailed empirical research of their own into contemporary women's lives (though both of them had already completed invaluable historical studies of female industrial workers in Chinese cities), base their survey of this aspect of the changing Chinese society on magazine debates and discussions, stories, novels and films.

Since 1978, with the economic reforms spreading in China, sociology, as a branch of learning in social sciences, has gained a new lease of life after having been banned for nearly 30 years. Partly because of the absence of general information about many aspects of Chinese society, and partly because of the prevailing philosophy of science in Communist China, the main form of acceptable sociological research has been the large-scale statistical survey (Rosen & Chu 1987). Among the topics in which great strides have been made are surveys on family life and household organization. In 1982, sociologists in the Chinese Academy and other local academies began their first large-scale social survey on family, marriage and fertility in five big cities. Following this survey, there were several large surveys as well as a number of smaller research projects on family and marriage in both urban and rural China (Unger 1993). In recent years, interest in family studies in China has been moving away from general research towards more specific topics, such as the problems of the elderly, working couples, divorce and so on. The Sino-Japanese Working Women Survey is one of these, and focuses on the relations between women's employment and their family life.

Few sociologists, either Chinese or non-Chinese, have thus been in a position to undertake sociological research in general, or research on urban women's family and working lives in particular, in a more interactionist or ethnographical framework. It is only in very recent years that research based on naturalistic observation in Chinese urban contexts has begun to be carried out and published in the West (Bruun 1993, Jankowiak 1993). The situation is a little different in the case of Japan, where clearly such political considerations do not apply. There is no bar to either Japanese or Western sociologists carrying out ethnographic or naturalistic research in Japanese towns and cities, and indeed there are some excellent studies on the family and working lives of Japanese women from within such frameworks (for example Lebra 1984, Imamura 1987, Kondo 1990, Lo 1990). To our knowledge, however, such studies form the exception in two senses: methodologically, in that the dominant paradigm of research in Japan is also the survey, and substantively, in that most research on working lives concentrates on men, reflecting the gendered segregation of spheres in Japan on which we will have much to say later in the book.

In order to obtain comparable information on societies of East and West, therefore, we have restricted ourselves to survey data sources. As one of the very few sociological studies on any topic that provide comparable data on China and Japan, the Sino-Japanese survey is a rich and unique source of information which deserves to be known outside of East Asia. Our procedure in this book has been to allow the Sino-Japanese survey to set the terms on which our comparison of societies of East and West could be based, and to draw on SCELI in particular, and other survey sources on Britain and the United States more generally, to provide material as comparable as possible to that of the Sino-Japanese survey. The result, we believe, is a unique contribution to comparative sociology, although, like any other contribution to scholarly work, one that will be improved on as a greater variety of detailed research on women's lives becomes available. We leave the reader to judge how successfully the various data sources we have used convey the different life-worlds of mothers of young children in the four societies.

Overview

The rest of the book falls into five chapters. In Chapter 2, we provide some historical and institutional background on the four societies. The emphasis is on the differentiation of the household and the enterprise in the course of industrialization, and our aim is to show that this apparently universal process actually took different forms in different societies, with important implications for the development of gender roles. Britain and America represent the standard cases for the modernization theory of industrial society. The household and the enterprise develop as "separate spheres" for men and women; husbands are expected to take the breadwinner role, seeking permanent and stable life-long employment, while wives take primary responsibility for the household and children. When women enter employment, they do so with the background assumption that it will be temporary and secondary, and they are treated as more marginal to the affairs of the enterprise. Nonetheless, both husbands and wives have private lives in their households; each has responsibilities to both paid work for the enterprise and unpaid work for their household, and these may come into tension with each other. In Japan, this segregation of spheres is more intense: the commitment of men to their enterprise, especially in the case of employees in large corporations, is more total, as is the responsibility of wives for household affairs. Enterprises have many characteristics of patriarchal households, and only men are full members. Women's employment is not necessarily less in quantitative terms, but is even more marginal than in Britain or America. In China, the communist regime developed a form of work organization which combines pre-industrial elements with aspects of the Soviet model; the work-unit is a multifunctional organization rather than a profit-making enterprise, and forms a basic social identity for all adults, men and women alike.

The following chapters put empirical meat on these abstract bones. Chapter 3 presents material on the paid work of women, especially those who are in employment while their children are below school age, in the four societies. Information is given on the labour force participation, occupations, earnings and hours of work of such women, distinguishing in particular between full-time and part-time employment (except for China, where part-time work is not an available option). Since we are dealing primarily with mothers of pre-school

14

children, we also provide information on child care facilities and actual patterns of child care.

Chapter 4 moves into the household, and examines the division of domestic labour between wives and husbands in families with pre-school children. Clear differences between our four societies emerge from this survey data: the degree of gendered role segregation is greatest in Japan, where husbands do virtually no work in the home, and least in China, where the amount of sharing of domestic tasks is greatest. Britain and America lie between these two poles, with America closer to the "desegregated" pole and Britain somewhat closer to the Japanese pattern. One important differentiating factor lies in the role of grandparents, since the proportion of multi-generation households is much greater in the Eastern societies than in the West.

Chapter 5 takes up the theme of the norms governing gender roles in the four societies. If women are supposed to have primary responsibility for home and children, especially before children go to school, then their employment outside the home must in some way be problematic. We examine debates on the morality and expediency of mothers working in each society, and present survey material on women's (and in some cases also men's) attitudes and beliefs concerning women's employment and the combination of motherhood and paid work.

Finally, in Chapter 6 we return to the theory of convergence of industrial societies. We try to discern trends of stability and change in gender roles in the four societies. While there may be an overall tendency towards greater participation of women in paid employment even while they have pre-school-age children, assumptions about standard terms of employment continue to create differences between men's and women's work. In Britain and America there appear to be slow trends towards greater male involvement in household work. In Japan, however, such change appears infinitesimal, although recent shifts in women's attitudes may foreshadow greater tension and social changes in the future. China is, if anything, moving in the opposite direction, with the economic reforms creating conditions for limiting women's work and re-establishing more segregated conjugal roles. A final section reconsiders the convergence theory in the light of trends towards globalization.

Chapter 2

Family, employment and urban society

Introduction: household and enterprise

The differentiation of the household and the enterprise is a profoundly significant process and a basic element of industrialism. In all agrarian civilizations, the majority of the population gained their living from agriculture, apart from a relatively small, mostly urban, population composed of those working in trades and services, those concerned with exchange and commerce, and ruling groups whose power and privilege exempted them from direct productive labour and allowed them to occupy themselves with the arts, scholarship, military pursuits and the business of rule. For all these classes or strata of the population, the household was the elemental institution of daily life. It was the social unit in which productive activity was organized, as well as being the unit in which a familial group (however defined) resided and sought its everyday sustenance. Men and women, young and old, adult and children, all had a role within the doings of the household. In this "domestic mode of production", whether agricultural or artisanal, there was no clear way in which productive activities and roles could be distinguished from others. All activities were interconnected within the framework of the household.

This is not to claim that households were self-sufficient. In some isolated rural areas, local communities achieved a high degree of self-subsistence, neither dependent on the wider society nor producing anything which anyone else might want. Such a situation was rather rare. The very existence of urban households points to the transfer of resources between households through barter, exchange, taxation and other forms of appropriation. These processes drew households into complex chains of interdependency, in which, for example, peasant households delivered "surplus" produce to markets, receiving (depending on the level of monetarization of the society) cash with which to buy needed items that could not be produced within the household or the community, and with which to pay rents and taxes and meet other obligations. Ruling groups, in turn, would receive such "surplus" in the form of produce or cash, which would be used, not only for their own households, but also for the material basis of political rule.

Yet underlying all these complex chains of social interconnection there remained the manifold households in which men, women and children lived and worked. Such households were normally based on core elements of the kinship system, which varied with the particular institutions of the society concerned. Anthropologists have distinguished a number of types of family structure, which will become important for our comparative study. In Britain and America, the normal basis for a household has been an *elementary* (or *nuclear*) family of a single married couple with their young or older unmarried children. In many Eastern societies, and especially China and Japan, it has been considered desirable, though not always practicable, for the household to be based on a *paternal stem* family of three generations, an older married couple, one of their sons and his wife and children; or alternatively a *grand* or *joint* family, in which all of the married sons and unmarried sons and daughters would remain residing with their parents until the aged parents died. In addition to the kinship-based family unit that formed the core of the household, others might also be resident, sharing the work and the sustenance of the household, who were not immediately part of that narrowly defined kin group. They might be more distantly related kin, adopted kin, servants or employees, transients or long-term residents, but they would count for the period of their residence as members of the household with their appropriate roles and designated activities. Membership of a household should not, however, be seen as a static and fixed characteristic. Households were "in a constantly changing dynamic situation" (Pahl 1984), and might exhibit great diversity even within the same society with shared and institutionalized norms of household formation.

The primacy of the household was compatible with varying degrees of wage labour. Households differed greatly in the resources for production available to them. Households-as-enterprises, with access to adequate means of (re-)production, might have labour requirements beyond those that could be met by household membership, and the wage-form was one way in which labour could be transferred between households. Labour would be supplied from households with less access to their own means of production. Other forms also existed: co-operation and mutual aid between kin and neighbours, for example, was common in pre-industrial societies. Even when the wage was the form for transferring labour, this did not imply regular employment. The household-as-enterprise's need for additional labour was often seasonal or temporary, occasioned by the harvest or spring-cleaning, or by the illness or incapacity of a key household member. There were also some kinds of productive activity that required a scale of organization considerably larger than even the largest household, such as mining, ship-building and public works, though forms of unfree or semi-forced labour, such as slavery or corvée, were often used for such purposes.

The process of industrialization, from this point of view, can be regarded as the process by which more and more households lose access to their own means of production and can only survive by supplying the labour of one or more of their members to enterprises. Such households, to use the Marxist terminology, are increasingly proletarianized. The reverse side of the same coin can be seen as the process by which households-as-enterprises increase their stock of means of production, and attain a scale of operations which allows the enterprise to become an economic entity separate from the household of the owner. This process is not simply one of spatial separation of "workplace" from "residence", which in capitalist industrial societies eventually affects the vast majority of employers and employees alike. It is also one of the differentiation of one social, economic and legal entity into two, as the enterprise takes on an economic and legal identity of its own. Developments such as partnerships, joint-stock companies and limited liability intensify this differentiation, as the enterprise becomes a legal personality distinct from that of its individual owner(s), the property of the enterprise becomes distinct from the property of the household(s) of its owner(s), and the accounts of the enterprise become distinct from the household accounts of those who own it or work in it.

Another aspect of this differentiation of the household from the enterprise, which will concern us most directly in this book, is that it

19

is often accompanied by the emergence of a doctrine of "separate spheres". Even if gender had long been a major basis for the division of tasks within the household, and even for the demarcation of activities inside and outside the household, it remained clear to those involved that all those tasks were essential to the working, even the survival, of the household, and bound the members together in relations of mutual dependence (Segalen 1983). Once households lost much of their capacity to produce what they needed to sustain the existence of their members, they became dependent on acquiring claims to the resources they need from outside the household. In capitalist societies the primary way in which this is achieved is through one or more members of the household working for wages, generating cash to buy what the household needs. For various reasons, which we will examine later, the primary duty of earning money to sustain the household tended to fall on men, in the role of "breadwinner". But there remained much that needed to be done in the household, even when narrowly defined "productive" activities had been transferred to the realm of enterprises. For earnings to be transformed into household survival, goods had to be shopped for, meals cooked, clothes cleaned and maintained, homes kept in a fit state for living in, children tended and taught, sick and elderly dependants cared for, and all of these activities took time and effort. These tasks were defined as the responsibility of women. Yet, as industrialism took root, it was labour in the wage economy that was increasingly defined as "real work", while the labour of the "housewife" became less visible as "work" (Boydston 1990). The doctrine of "separate spheres" contained the ideological distortion that the growth of the factory system had caused a "separation of home and work", as if all those burdensome (possibly increasingly burdensome (Cowan 1989)) tasks allocated to the housewife were not really work at all.

Any process of differentiation raises issues of integration, of the interrelationship and interaction between the differentiated entities. Households and enterprises remain part of the same social and economic world, and somehow they have to relate to each other (Pleck 1976). In what follows, we briefly sketch out the major aspects of the interrelationship of these two social entities, first as they affect the enterprise, then as they affect the household.

An enterprise requires a labour force commensurate with its scale of operations. Each enterprise has to gain access to the labour force it needs within the political and legal framework that governs its operations. In capitalist societies, the main form in which a labour force is acquired is through waged labour. The enterprise needs to design and package the work so as to offer it to an envisaged workforce. It needs to decide the terms on which it is prepared to employ workers, among which is the length of time the employment will be expected to last. The enterprise could, as economists put it, enter the spot market for labour, hiring employees by the hour or the day at a wage that will clear the market. At the other extreme, the enterprise may, expressly or by tacit understanding, take on employees for the whole of their working lives. The enterprise must decide what level of skill it requires in its workers, and whether it expects to find that level of skill already embodied in workers before the employment begins, or whether it is prepared to train and educate employees to the required level. The enterprise needs to be able to come to an understanding with its employees over wages, hours and conditions of work. According to how all of these factors are settled, specific members of specific types of households will be more likely to be potential employees (Siltanen 1994). The enterprise thus needs to decide whether or not to take these household characteristics of its employees into account as relevant factors influencing the terms of employment. For example, if the workforce consists mainly of married men with dependent children, it must be decided whether this fact is to influence the wage or the conditions, perhaps by paying a "family wage" which will allow the man to support his wife and children. If it is to employ predominantly married women who are socially expected to bear major responsibility for the care of children, the enterprise has to decide whether to provide crèche facilities, maternity leave or flexible hours. Alternatively such factors can be treated as irrelevant to the employment relationship, and all workers dealt with as if their lives outside work, even whether they live or die, were their own private affair.

Households on the other hand must develop, explicitly or implicitly, what Pahl (1984) calls "household work strategies". Given that members of a household have a certain capability (in terms of skills and time) to devote to work, and given that they also have a set of needs that can only be met by work, they must somehow allocate their efforts between different kinds of work. Different combinations of household activities can be imagined, in which one kind of work can be seen as a substitute for another. One household might try to earn more money in order to buy vegetables, whereas another household might use garden or allotment space to grow the vegetables needed for household consumption ("self-provisioning", as Pahl calls it), possibly even producing a surplus to be sold or bartered. One member or more might find a job that will bring wages into the household. One or more might refrain from wage labour in order to concentrate on unpaid labour, including that of self-provisioning, in the household. Household members might devote their energies to "informal" money-earning activities that lie on or over the edge of illegality, in terms of taxation law and social security regulations. Or some or all of them might become self-employed, reconstituting the older form of household-as-enterprise as a small family business. Whichever household work strategy is employed, the members of the household will find themselves in specific and varied relationships to the enterprise sector of the industrial economy, thus creating interlinkages between enterprise and household. And once again, questions of gender lie at the heart of the matter.

Such, in broad outline, is the social problematic brought about by the differentiation of household and enterprise. In general terms, what we have described so far is common to all forms of industrialism. But we are here concerned with the possibilities for convergence or diversity in industrial societies, and to examine this question we must go into further detail on each of our chosen societies. This is the task of the rest of this chapter.

China: revolutionary transformation

Gender and work in pre-industrial China

Before the end of the imperial era, the structure of Chinese rural society approximated closely to the model of agrarian patriarchy as summarized by Mann (1986). The vast majority of the population of China lived in the countryside and gained their living from agriculture. The land was typically worked by relatively small family units, with a clear division of labour based on gender. Women were "inside people", responsible for the internal functioning of the household. The corollary is that men were responsible for the external relations of the household as well as for outside work in the fields. Thus, marketing was the preserve of men, as were kinship, religious and political activities. The affairs of the clan, the temple and the village were in the hands of men.

To a variable extent, both regionally and temporally, working people also hired themselves out to employers, especially to farmers with greater land holdings, as wage workers (Huang 1985). The temporary and occasional nature of seasonal hired labour stands in contrast to the permanent dependence on capitalist labour contracts which is the fate of more proletarianized workers, whether agricultural or industrial; the predominance of peasant farming, for self-sufficiency and for the marketing of surplus, reveals the failure of a capitalist dynamic to take root in the Chinese countryside. There was therefore little basis for a sharp distinction between (paid) productive labour and (unpaid) reproductive work which could overlay the admittedly sharp distinction of gender roles in Chinese rural society.

The structure of urban society in imperial China was, from the point of view of gender roles, not greatly different. The wider society was much more stratified than was the case in the villages, because the upper strata and classes were more heavily represented. But this whole structure could be described without mentioning gender, since it was also a patriarchal structure, excluding women and confining them to activities inside the household.

There were also large sections of city populations who, although employed for wages, were not using those wages to support families in which reproductive needs were met on a private basis. Instead, many men and women were living and working in contexts that did not clearly distinguish between production and reproduction. Single and married male apprentices and journeymen, who might be sojourning in the city, lived on the job in the master's household (Skinner 1977). Similarly, servants, both male and female, lived as part of the households to which they were attached.

In addition, as Max Weber had already pointed out, mercantile and business enterprise did not rest on a clear accounting distinction between the finances of the business and those of the household. Instead, he argued, business association and credit were to a large degree dependent on the kinship group, and directed towards the financing of family members' preparation for the imperial examinations and, if successful, for bureaucratic office, out of which the whole kinship group might expect to benefit (Weber 1968). More recent research has cast doubt on the universal validity of Weber's generalization, and revealed the growth of rational capital accounting in Chinese commerce (Rowe 1984). But the majority of businesses remained "near perfect examples of the 'household economy'" (Rowe

1989), suggesting a lack of clear division between business and household accounts and finances. Once again, this stands in marked contrast to the more strictly capitalist orientation of trade and commerce that appeared much earlier in the West, with a stricter division between capital accounting in the business seen as a legal personality and income–expenditure accounting in the household to meet private family needs.

To sum up, the main structural aspects underlying gender roles in late imperial China include the following: (1) the patriarchal family and kinship system; (2) the exclusion of women from all significant extra-familial occupations, including crafts, mercantile trade and commerce, and, of course, the imperial civil service; (3) the lack of a widespread institution of the capitalist labour contract and capital accounting; and (4) the low degree of institutionalized differentiation of productive and reproductive activities.

Capitalist industrialization and gender roles

It might be thought that the development of modern industry in many Chinese towns and cities from the end of the nineteenth century would have changed this situation drastically, and introduced the "normal" capitalist distinction between capitalist production and private reproduction. To some extent this appears to have been the case, but in the fifty-year experience of capitalist industrialization the separation of household from enterprise had many anomalies and was far from complete.

First, the growth of modern factory production was indeed very rapid but, as it started from a very low level, continued to employ only a small proportion of the workforce of cities (Hershatter 1986, Honig 1986, Riskin 1987). Secondly, the workforce in modern capitalist industry was disproportionately female. This was not necessarily the case from the initial establishment of factories, but the difficulty of maintaining control over and preventing political activity by male workers (and also the relative cheapness of female labour) led employers to substitute women workers as far as possible. This process proceeded fastest in Shanghai, China's largest industrial city. As early as 1929, 61 per cent of the workers in Shanghai's industries were women, and in the largest industry, the cotton industry, 76 per cent were women (Honig 1986). In the northern city of Tianjin, however, the feminization of the workforce occurred later and more slowly: in the cotton mills, for example, women were only 9 per cent of the workforce in 1929, and it was "not until the Japanese occupation, and the Japanese takeover of millownership, that the percentage of women rose to 39 percent, and in 1947 it was barely one-half" (Hershatter 1986: 55).

Many of these new industrial workers, and especially the women, were provided with housing, clothing and food by the factory, and lived in factory dormitories. Honig, in her study of women in the Shanghai cotton mills, shows how women recruited as contract labour were controlled and restricted by these terms of employment. "She had no options – she lived where the boss told her to live, she ate the food he or she provided, she left the dormitory only when the contractor allowed her to" (Honig 1986: 105). From the point of view of the contract workers, this system of course did not involve a normal capitalist labour contract, since they did not receive their wages, which had to be handed over straightaway to the contractor, and it is also clear that the reproductive functions of shelter, clothing, cooking, cleaning and so on, were not carried out on a private family basis. On the other hand, it is also clear that many other women workers, who were not recruited into the contract labour system, did receive their wages, and did use these wages to contribute to the maintenance of private family households, in which the domestic labour of reproduction was carried out by household members (Honig 1986).

Some non-contract labourers also lodged in factory accommodation, as Hershatter shows in her study of Tianjin industrial workers. In a manner similar to the early industrialization of Britain and other Western countries, the cotton mills of Tianjin were "planned communities complete with a full range of welfare services. The Yu Yuan Mill, for example, was lauded in government and academic surveys for its dormitories, dining hall, clinic, schools for workers and their children, consumers' cooperative, bathhouse, athletic field, and martial arts society, as well as its paid maternity leave, disability benefits, funeral subsidy, and the bonus paid to workers so they could purchase melons in the summer" (Hershatter 1986: 165).

Not that this paradise was either universal or charitable. As Hershatter points out, this closed environment was the employers' attempt to impose factory discipline, and it was an attempt that was vigorously resisted. No more than a quarter of mill workers were in fact dormitory residents in the 1930s, and even those who were registered as such often found other private accommodation where they could be more free from company controls. Nonetheless, these employers had, in their efforts to control their workforces, created a model that could be built on by their communist successors. Hershatter points out that the role of factory dormitories began to change as early as 1946, when mills re-opened after the end of the war with Japan. More families moved into factory housing, which became less a strategy of employers' control, and more a useful service to workers and their families (Hershatter 1986).

These forms of industrial community catered for only a small proportion of the total population of pre-communist Chinese cities. The majority of the workforce would, as before, be engaged in pre-industrial activities of handicrafts, trade (including retail shops, stall-keeping and peddling), personal services, transport and communications, and a significant proportion of the urban population lived in great poverty with no regular source of livelihood. Even in the modern industrial sector, the majority of workers lived in households which, in relation to their employers' business, must be considered as private.

Production and reproduction in the communist urban work-unit (*danwei*)

Once the Chinese Communist Party took control of the whole country in 1949, the new leadership was faced with a colossal task of reconstruction after the damaging war against Japan and the civil war against the Nationalists. We do not have space to recount this process in any detail here (see, for example, Meisner 1977). Instead, we move directly to a description of the main new form of work organization that was set up by the new government, and its implications for women's employment. For reasons that will become apparent, rather than referring to this organization by the capitalist term "enterprise", we use the Chinese term *gongzuo danwei* (work-unit), or just *danwei*.

The *gongzuo danwei* is a unique form of organization and is the basic building block in Chinese urban society, and it is not possible to understand the development of women's and men's participation in the labour force in Communist China without an examination of its main features. A *danwei* can be a factory or factory complex, an administrative agency, a school or university, a hospital, a publishing

26

house, or any other of a host of apparently specialized organizations. Almost all urban Chinese belong to a *danwei*. The operative word here is "belong"; as Hebel and Schucher (1991) rightly stress, the concept of "membership" is fundamental to understanding the significance of the *danwei*. Up until the reform process was launched a decade and more ago, it was an unchallenged basic principle of social life that, once an individual was allocated to a *danwei*, he or she remained a member for life. Unlike in the case of a capitalist enterprise, employment in which is eventually terminated by retirement if not sooner, membership in a *danwei* is not affected by the capacity of the member to continue to perform specialized work functions. Whether ill, disabled or retired, a worker continues to be a member of the *danwei*.

The *danwei* is thus not merely (if at all) an enterprise in any sense current in Western societies. Every *danwei* does have a specialized function in production, administration or service provision. But this specialized function by no means exhausts the responsibilities or social functions of the organization. Li Hanlin, one of a number of writers (Lu 1989, Hebel 1990, Hebel & Schucher 1991, Henderson & Cohen 1984) who stress the multifunctional nature of the *danwei*, identifies the following categories of functions performed by the *danwei*, apart from its ostensible specialized function, such as production of goods in a factory or delivery of medical treatment in a hospital: *political* functions, including ideological propaganda, implementation of political decisions and political and social control; *socialization* functions, inculcating specialized and political role-expectations in members; *educational* functions, including the specialized training and upgrading of members' qualifications and the primary and secondary schooling of members' children; *social security and social welfare* functions, including the provision of services, the improvement of material conditions, the provision of housing and support for the elderly; *regulation of private affairs*, such as family planning and birth control, finding jobs for children of members, mediation in marital discord, brokering marriages and cultural provision for free time; *participation in local development*, through "friendly" interaction with local government (Li 1991). It is not surprising that the *danwei* is often referred to as a "small society". One of the key social identities of any individual is membership of the *danwei*. Every member has a status within the hierarchical structure of the organization, and a location within a network of personal relationships centred on the unit. In many large-scale work-units, individuals can meet almost every normal requirement that the Chinese economy and society can provide within the confines or under the auspices of the *danwei*.

In practice, work-units vary considerably in the degree to which they can embrace the whole lives of their members. Work-units can seldom provide housing, for example, for more than a proportion of their members, and many *danwei* members must rely on housing supplied by the city government or live in privately owned housing. Andrew Walder, drawing on the results of the One Thousand Households survey carried out annually in Tianjin, charts the degree to which the respondents' families lived in housing of different kinds. About a third of respondents in the 1986 survey lived in housing provided by the work-unit of a family member, 44 per cent lived in housing provided by the city government, and just under a fifth lived in privately owned housing. However, asked about the possible source of a future apartment, two-thirds of those respondents who could envisage such a possibility felt that it would most likely be provided by a work-unit. Although there was no clear association between the size of a work-unit and the percentage of respondents living in housing provided by the work-unit, there was a significant relationship between the provision of work-unit housing and the rank of the work-unit, with the highest-ranking units providing seven times the proportion of housing afforded by the lowest-level units ("rank" here refers to a unit's position in the relevant ministerial hierarchy, from central to local) (Walder 1991). Similarly, Walder found great variations in the extent to which work-units provided a variety of services, with 86 per cent of units offering meal halls, showers and a health clinic, while a quarter or less offered a sports field, a barber shop or a free bus service.

Nonetheless, despite this great variety in the scope of work-units, it is clear that in general the Chinese urban *danwei* does not correspond to the type of the capitalist enterprise. First, the system of life-long membership of the *danwei* contrasts sharply with the employment contract in capitalist enterprises. As the economic reformers have often bemoaned in recent years, *danwei* membership substitutes for the formation of a labour market, as, of course, it was intended to do by those who felt that they were engaged in the building of a socialist society in which labour would cease to be a commodity. From the point of view of the *danwei*, labour is merely one of the activities of members, not their sole function. Secondly, although the "non-productive" functions of the *danwei* clearly can be seen as a cost, which a poorer work-unit might not be able to afford, the minimization of labour costs is not and cannot be a prime objective of *danwei* management. Although it would not be accurate to identify the *danwei* as a complex form of household, expenditure on some such "non-productive" functions does bear some resemblance to the living expenses of a private household attempting to maximize its living standard within the constraints of its income. Thirdly, the activities which in capitalist societies would be classifiable as "reproductive", because they are not accounted for in the profit-seeking enterprise of the firm, are in China not clearly separable from the substantive, or "productive", purpose of the *danwei*. Thus, for example, a proportion of the time of administrators in a branch of a work-unit might be spent in attempting to solve the housing problems of members whose family circumstances had changed, a matter which in most capitalist enterprises or other employing organizations in capitalist societies would be treated as the private affairs of the employees and their families and none of the organization's "business".

However, it would be wrong to maintain that there is no distinction between the *danwei* and the households of its members, or to suggest that the *danwei* is one large complex household. Members of work-units do still live in private households and carry out many household activities on a private family basis. A high proportion of workers live in apartment blocks situated at some distance from the unit in which they work, whether or not their housing is provided by the work-unit. So, apart perhaps from their mid-day meal, much of their daily life outside working hours is carried on independently of their work-unit. But even if the family lives in rooms on the premises of the *danwei*, there is still a boundary between the member's household and the *danwei* as an organization. In terms of the division of space, the territory of the household is still bounded, even if the degree of privacy afforded by walls and doors is not very great, and even if some components of the household's space, such as cooking facilities, have to be shared among several households. Furthermore, many household functions can be and are carried out on a private family basis, even if the *danwei* also offers facilities collectively. For instance, the cooking and eating of meals can be either a private household matter or a collective activity within the *danwei*. Those who live within the *danwei* compound may eat some of their meals in unit canteens, or collect cooked food from canteens to take back to their rooms to eat. But, partly for reasons of expense, partly for reasons of family cohesiveness, partly because of food preferences, families may prefer to cook their own food in the kitchens either within or attached to their own apartments. The budget of the family household also remains distinct from that of the *danwei*. Although many needs may be met collectively and consumed as social goods, thus forming part of the social wage, many other needs are not met collectively, but rather, as is typically the case in commodity societies, purchased on the market. The money wages which must sustain households are typically very low, but, due to the fact that a higher proportion of needs are met collectively than is common in capitalist societies, and to the fact that even those goods that are commoditized are nonetheless subsidized by some level of government or by the work-unit itself, standards of living of families are actually higher than might be expected on the basis of the money wages themselves. The relationship between the socialized budget and the household budget is markedly different from that common in capitalist societies, but this by no means signifies that the distinction has been eliminated.

The boundary between the private household and the *danwei* can be thrown into sharp relief by casting a brief glance at an alternative urban structure that emerged in Chinese cities in 1958, blossomed quickly and equally quickly disappeared – the "urban people's commune". Designed as an "integrated unit of administration, living, and production" (Schurmann 1968: 388–92), urban communes were urban units capable of meeting in a socialized manner all the needs of the members, whose numbers could run into the tens of thousands. Organized around a nucleus of a productive unit, such as a large factory, a commune would also comprise agricultural brigades, public canteens, kindergartens, nurseries, wet-nursing stations, schools and even a university, as well as administrative departments taking on all the functions of local government as well as the management of the productive activities. The intention was to collectivize all aspects of life in order to raise production and build a socialist society. This meant that the distinction between private household and public organization was blurred to a considerable extent.

> Collective life, it was said, replaced individual life. Families contributed their tools to the commune. Meals were taken in common in the public dining hall. With more people eating collectively, the commune was able to cut its coal costs by 50

percent. Collective shopping made it possible to cut down on the number of sales people. Children spent more time in nurseries and kindergartens . . . The ordinary citizen found himself [*sic*] in the grip of a new way of life. Private life was decried as old-fashioned, women were mobilized for labour, and collective life supplanted home life. The street, not the home, became the central focus of daily life (Schurmann 1968: 388–92).

Further research would be needed to ascertain the degree to which Schurmann's generalized description fitted the reality in different actual urban communes, but it is clear that, in intention at least, the urban people's communes implied an even more radical fusing of public and private, of household and organization, than is seen in the structure of the *danwei* and its relation to the households of its members.

The *danwei* and women's labour force participation

What consequences have the structure and functions of the *danwei* had for the employment of women? First, virtually all women in urban China between the age of completing full-time education and the age of retirement are in the labour force, and are members of an urban work-unit (State Statistical Bureau 1988). Secondly, virtually all of these women are in full-time work; there are no established arrangements for part-time work in China. The bare consequence of these two facts is the complete contrast between the pattern of economic activity of Chinese women and the pattern typical of capitalist industrial societies. Despite considerable variations, it is no caricature to suggest that the female population of working age in capitalist societies is distributed at any given moment into approximately equal thirds: those who are full-time housewives; those who are employed part-time; and those who are employed full-time. In China the first two categories are almost non-existent; nearly all women of working age work full-time.

It is evident that the structure of the *danwei* does not pose any obstacle to the labour force participation of women. Far from it; one of the policy objectives of the Chinese regime has been to encourage women into the labour force. As Schurmann points out, one of the major purposes of the urban commune movement of 1958–61 was to draw women into the labour force outside the home, from which they had traditionally been largely excluded (Schurmann 1968), and the drive to mobilize women into the labour force continued apace in subsequent years. The Chinese Communist Party was committed to a programme of equality of men and women (Croll 1978), and the language of gender equality was to the fore in this labour mobilization effort, although for many years the older generations of women were not touched by this movement out of the home and into the work-units (Davin 1976), and even today there are many elderly women who have never worked outside the context of the family. The younger generation, and certainly those born after the establishment of the communist regime, have been drawn into the labour force by, if nothing else, the low-wage policy of the government, which makes it next to impossible for a family to survive on a single wage. This by no means excludes various forms of gender-related segregation in work. Of these, perhaps the most significant is the degree to which women are under-represented in the relatively advantaged state-owned sectors of industry and over-represented in collective work-units, which are on average smaller and less able to provide their members with services and benefits on the same scale as state work-units (All China Women's Federation 1991, Whyte 1984). Other aspects of occupational segregation and inequality also exist, and these will be touched on in Chapter 3.

In general, crude measures of gender inequality in urban China reveal, first, no greater inequality than in industrial capitalist societies, in fact possibly greater equality, and, secondly, a marked reduction in inequality over the period of the building of the communist regime, up to the mid 1980s. The argument of this section is that the relatively less sharp separation of productive from reproductive spheres in urban China, as embodied in the structure of the *danwei* outlined above, has provided one of the most important structural conditions underlying the degree of gender equality that has been achieved since the 1950s. First, the abolition of a labour market and the establishment of life-time membership of a *danwei* mean that labour is not (or not only) considered as a "cost" from the point of view of the leadership of the work-unit, thus allowing almost universal adult participation in the workforce for both men and women. Secondly, the welfare and "household-like" activities of the *danwei* help to provide the conditions that make this universal female labour force participation practicable from the point of view of families. For example, as we will see in later chapters, the contribution of the *danwei* to the provision of child care facilities has been one important factor in the lives of mothers of young children.

Although for brevity this section has had to slide over the twists and turns of political and economic policy in China since the establishment of the communist regime, this procedure necessarily oversimplifies the complexity of developments in that country. Far from there having been a continuous policy line underlying the construction of the urban *danwei*, it is far more plausible to analyze developments since 1949 in terms of competition and tension between a number of different lines and different conceptions of socialist society (Solinger 1984). This competition continues. We have said nothing in this section about the reform process that has been introduced by Mao's successors since the late 1970s, preferring to set out the main specific features of the industrialization process in China and how this has affected the roles of men and women. This omission will be rectified in later chapters.

Japan: Confucian capitalism

The Tokugawa household

The characteristics of pre-industrial economic and domestic organization described earlier were apparent too in Japan. In Tokugawa (1603–1868) and Meiji (1868–1912) Japan, and indeed for major sectors of Japanese society well into the twentieth century Brunner's concept of the "whole house" applies usefully to the fusion of domestic and production functions. Rodney Clark (1979) noted that the house was the fundamental unit of domestic and economic organization in each of the four orders of Tokugawa Japan (the aristocracy, the samurai, the peasants and the merchants). Every person had to register as a member of a house and was legally subordinated to the househead. The household was an enduring corporation. Property did not belong to the househead; "the househead merely managed the property for the sake of the house, its current members, its generations of ancestors, and its unborn posterity" (Clark 1979: 14). Because of the late impact of capitalist relations through much of Japanese society and the persistence, in sometimes changing forms, of many traditional values, attitudes and institutions despite ostensible changes in the institutional superstructure from the Meiji period onwards, the influence of these patterns can be traced down to the present day. They are evident, for instance, in the continued importance of the family enterprise sector in agriculture, small industry, retailing and services and in the unique pattern of organization of the large-scale Japanese company. These patterns, too, are of the greatest importance for understanding the structuring of gender roles in Japanese society.

The principles of this fusion of household and economic organization in Tokugawa Japan are exemplified in Clark's (1979) description of the merchant family and enterprise in which the two were melded into the same corporation. The assets of the business and the family were indistinguishable. "Families did not so much own the businesses as with the European business family: the house itself was the business . . . the liabilities of the business were the obligations of all the house members jointly." Kinship provided the essential basis of trust and the channels of knowledge required to function effectively on the wider business scene. Successful merchant enterprises recruited extra staff by utilizing fictive kinship through the adoption of young men who married the daughters of the house. Apprentices taken into the house were regarded as members of the family for whom the master had a parental responsibility. Clark (1979: 14f) summarizes as follows:

In short, outsiders were recruited into the business house in return not for contractual rewards but for the benefits of a long, possibly even life-long association with the house in a relationship which was analogous to, and sometimes almost identical with, that of a family member.

Peasant agriculture was the dominant mode of production for the majority of the population until the middle of the twentieth century and most agricultural units were based upon family enterprises. A vivid account by Alice Bacon in 1902 describes in detail the relative egalitarianism of peasant family life at that time and contrasts this situation favourably with the more restricted social and economic life of urban and higher status women. Women worked along with their husbands cultivating rice, harvesting, and marketing, as well as caring for the silk worms, spinning and weaving and organizing the home itself. Alice Bacon observed a lack of social distance between peasant spouses, a degree of consideration of husbands for wives, and relatively democratic domestic decision-making based upon the joint contributions of the spouses in domestic production. Modern research has confirmed and elaborated upon this picture of the role of women in rural production in Japan, has emphasized the resistance of the peasantry to the official samurai restrictive codes on women, and contrasted the situation with that of China where footbinding symbolized the more restricted role of women and where women's economic role was given far less recognition in the rural family and community (Tsurumi 1990).

In contrast to the relatively egalitarian peasant family, women in the higher reaches of the Japanese status structure during the Tokugawa and Meiji eras occupied a more marginal and confined position in the family economy. Historians have traced the deteriorating position of women in samurai and aristocratic positions during the Tokugawa era. A marked difference in gender spheres was evident in the roles of husband and wife in these more elevated social circles. The home or household was the primary locus of the wife's activities. According to the relative degree of wealth of the family, she managed or undertook domestic affairs and was trained, and acted, as the chief or only servant, assistant and valet to her husband. She had almost total responsibility for administering the routine family expenses and seeing to the upbringing and education of the children. She would also engage in sewing and cultivating the silk worm. "Her sphere is within the home", although unlike in other Asian countries at the time she could come and go through the streets by herself in safety and security (Bacon 1902).

Alice Bacon's account of domestic service in wealthier homes in Japan at the turn of the century is a revealing illustration of the continuation and strength of feudal values, of the lack of penetration of commercial influences in Japanese society at this time, of the relevance of Brunner's concept of the whole house in pre-capitalist society and of the lack of differentiation of home and workplace. It also echoes themes about the nature of Japanese society which are present even today in contemporary analysis of a much more advanced industrial society. Servants were numerous and cheap to maintain. Wages were low but the servants were supported out of the household's revenue and resources. They became members of the household, took their position in society from their involvement in the household and ostensibly and palpably put the interests of the house above their own. With their fortunes clearly related to those of the house they could be entrusted with considerable discretion to pursue the interests of the master and household. Pay was low but was enhanced by the semi-annual giving of gifts. Male servants were however paid much more than female ones. The pace of life was leisurely and in the evenings the servants participated in shared activities. Comparing domestic service in the USA with that in Japan, Bacon argued that the relationship was much more contractual and limited, with servants in the USA having their own home separate from the master's house. American servants with their limited-time engagements and limited-cash based loyalty to their employers required much more instruction and supervision and could not be left to get on with the job to the same degree as in Japan. Outside of the employment relationship they were free to get on with their own lives whereas the Japanese servants led their daily and yearly lives within the context of the master's household.

The cash nexus, the commercialization of relations of production and the separation of the home and the workplace made only limited inroads in late nineteenth-century Japan. Alice Bacon noted the continuation of feudal attitudes with the general aversion to commercial relations in turn-of-the-century Japan. Professional and trade services were not charged on a fee basis. No price was stated or implied but recipients offered gifts subsequent to the service being rendered proportionate to the service and the social standing of recipient and service provider. An important role of the mistress of the house was to ensure that the offering of gifts at the New Year and other festivals ensured appropriate recognition and continuation of such relationships. Such considerations extended also to presentations to servants as well. The mistress of the wealthier household thus had her role based in the domestic sphere but nonetheless she was not exclusively confined to it, since her role as domestic manager ensured that she handled necessary economic relations with other households that provided services. These other households such as trades operatives, teachers and doctors were also organized through a domestic structure that fused with economic production, with apprentices, journeymen and students living in their master's house.

The similarity in themes between this discussion of the domestic household economy in turn-of-the-century Japan and contemporary discussions of the large Japanese firm are quite remarkable. The long-term attachment of employees to the firm, the apparent lack of individual social time and space for employees, the low portion of remuneration paid in wages compared to bonuses based on the

general fortune of the enterprise, the initiative and discretion exercised by subordinates, the higher wages paid to males – all these
features have been held to be characteristic of the contemporary
large-scale Japanese firm, suggesting that very powerful cultural values have persisted and found expression in important institutions in
the present day. In this sense, however much the modern Japanese
business corporation is a contemporary creation, nonetheless it still
exhibits characteristics inherited from the pre-capitalist household
economy. Male employees in large companies in particular find
themselves very much in a work situation governed by such norms
with very little time to themselves and their families outside of their
work obligations.

Despite her recognition of the role of the mistress of the wealthier
household in the domestic and urban economy, Alice Bacon generally believed that urban life narrowed the range of gainful occupations and spheres of action for women. Samurai norms tended to
confine women to household roles. The urban economy as a whole
offered women fewer economic and overall opportunities for equivalence with men than was the case in the countryside. The cities at
this time were still largely the product of the Tokugawa era based
upon the castles of the *daimyo* (feudal lords) and the administrative
and service needs of the government. Industrialism still had to make
its impact. Houses had pleasant gardens and there were ample parks.
Samurai values continued even after the official abolition of the rank
in 1872. Nonetheless Alice Bacon does provide evidence for there
being a range of occupational pursuits by which lower status urban
women could gain a living or supplement the family income. These
largely related to teaching the necessary skills of the feminine role,
such as flower arranging and painting and the tea ceremony. The
geisha and prostitution were other urban occupations catering to the
needs of men which could also provide a living. These occupations
were organized on a household basis. Young girls were often taken
into the homes of providers of these services on contract from their
parents and trained in their profession. Geisha trainees were often
adopted by the owners and managers of the establishments.

In understanding domestic and economic organization and the
gendering of these institutions in Tokugawa, Meiji and contemporary
Japan it is important to make some further observations about the
place of women in Japanese society. Despite the variations evident in
gender roles that have already been recounted it can be argued that

women are regarded as marginal and peripheral to the major institutions of Japanese society. Patrilineal kinship places the emphasis of family authority and succession upon the senior male and son. Families achieve their continuity through the male line. Because of exogamy and patrilocal marriage daughters will be lost to the family of origin. Daughters are a cost to be borne; the investment of time and resources in them as children and young persons will accrue to another family – that of her husband and his parents. In old age parents would look to their son to care for them, rather than to their daughter who would be caring for the in-laws. At marriage a woman traditionally had to be endowed with a considerable dowry of furniture, clothing and domestic resources so that she would not be a burden on her family of procreation after marriage. This perspective is of importance for understanding the plight of young girls described above and in the subsequent industrial economy. Brinton argues in the present day (1993) that similar attitudes account for the differential educational strategies of parents towards their sons and daughters. As will be seen too their position in the contemporary occupational context is often perceived in a similar light.

The first industrial workers

Women participated to a greater extent than men in the first industrial enterprises in Meiji Japan. Morishima (1984) notes that some of the first industrial workers in the new silk and cotton mills of the 1870s were the daughters of former samurai impoverished by the abolition of their former legal status and the economic changes of the times, who like many of their parents were more innovative than the traditional merchant class in leading the country to meet the new economic challenges of the West. Tsurumi (1990) has given a more recent and detailed account of the hard but relatively good working conditions that these pioneers experienced, as the Japanese government and business leaders established pilot projects designed to learn the technology and social relations of machine production so as to fight off the competition from Western producers who had gained inroads in the Japanese market through the unequal treaties of 1858 and 1866. There are suggestions that these early industrial enterprises were run on lines akin to the traditional patriarchal family model (Tsurumi 1990).

But it was peasant families who were to provide the bulk of the recruits for the predominantly female labour force in the growing textile industries which were the first internationally competitive Japanese industries of the new era. By 1907 women constituted 61 per cent of workers in factories employing ten or more people (Gleason 1965) and 80 per cent of the 255,000 people employed in the textile industry (Garon 1987). Their pattern of involvement in this new form of employment was very different from the much discussed unique contemporary pattern of life-time employment for males in large organizations. Most were recruited as young single girls from rural villages by labour bosses with annual contracts with their parents or brothers to whom the payments were made in advance. They worked for two or three years before returning to the village or merging into urban life. Conditions varied but they often worked 12-hour shifts and usually lived in supervised dormitories with little personal free time or space. In contrast male employees often lived in the locality or were provided with company married housing. Women were generally paid less than male employees. Morishima notes that although employed in the largest establishments female employees earned only half of male wages in the first quarter of the twentieth century. Some possibly found these conditions, with a degree of independence and passable food, superior to village life (Garon 1987), but health and accident risks were probably higher at work (Tsurumi 1990). It is not surprising that under such a system there was considerable labour turnover. Contracts became increasingly exploitative (e.g. the retention of part of the wages as forced savings only to be released upon satisfactory completion of the contract) as employers sought to restrain the workers from leaving employment and employers increasingly looked further afield to poorer and often famine stricken locations for naive single female recruits. Hazama Hiroshi observed that although "this system gradually disappeared in the twentieth century . . . for a long time when a young woman became a factory worker the decision required a resolution similar to that of selling herself into prostitution, as the social status was nearly as low" (quoted by Brinton 1993: 26).

Gender and the life-time employment system

As new heavier industries began to grow in the early years of the twentieth century, men increasingly became a more significant element in the industrial workforce. But there was little sign at this stage of the emergence of the pattern of life-time employment commitment. There was considerable labour turnover as workers moved to where they could obtain the highest earnings, influenced possibly by the Tokugawa tradition of artisan independence and itineracy. The modern system of life-time employment in the larger business organizations for many male employees began with key graduate managerial employees in the early decades of the twentieth century and with key skilled workers whose employers offered employment security in order to retain and enhance their scarce skills. The system only became widespread by the middle of the century as modern industry became a much more dominant sector in the economy and as trades unions sought to ensure the provision of similar terms for their members (Clark 1979).

The major features of this system are the hiring of a core of key male workers who are engaged from the time of university, school or college graduation until their mid fifties. They devote long daily working hours throughout their adult lives to one employer. Identification with the organization is profound and the abandonment of commitment to it is rare, regarded socially as disreputable and would make re-engagement with another large organization unlikely as it would reveal a lack of loyalty. Seniority is another important aspect of the system. Length of service is associated with rising pay and social respect. Pay is much more determined by age seniority than is the case in the West where individualized employment and pay contracts make occupational progress more independent of the ascriptive characteristic of age. Pay and status differentials are much less than in the West. Basic pay is relatively low and annual bonuses based upon the overall performance of the enterprise are much more important. Compared to the West employees are believed to identify much more with the employing organization, to be more enthusiastic workers and to be entrusted productively with much more discretion and self-motivation. Because of the guaranteed security of employment they are believed to be more willing to change to more productive employment practices and new technology and to make current sacrifices, e.g. reduced annual bonuses, when necessary for the good of the enterprise and firms, and because they do not fear the subsequent loss of their employees firms are more willing to invest in the training of their workers (Dore 1973, 1989, Vogel 1979).

Although there is not unbroken continuity with traditional cultural values and forms of social organization it is clear that the modern form of business organization in Japan draws heavily upon traditional Japanese social structure. Several influential commentators have observed how elements of traditional social relations have been incorporated into new structures in the contemporary era. Chie Nakane (1970) has observed how persistent key features of Japanese social relations such as household and workplace orientation, deference to seniors and superiors, sensitivity to group norms, and patron–client relations, have been drawn upon to find new expression in contemporary institutions. Underlying the apparent changes in society since the Meiji era she sees underlying continuity in many patterns of social relationships and social organization. Morishima (1984) has also noted the resemblance between the modern day dedication of the corporate employee and the loyalty and devotion expected of the samurai to his lord.

The large Japanese company has other significant resemblances to the household-economic units of traditional Japanese society. Employees have a much wider interest in the company than a narrow employment contract. In the absence of well-funded state social security schemes they look to the company as the major basis of their social welfare. Companies provide assistance with housing costs through cheap mortgages; sometimes they provide company housing, although usually for male householder heads and not females. Medical schemes cover health requirements and employers' welfare benefit packages are reckoned to be of greater value than those provided by American companies. Companies often take much of their employees' evening time in business-related socializing and many people take their holidays under company-organized schemes (Vogel 1979). It is not uncommon either for employees to do "voluntary" overtime in the evening to help in pressing business. And some people do not take their holiday entitlements. Most male employees in large business organizations retire in their mid fifties with a small company pension which they enhance through working for related subsidiaries and contractors at reduced levels of remuneration. Discussing its nearly all-encompassing nature Morishima remarks of the large-scale Japanese company that

> it is not just a profit-making organization; it is a complete society in itself, and frequently it is so all-embracing that all the activities of the daily life of the company's employees can take place within the company framework (Morishima 1984: 120).

For those Japanese men enmeshed in the life-time employment system in large-scale business and government organizations, their adult and retirement life chances are intimately dependent upon their intense commitment to the enterprise. They receive many benefits from the system at the cost of the investment of a large portion of their time, selves and social life. Their participation in this system is however also dependent upon the more marginal involvement of other sectors of the population, women and men in other business sectors, female employees in their own organization and their own spouses. The system can only function because of the cushion of flexibility provided by the latter groups of people. Female employees and sub-contractors provide the necessary slack. When business is booming the employment of women and men on part-time or temporary contracts and the sub-contracting of work to subsidiaries or associated companies provide the necessary additional resources to meet demand requirements. When there is recession the core elite of workers on privileged employment terms can retain their jobs and perhaps experience reduced bonuses or pay levels, the hiring of core workers can be reduced, work for sub-contractors and subsidiaries can be cut back and women and temporary employees can be encouraged to sever the employment relationship. The majority of Japanese workers thus do not qualify as core permanent employees of large-scale companies. Many men work in the family enterprise sector or in small firms where their employment rewards are lower and their time obligation greater or similar in scale.

Female employees of large companies occupy the converse position to that of male employees. Their position is much more marginal, temporary and peripheral. They may be recruited as full-time workers after graduation from the educational system but they are expected to leave employment after marriage or childbirth. They thus subsequently lose out in seniority rights and can only re-enter employment as temporary or part-time employees. Contemporary gender inequalities in wages are uniquely high in Japan among industrial countries (Brinton 1993). Japan is also unique in the fall in women's pay levels following marriage (Roos quoted by Brinton 1993). Young female employees are not regarded by large firms as likely long-term employees. A woman's career is seen as being based in the home as a wife and mother. Firms frequently manifest a paternalistic attitude to their young female employees. If housing is provided for single employees it is only available for males and not women (Brinton 1993). Young women living in their own house are regarded as morally dubious and experience difficulty in finding employment (Brinton 1993) as though continuing the traditional attitude that a woman's social position can only come from her father or husband. Employers of young single women often regard themselves as being *in loco parentis* and perceive the right and proper next stage for them to be marriage. Financial inducements in the form of severance payments frequently add to the pressures on young women to terminate their employment upon marriage or childbirth (Lam 1992).

The system of life-time employment in large Japanese business organizations thus can only exist through its relationship to the wider business system, labour market and domestic economy. An understanding of the core institutions of the modern sector of the economy and labour force also requires consideration of the remaining sectors of the economy. The domestic household, small family and small non-family firms and enterprises and self-employment absorb the energies of, and provide the institutional framework for, large parts of the remainder of the economically active sections of the community. We shall be returning to a discussion of the household, and of Japanese women's place within it, in Chapters 4 and 5, and to the question of the small family firm at various points throughout the book.

Britain and America: androcentric capitalism

Britain: the first industrial nation

The model of self-sufficient household production stands in most need of refinement in the case of Britain. As far back as the thirteenth century, wage labour was widespread, and many households relied on it for part of their livelihood. In fact, in contrast with the fetters of serfdom, working for wages was seen as a kind of freedom. However, in contrast with the independence given by ownership or tenancy of a farm, or the management of a family household in some branch of handicraft industry, wage labour came to be seen as tantamount to poverty, and by the seventeenth century was avoided if possible. The ideal, for an adult man, was to be head of a household that was also a productive enterprise, with women, children, and possibly servants or employees all engaged in the labours of the household. The proportion of men who could fulfil this ideal is uncertain. More common, perhaps, was the situation summed up by Pahl (1984), in which households combined self-provisioning, wage labour and various kinds of side-employments in a strategy of getting by. Regular wage labour for the majority was uncommon until well into the nineteenth century, and even then irregular employment was the lot of many.

However extensive the incidence of wage labour may have been on the eve of the "industrial revolution", the increasing proletarianization of British households undoubtedly constituted a major structural change in society between the eighteenth and nineteenth centuries. Small farms declined as land was enclosed and tenancies and less profitable independently owned farms were incorporated into larger capitalist agricultural enterprises, creating an even larger pool of landless labourers seeking work. The growth of factory production sounded the death-knell for independent artisanal households, many of which had already become dependent on a partly concealed form of wage labour in the cottage industries of the eighteenth century. Gradually, households became completely dependent on the wage labour of their members, regular if they could get it, sporadic or seasonal if not.

This process removed much of the possibility of integrating production and consumption within the household. Household members had to go "out to work", leaving their homes each day to work under the new disciplines of industry. The labours of household management, ensuring the day-to-day survival of the members of the household, still had to be carried out, but appeared to have no economic significance, since the wage of the household's wage-earner(s) appeared to be payment only for the work performed for the employer (Seccombe 1986). Journeymen working at home under the domestic outwork system had recognized the significance of the work of wives and children for the economic survival of the family. Women should earn their keep; men would not marry dependent women (Pinchbeck 1969, Hewitt 1958). Women had an essential, if subordinate, place in the family economy. With the growth of the wage and factory system, the question necessarily arose whether the woman's contribution in future was to be in the form of wages earned, or in the unpaid fulfilment of domestic duties (which came to be known as "housework"), or both. If the last, how was this combination to be managed? The problem of the dual burden had been born.

The problem was "solved" in many households by the simple fact that the household could not manage on the wage of a single earner.

This was true for many households throughout the nineteenth century and remains the case in the supposedly more affluent twentieth century. The parameters of this "solution" differed, however, for much of the nineteenth century from those that obtained later. The main difference was in the availability of children, part of the problem as well as part of the solution. A high birth rate, even mitigated by a high rate of infant mortality, created for most families an extended burden of child care, since a couple might expect to have one or more infants in the family for the best part of 20 or more years. But three-quarters of these infants grew into older children, and before the introduction of compulsory schooling (and to an extent even afterwards) these children were labour resources for the household. They could be sent or taken out to earn wages (Smelser 1959), a possibility that was progressively restricted by legislation in the first half of the nineteenth century. Or they could be utilized at home as household workers, cleaning, cooking and taking care of infants. If a family did not have an appropriate child of the right age, it could hire one from another family (Hewitt 1958). The use of children in the household could thus ease the burden for those married women whose family economy required them to be in employment.

The solution to the problem of the allocation of household labour resources, between wage-earning, self-provisioning, child care, and so on, was clearly a private matter for the household members. This can be seen in the case of child care. Attempts were made from the 1850s to establish crèches or nurseries for the children of employed mothers, partly as a response to concerns about the health of such infants and the high rate of infant mortality (Hewitt 1958). Some such attempts were made by philanthropic groups of ladies, some were made by employers, such as Courtauld at Halstead (Lown 1991). The majority of such establishments failed quickly. Few of them were free of charge, and working mothers found it cheaper to make their own private arrangements. They also often resented middle class meddling in their methods of child care. The only major nineteenth-century attempt at collective housekeeping and child care was promoted by Robert Owen at the New Lanark Mills, an initiative which sparked off an Owenite movement among women in the 1830s. This too was short-lived, and by 1845 this move to shift the boundary between the private family household and the wider public realm was dead (Taylor 1983). Some paternalistic companies became involved in the provision of services to employees and their

45

families, such as housing, education, medical services and pensions, but the majority of businesses took the view that the welfare of employees was not the employer's responsibility.

The regularity and continuity of married women's employment seems to have varied widely. It used to be thought that women gave up employment on marriage. This is, however, the projection back into the early part of the nineteenth century of norms which later became strong among the middle classes and the ranks of skilled workers or labour aristocracy. An alternative view is that married women alternated periods in and out of employment according to the needs of the family (Tilly & Scott 1989), and would give up paid work if at all possible (Roberts 1986). However, Lown (1991) provides evidence that millworkers for Courtauld's in Halstead remained millworkers for their whole working life from the age of 12 until ill-health forced them to give up, with only very short breaks for marriage and childbirth. It is unclear how typical Halstead was. Apart from anything else, the continuity of employment would have been affected by fluctuations in the demand for labour, and households would have had to respond flexibly to changes in employment opportunities in the local area and beyond. Whatever the more typical work history was for married women in the nineteenth and early twentieth centuries, it was strikingly different from what has emerged in the latter half of the twentieth century.

The employment of married women outside the home was a controversial issue in the early phases of industrialization. It entered the wider public realm in the 1830s, in the wake of investigations by government officials into matters of health and safety affecting women and children in the mines and factories. By the 1840s, the terms of debate had centred around a number of issues concerning the relationship between employment and family life: whether operatives married at too early an age; whether factory girls were more exposed to early pre-marital sexual experience and to the risk of bearing illegitimate children; whether married women who were out at work for 12 or more hours a day could also adequately perform their duties as wife and mother; whether the employment of mothers was a contributory factor to the high rate of infant mortality; and, more generally, whether the employment of married women was destroying the basis for proper family life (Hewitt 1958).

Victorians who were exercised about these matters and who campaigned to restrict or ban married women's employment tended not to realize that such employment was primarily necessitated by the insufficiency of married men's wages to support a family. This is partly because the campaign was joined by sections of the male workforce whose higher level of organization allowed their voice to be heard. Skilled working men in a number of trades began to argue in the 1840s that their trades should be closed to women. Fearing that the employment of women would force down their relatively higher wages, these men took up the religiously tinged patriarchal discourse of the middle class or aristocratic defenders of family values (Davidoff & Hall 1987). Whether or not we interpret the skilled workers' use of this discourse to oppose women's entry to their trades as a form of patriarchal cross-class solidarity (Lown 1991), the result was the progressive establishment of an ideal norm that a man's wage should be sufficient to support his wife and children without the need for the wife to engage in paid work (Seccombe 1986), an ideal which, even though the majority of men could not attain it, has had profound consequences for the development of wage differentials and public policy (Land 1980).

The ideal of the male breadwinner wage was one component of a more general process of occupational segregation by gender and of sex-typing of jobs that became established through the nineteenth century and has never been broken down in the twentieth (Bradley 1989, Hakim 1979). It can be seen most clearly in those industries that employed both married men and married women, even husbands and wives. Lown's (1991) description of men's and women's employment in Courtauld's factory at Halstead, or Osterud's (1986) account of the Leicester hosiery industry, even if patterns of gender segregation differed greatly in detail from industry to industry and between regions of the country, establish most of the basic structural principles involved. One of these is that employers, on the basis of assumptions about married women's family life, especially the assumption that a married woman would be primarily supported by the wages of her husband, forced most aspects of women's work into a pattern close to a spot market for labour (casual, irregular or seasonal labour, fluctuating demand resulting in frequent layoffs, piecework payment system), while at least some men were offered work on a more permanent basis, with greater opportunity for training and for promotion through internal labour markets, within a male gendered culture of paternalism (Joyce 1980). The other is a tendency towards ever-finer job segregation by gender, both promoted by employers as a way of dividing the workforce and campaigned for by men as a statement about their masculinity and their rights to more advantaged employment. As Osterud (1986: 65) concludes: "The interaction of family relations and capitalism over the course of industrialization led to the development of a gender system that simultaneously relied upon and restricted women's labour."

We have concentrated on the nineteenth century as the main period of British industrialization, and the working through of the implications of the separation of household and enterprise for the employment and family life of men and women. The main structural features which were in place by the later nineteenth century continued to underlie the increasing scale of organization and bureaucratization of employment that characterized the late nineteenth and twentieth centuries. As new office, shop and service occupations came to form an increasing proportion of all employment, the principles of gender segregation and sex-typing continued to operate. So did the distinction between male career hierarchies through internal labour markets and female temporary or short-term employment with no or few opportunities for advancement. These tendencies can be seen clearly and explicitly in the growth of office work (Zimmeck 1986). Especially in government employment, but also to a lesser extent in the private sector, the rapid expansion of clerical work was constructed on explicitly gendered lines. Single women were taken on as typists, filing clerks and telephone operators on the assumption that they would leave employment on marriage. In some organizations and occupations an explicit marriage bar was operated. Women thus had little hope of promotion into higher ranks of office work or management. Men, on the other hand, were allocated jobs within minutely specified hierarchies, and had at least the formal possibility of climbing the ladders thus constructed, to remain in the organization's employment for their whole working lives, and to qualify for a retirement pension at the end of it. Internal documentation of the civil service shows that this principle of women's lower eligibility was justified in terms of the need to provide men with a breadwinner or family wage, while women only needed a single person's wage. Women's work was often paid on piece rate, while men's jobs attracted scale rates which rose with age and experience. The upshot was that the considerable expansion in women's employment up to 1939 was predominantly a growth in the employment of single women. Despite frequent challenges from individual women and from some trade unions in which women were well represented, such gender-specific employment systems continued in existence well into the post-war period, and even the equal pay and equal opportunity legislation of the 1970s has been rendered less than fully effective by the high degree of gender segregation in employment, and by the strength of sex-typed cultural images of occupations that have been built up over many decades.

Employment patterns thus have continued to reflect assumptions about the family status of employees, rather than being completely universalistic. At the same time, assumptions about the household division of labour and the separation of private household from capitalist enterprise have, until recently at least, continued to have a systematic relationship to the gender segregation in employment. Child care, in particular, has remained the responsibility of the private family, and particularly of mothers, except in the emergency of wartime when the nation's need for the labour of married women induced the public provision of child care facilities. The patterns of commercialization of domestic services and household technology have also assumed the continuity of the private household as the main site of family life (Cowan 1989). Services to the household are predominantly delivered through the market, and paid for out of the wages of household members, apart from those services that are made available on a collective basis by the state; relatively few services are provided by capitalist enterprises to the households of employees. As we will see in more detail later, there is still a widely accepted and strong belief that women with young children should not be in employment (although actual practice is ceasing increasingly to reflect this), and that women's employment in general should be adapted to fit in with their domestic responsibilities.

America: the first new nation

Much of what we have written on Britain could equally, with few alterations, be said of America, as the theory of industrial society would lead us to expect. The basic contours of the separation of household and enterprise in the course of capitalist industrialization are manifested in the case of America, with very similar consequences for the employment of married women and for the development of the dual burden. In America, as in Britain, women were drawn into employment in the early factories, especially in textile manufacture, at lower wages than were current for men, but these were mainly unmarried women, and waged labour by married women remained unusual throughout the course of industrialization. One finds the same assumptions about the breadwinner wage, about the wife's primary economic support deriving from the wage income of her husband, about the separate spheres of men and women with a strong emphasis on feminine domesticity, about the lack of economic significance of domestic labour (Boydston 1990) and about a sharp domestic division of labour (Matthaei 1982, Kessler-Harris 1982). Domestic service was likewise very widespread, with even relatively poor families hiring help for some domestic tasks such as laundering, until the scarcity of domestic help and the growth of household technology left the remaining domestic labour in the hands of the housewife (Komarovsky 1964, Rubin 1976, Cowan 1989). On the side of employing companies, one also finds the same developments in employment practices: the gradual emergence of internal labour markets in which promotion careers are mainly restricted to men; a preference for the employment of single women, even to the extent of marriage bars in many occupations from the later nineteenth through to the mid twentieth century (Goldin 1990); and the strong assumption that the general welfare of employees and their families is not the concern of the employer, whose responsibility ends with the payment of the wage. However, there are also some important differences between Britain and America which we will now briefly outline.

One major difference is that a far higher proportion of American households could avoid dependence on wage labour later into the process of industrialization than was the case in Britain. The abundance of land allowed for the establishment of new farms, whose owners and families could thus exist on a combination of self-sufficiency and commercial production, right up to the end of the nineteenth century and beyond. In the villages and small towns that serviced such farms, artisan production from wood, leather and the output of agriculture could also continue well into the main phases of industrialization. The colonial and republican traditions placed great emphasis on economic independence and the resistance of proletarianization, and many men and women were determined to retain this independence for as long as possible. This implied a work organization that resembled the household interdependence of pre-industrial times, at first on a patriarchal basis, later on more egalitarian principles (Matthaei 1982, Osterud 1991). In some areas, unmarried farm daughters worked for a while in the early textile mills, but expected to marry farmers and withdraw from paid labour (Kessler-Harris 1982). This possibility of retaining economic self-sufficiency and the involvement of married women in the labour of the household-as-enterprise may have contributed to the very low proportion of married women in the paid labour force at the turn of the twentieth century.

The second major difference lies in the legacy of slavery. Before abolition, wives of wealthier slave-owners could be relieved of labour by domestic slaves, while in less wealthy households the wife might work alongside indoor slaves in household production and housework (Matthaei 1982). Abolition created a large pool of propertyless black workers who first continued to work on the plantations in the southern states, then migrated in considerable numbers to the cities and to the north. There emerged a striking difference between the economic activities of white and black women: black women, at all levels of household income and educational attainment, had and continue to have a higher rate of participation in the paid labour force. Many reasons have been suggested for this: the higher unemployment and lower incomes of black men; the greater discrimination against black men compared to black women; and possibly that slavery left an indirect legacy of making paid work less socially stigmatized among black women than among white women (Goldin 1990). Whatever the reason, the higher labour force participation was also accompanied by racial concentration in various occupations: black women were, at the turn of the century, more likely to be engaged in agriculture and domestic work such as laundering, while they were virtually excluded from the mills, from clerical work and from shop work (Matthaei 1982). Later in the twentieth century, sociologists have pointed to the higher proportion of female-headed households among blacks which, together with a higher employment rate, results in distinctive patterns of the dual burden compared with whites.

Aside from distinctions between black and white, the ethnic diversity of the American population, resulting from waves of emigration from Europe and then from all over the world, also created differences in the experience of women. However, at the start of the twentieth century, these differences mainly affected single women, whose labour force participation varied considerably from one ethnicity to another. The overall labour force participation of white married women, on the other hand, was equally negligible at around 3 per cent, whether native-born, foreign-born or second-generation immigrant. Occupations of those women who were in the paid labour force also varied according to ethnicity, with native-born women dominating teaching and clerical work, Italians, English and Irish women working in the textile mills, Bohemians, Russians and Italians in tobacco and cigar factories, and so on (Matthaei 1982).

As befits "the first new nation", Americans were more inventive in finding alternatives to life in the nuclear family household, which were intended to change the conditions of work for women (and in some cases men). Some colonies experimented with forms of communal organization, but these did not last long and the private family homestead based on the nuclear family became the dominant household. In the early nineteenth century, utopian communities such as those inspired by Charles Fourier were established, organizing domestic labour on a communal basis. Religious communities made similar organizational innovations, although tending to retain the sexual division of labour, with groups of women collectively performing domestic tasks. Groups of relatively privileged women also attempted to establish collective housekeeping schemes. All of these innovations met with failure (Cowan 1989), but it is striking that it was in America that they were attempted, as part of a conscious effort to break from Old World patterns of development.

Despite these manifestations of an incipient "communism" in America, the prevailing temper was a commitment to free market private enterprise with *laissez-faire* government, and this entailed a sharp division between the private household and the profit-seeking enterprise, with little government involvement in the relationship between them. In the very early stages of the establishment of textile factories, some companies followed the "Waltham system" set up by Lowell, in which young unmarried women were installed in boarding houses owned by the company, but this model had a short life-span, and in any case found its justification in the preservation of morality among factory girls and in training them for their future married life (Kessler-Harris 1982). The Waltham system was also contrasted with the proletarian degradation believed to be characteristic of textile towns in England, but this did not prevent companies from abandoning the system and reverting to an arm's length relationship to the private lives of employees and their households. From then on, the household activities of employees have been left as their private affair, with companies refraining from the more interventionist stance of those more paternalist employers in Britain. An exception might be found in the interest that companies have taken in the family circumstances of their middle and higher management employees, whose wives found themselves "married to the job" (Whyte 1960).

The commitment to free enterprise and *laissez-faire* is also manifest in the reluctance of government to become entangled in the private contract between employer and employee. As far as the employment of married women is concerned, this can be seen in two areas. One is protective legislation, which came much later to America than to Britain, and was often judged unconstitutional by the courts, as were attempts at equal pay legislation. The other was the subject of child care, with community child care centres which might ease the load on mothers again challenged as to their constitutionality, and even during the Second World War modest proposals to respond to the war crisis and the need for increasing female employment came under severe criticism. As Chafe (1991: 143) remarks: "So deeply held were views on the proper place of women with young children that, even faced by the necessity of war, America did far less to provide young female workers with community child care facilities than was the case in Britain."

Conclusion: household and organizational membership

The differentiation of household and enterprise creates two "poles of membership" for individuals. When household and enterprise are one, it is clear which group an individual is a member of, and what rights and obligations follow from such membership. When they divide, the individual's membership is also divided, and the possibility emerges of tension in the rights and obligations of membership. However, this highly abstract formulation conceals the concrete variation in the terms of membership that have developed in different societies. In this section, we will examine how cultural variations in the principles of membership of households and of enterprises are structured along lines of gender in our four societies.

Household membership is primarily determined by kinship, and the extent and nature of the rights and obligations of membership are deeply affected by cultural conceptions of kinship. In Britain and America, household formation has long been based on neolocal marriage, each new married couple setting up their own household and bringing up their children within it until the children in turn leave to set up households. Each household thus contains only one elementary family, and any recent census material will show that this is not just a normative prescription but also a statistical fact. Each of these elementary families is, as Parsons put it, "structurally isolated", in the sense that the culture provides no strong basis for forming social groups based on the kinship relations between elementary families. Social contacts and felt obligations between members of extended families may well continue to be strong (Litwak 1960a, 1960b, Finch 1989), but this does not affect the independence of each elementary family which may take pride in being able to solve its own problems without outside aid. If it cannot solve its own problems, an alternative is to dissolve the household through separation of the partners, with or without legal recognition through divorce. This alternative is becoming increasingly common, and, despite much official and public commitment to life-long marriage, the reality for many is that membership of the elementary family household formed by marriage is temporary. The growth of customs such as cohabitation (widespread) and fixed-term marriage contracts (still relatively unusual) indicate awareness of this temporariness.

It is widely observed that membership of the household is more central for women than for men. There is no male counterpart to the maxim that "a woman's place is in the home". Women have primary responsibility for household affairs, such as shaping the environment in the home, housework and cooking, child care and the care of sick or dependent household members. Motherhood is highly institutionalized, fatherhood not, giving rise to considerable recent debate about the norms and behaviour appropriate to fatherhood. Single-parent households are far more commonly female-headed than male-headed. Women are the core of the nodes that link households to each other, either through kinship, friendship or mutual aid. The belief that men are dispensable from households is not infrequently expressed.

China and Japan differ considerably in a number of aspects of household membership. In both, the residues of traditional patrilocal or virilocal marriage customs are still strong, giving rise to a significant proportion of patrilineal stem family households in both societies, even in urban settings. Practical considerations, such as housing scarcity, also result in multi-generation households, including matrilineal stem families. Joint households, bringing together two or more married siblings, are not unknown. Even where households are based on elementary families, movement of members between households is not uncommon, such as when a Japanese young wife goes back to her natal household for childbirth (Lebra 1984), or when a Chinese child spends weeks, months or even years in the household of grandparents or a parent's sibling. The conception of the extended family as a group with common interests is still strong in China, resulting in a considerable degree of mutual aid, interlinked budgets and extended family catering arrangements. The expected commitment of all household members, even all members of extended family groupings, to a common cause to which individual interests should be subordinated is part of what underlies the relatively low incidence of household dissolution through separation or divorce. Even the increase of divorce rates to levels which, by Western standards, are still very low is often perceived as a major social problem. Membership of households and of inter-household groupings is thus conceived of as permanent and all-embracing.

In Japan, the association of the household with the woman is even stronger that in the West. Women are often entirely responsible for all household affairs, including budgeting and expenditure of all kinds. Husbands play little part in the internal life of the household, and are often absent from it for long periods. In traditional houses, men used to have a formalized place within the house (the reception room) that was theirs, but in modern apartments there is no room for this, and men have no specific location within the house. Women talk of husbands who do not know where things are kept in the house, even their own clothes (Lebra 1984).

In urban China, an essentially similar traditional association of the women with the household and the man with external affairs has been considerably modified by a combination of political pressures, economic transformation and household logistics. Political emphasis on gender equality and campaigns against "feudal" patriarchal attitudes, universal employment of women, relatively equal wages for men and women, and the practical need for all members of the household to pull their weight in household affairs have resulted in a decline in the gendered conceptions of household obligations.

Just as we find societal variations in the nature of household membership, so the implications of "membership" of enterprises also vary considerably between the four societies. Again, Britain and America can be treated as essentially similar. Employment in these societies consists of a combination of market relationships and bureaucratic organization (Ouchi 1980). A person who is temporarily employed by the hour or the day to do a specific task can scarcely be called a member of an organization; the relationship is a purely market one, and nothing but a "cash nexus" holds the parties together. Some employment has been and still is of this nature, but more typical is a contractual relationship of some considerable length of time, whether fixed or indefinite. Employment of this kind renders the employee a member of the employing organization, with a specific place within its structure of authority. Long-term membership involves socialization into the ways of the organization, which may result in employees conceiving of sharing interests with the organization. Such a conception may be encouraged by the organization's management as a method of control.

Membership of an employing organization is understood to entail limited and specific obligations. Hours of work may be laid down by law or as the result of bargaining between employer and trade union, the work that can be expected may be more or less precisely specified in a job description. Beyond these specified obligations the organization has no claim on its members. However, the very difference between spot market employment and organizational membership is that in the latter case there is a grey area in which the enterprise may expect additional commitment, a preparedness to work for longer hours or on additional tasks if necessary. Nonetheless, even this grey area has conventional limits. It is recognized that members of employing organizations have also a "private life", theirs to organize as they see fit, which may not be infringed upon by the enterprise.

As we have seen, the distinction or continuum between spot market employment and long-term membership of an enterprise has gendered implications in Britain and America. As careers within organizations developed, the assumption that women's primary responsibility was to the household and its members was used as a justification for restricting organizational membership to men. Women might well be employed, but their "membership" of the organization was seen, by the employers and often by themselves too, as temporary. They were not expected to be able to give that extra diffuse commitment to the organization that full membership required. The present-day legacy of that gendered development is still strong, though more so in Britain than in America. Women are more likely to give up employment on marriage or childbirth and to return to work on a part-time basis, and those discontinuous work histories are seen by employers as less appropriate for long-term career building than the continuous commitment of men. Men may well have a private life outside the enterprise, but their lesser involvement in household affairs makes it more possible for the enterprise to invade that privacy when it feels it is necessary than in the case of women. As organizations become increasingly "greedy" (Coser 1974), these implications for the boundary between enterprise and household become more marked.

Employment in Japan also has aspects of market relationship and bureaucratic organization. However, it also often exhibits features that differ markedly from either of these forms. For many employees, especially of large companies, joining an organization is more like becoming a member of a moral community than a member of a bureaucratic organization. A number of writers have used different terms to capture this distinctive form of relationship, all of which align it with a form of kinship. Thus, Hsu (1975) sees the relationship of members to a wide range of organizations as a combination of contract and kinship for which he coins the term "kintractship". Murakami (1984) sees the corporation, and many other organizations in modern Japan, as having features in common with the traditional Japanese *ie*, which was, until its legal abolition in 1947, a synthesis of a patriarchal family household and an enterprise. And Ouchi (1980) draws on Durkheimian sociology in referring to the large Japanese corporation as a "clan". Membership means the embracement by the organization of the whole person of the employee, and the embracement by the employee of the culture, goals and values of the organization (Deutschmann 1987). Recruitment into the enterprise takes into account a range of personal characteristics beyond those related to the technical demands of the work (rather like adoption into an *ie*, a common form of recruitment in earlier times), training is more like socialization and moral integration into a cultural world (Rohlen 1974), and the commitment required of the employee virtually obliterates the distinction between company time and private time referred to earlier in the case of Britain and America. Similar "familial" features have also been remarked in the case of employment in small family businesses (Kondo 1990).

The gender implications are clear. Women, whose primary commitment is to their families, are unsuitable persons for incorporation into the moral community of the corporation. The corporation requires the commitment of the whole being of its long-term members, which women cannot reasonably be expected to supply. Women are appropriate only to fill temporary roles as routine workers until marriage, and thereafter, if family needs demand, as peripheral ones requiring no great commitment. Otherwise, recruitment of full members to the "clan" is quite rightly restricted to men. Even after the passing of equal opportunities legislation, firms see nothing unusual in explicitly discriminatory recruitment and promotion policies, and women who attempt to break into the clan find themselves, even more so than in the case of many male-dominated occupations in the West, "in a man's world".

Finally, employment in China, at least up until changes were introduced in the early 1980s, had no element of market relationship at all, except for the fact that some of the rewards for work took the form of individual wages. Otherwise, membership of a *danwei* was a requirement for the vast majority of the urban population, having economic, political and welfare aspects. Membership of a *danwei*, as explained earlier, was (and for many still is) a primary social identity, an all-encompassing and life-long environment of social opportunity and social control. In this sense, it has aspects in common with the large Japanese corporation, and it is not surprising that the *danwei* too has been compared with a traditional clan (Li 1991). But the gender implications are entirely different, for membership of a *danwei* is a requirement for men and women alike. The question of the primary commitment to either household or enterprise, in the case of China up to the reforms, did not arise. It is almost as if household and enterprise had not become differentiated, but that both family household and work-unit had taken on aspects of the functions and characteristics of both. In fact, for that significant minority of members who live in housing within the walls of the *danwei*, there is no clear distinction.

Thus, in all four societies, industrialization has brought about divisions and realignments of different aspects of the lives of people, which have had profound consequences for the work of men and women. In all four societies, it is possible, at a stretch, to analyze these changes using the functionalist language of the differentiation of household and enterprise. But this differentiation has taken different courses, and resulted in different structural forms and cultural assumptions, and created different contexts within which women with young children may (or may not) find themselves confronted with the dual burden of employment and family life.

Chapter 3

Women in paid work in four societies

Introduction Maybe use some stat?

In the previous chapter we have sketched the differing historical, cultural and political factors that have influenced the shaping of gender roles in the labour force and the domestic sphere in each of the four societies. In this chapter we outline the major features of the contemporary paid employment experience of women compared to men in each of the four societies, assess how these patterns compare and contrast across the four societies and how they are related to the institutional system of the wider society. As a guide through this mostly statistical material, we propose that the four countries can be arranged along a continuum, marking the order of difference of gender inequalities in labour market experience within each country. These gender differences are least evident in China, followed by the USA, then Great Britain and finally Japan, where gender differences are most pronounced. The several sources of data that are examined in this chapter, and which deal with patterns of labour force participation and life course involvement in paid work, occupational distributions, occupational earnings and hours of paid work all combine to sustain this image of a continuum. The most extreme contrasts in these patterns are generally found between the two Asian societies, and while the USA is closest to the Chinese pattern there are also important divergences between the two Western cases which deserve attention.

Patterns of labour force participation

Figure 3.1 depicts the pattern of labour force participation of women of different ages in each of the four countries. China displays by far the highest levels of female labour force participation from ages 20–45, the phase of the life course of specific interest to us in this work. It peaks between ages 25 and 40 at over 90 per cent and has a median value during the age range 20–49 of 89 per cent. This is very high by international standards and considerably greater than the USA where the equivalent median is 76 per cent. The Chinese figure falls precipitately from age 40, and after age 45 is in a similar region to the three other countries. The Chinese graph exhibits what is generally regarded as a sign of advanced economic development, in that it does not display the "M-curve" of participation over the life course which used to be typical of industrial societies but which has been disappearing in Western industrial countries in recent decades. There is no evidence in this data of the withdrawal of Chinese women from paid work during the childbearing years.

The US graph also exhibits a flattened curve of labour force participation. As in China, there is no dip in the participation rate during the childbearing years and indeed it continues to rise through the age range 20–49, even if at a slower rate after age 25. The US pattern is similar to Sweden's, which is perhaps the Western society where

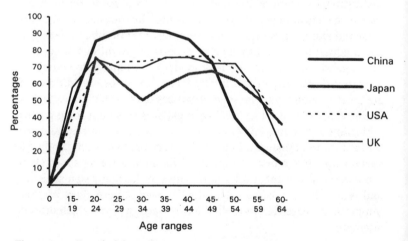

Figure 3.1 Female labour force participation rates by age in four societies (percentages)

women's labour force participation is least sensitive to age variations. The US rate of participation in the age range 20–49 remains considerably lower than that of Sweden (Brinton 1993), but even Sweden's levels do not reach those of China.

The graph for Great Britain still barely shows the classic "M-curve" with a fall in participation between ages 20 and 34. The fall of 5 per cent between the early and late twenties is small but places levels of participation in Great Britain below those of the USA by four percentage points during the age range 25–34. From ages 35 to 44 the rates for the two countries are identical at 76 per cent. That Britain's overall level of female labour force participation remains lower than in the USA was confirmed in a recent international survey that quoted the level for women under 65 to be 61 per cent in Britain and 64 per cent in the USA (Blanchflower & Oswald 1989). Both America's and Britain's female participation rates, however, fall below those of Nordic countries. The only Scandinavian country in the European Union, Denmark, has a higher rate, but Great Britain has the second highest figure of the 12 member states (OPCS 1993). According to a more recent report Great Britain had the highest female labour force participation rates in the European Union among women aged 20–59 (71.3 per cent in 1991), again with the possible exception of Denmark whose figures were missing (*Guardian*, 2 December 1993). In 1989 the UK rate was 67 per cent, the Danish 78 per cent and the EC median was 52 per cent (Meulders et al. 1993).

Japan displays the "M-curve" in a classic form with the steep dip in labour force participation by women after age 24. It falls to a subsequent minimum of 51 per cent at ages 30–34 but then recovers to converge on the other countries at the second maximum of 68 per cent at ages 45–49, although it is still below Great Britain (73 per cent) and the USA (77 per cent) at that point.

Because of variations in male participation rates a better gauge of gender differences in each society can be gained by comparing female participation rates to those of males in each age group in each society. Table 3.1 sets out these differences and demonstrates, particularly in the age range 20–50, that the magnitudes of gender differences are in the sequence following our proposed continuum. The divergences between male and female participation rates are very low in China, moderate in the USA, slightly higher in Great Britain and at their greatest in Japan. The median differences in the age range 25–49 are 7 percentage points in China, 16.0 in the USA, 19.9 in

Table 3.1 Gender difference in labour force participation rates in four societies (percentage points difference).

Age ranges	China	Japan	UK	US
15–19	2.0	2.4	3.6	0.8
20–24	3.5	0.2	11.6	6.0
25–29	6.0	36.2		15.8
(25–34)			24.3	
30–34	6.0	47.7		19.3
35–39	7.0	38.5		17.3
(35–44)			15.4	
40–44	8.0	31.5		14.0
45–49	23.0	29.5		16.0
(45–54)			19.9	
50–54	50.0	34.6		20.1
55–59	49.0	43.0	26.4	23.1
60–64	32.0	40.3	31.6	20.0
65–69	17.0	31.5		8.6
(65–74)			5.3	
70–74	17.0	24.4		7.2
75+	17.0	13.9		4.2
Medians age 25–49	7.0	36.2	19.9	16.0

Sources: International Labour Office, *Yearbook of Labour Statistics* (Geneva: ILO, 1992). Sheng (1991, Table 1).

Great Britain and 36.2 in Japan. The extreme cases are again the two Eastern countries, with China exhibiting relatively small gender differences in participation rates and Japan displaying relatively large ones. In the case of Japan these differences are at their greatest at ages 30–34, while many women are concentrating on domestic and child care roles, while in China they are at very low levels below age 45. Great Britain and the USA are in between these two extremes, with the USA again less distant from the Chinese pattern than is Great Britain. The dip in female participation rates in Great Britain in the age group 25–34 widens gender differences during this period markedly, whereas this is far less the case in the USA.

The female participation rates in Japan, Great Britain and the USA are heavily influenced by maternity experiences. The dips in labour market participation in early adulthood in Japan and Great Britain are associated with the birth of children, and the age of the youngest child is the best predictor of involvement or non-involvement in paid work. In the USA sources report that by the mid 1980s a half of women with a child under one year old were in paid work (Bergmann 1986, *too technical*

Hochschild 1990). Fuchs (1988) reports that in 1986 the same proportion of 50 per cent was apparent amongst mothers with youngest child under age 6. Official government figures for 1989 show that 58 per cent of partnered mothers with children below age 6 were in paid work (US Bureau of the Census 1991). The same figure is reported for all mothers of children under age 6 in 1991. For women with their youngest child aged 6–17 the figure was 74 per cent (Mishel & Bernstein 1993). For Great Britain the available statistics show slightly lower levels of participation. In 1989–91 48 per cent of mothers of children below 5 years old were in paid work or looking for it, as were 73 per cent where the youngest child was aged 5–9 (OPCS 1993). In Japan 34 per cent of mothers with children below age 6 were in paid work in 1987 (Saso 1990). This evidence, then, tends to be in conformity with the data presented earlier, suggesting that the Japanese situation diverges markedly from the cases of Great Britain and the USA, with a considerably stronger association of the mothering of young children with labour market withdrawal, and that the British pattern is slightly more distant from the Chinese one than is the American case.

This snapshot picture of female labour force participation in the four countries in the late 1980s and early 1990s needs also to be supplemented by an appreciation of patterns of change over time. The secular movement towards higher levels of female labour force participation and towards a flattening and eventual erosion of the "M-curve" is evident in the USA and the UK, as it is generally in Western industrial countries. This generalization, however, does not do justice to our Asian societies.

In China there is a sharp drop in female labour participation rates among women in their fifties, by which age it is lower than amongst women in the other three countries. In part this reflects the contrasting experiences of different cohorts of Chinese women. Women above this age are products of the pre-communist pattern and of the early years of the new regime. As fundamental social and economic reconstruction took several years after "Liberation" to take effect, it is only in recent decades that a cohort of women whose lives have been shaped by the new patterns of institutions and role definitions has attained middle age. In many ways the differentiation of female and male roles in the economic sector is minimized and delayed in China, unlike the other countries, until this phase of the life course. The drop in participation of women beginning at age 45 and becoming marked among women in their fifties leads, however, to a sharp divergence in male and female roles. The normal retirement age for women workers is 50. Women of this age are often eased aside from employment through early retirement schemes in small neighbourhood work-units or to make way for younger relatives, and spend this period of their lives in domestic roles, caring for elderly family members or grandchildren, and in voluntary public roles such as serving on street committees.

In the USA women's labour force participation rates have been growing throughout the twentieth century, and particularly in the second half of the century. Correspondingly the differences with male levels have been diminishing. From being 18 per cent of the labour force in 1900 (and most of these were unmarried women, as we have seen), women came to make up 43.5 per cent in 1983 (Bianchi & Spain 1986). Male participation in the labour force has been reduced largely through early retirement arrangements under privately and publicly funded schemes for men over age 55. Rates have remained consistently high amongst men in the prime working ages of 25–54. This is also the age group that has witnessed the most rapid growth among women in the post 1945 era. During the 1950s and 1960s this was largely the result of women over age 45 returning to paid work after childrearing responsibilities were completed. Since then the largest increases have been amongst women in their twenties and thirties, who have been postponing having young children or combining paid work with parental responsibility. Childlessness among women aged 25–39 rose from 18 per cent in 1960 to 28 per cent in 1986, and in the latter year 40 per cent of women in their late twenties were without children (Fuchs 1988). The participation rate for women aged 25–54 more than doubled from 35 per cent in 1950 to 67 per cent in 1983. The increasing likelihood of women returning to, or staying in work during this phase of the life course has led to the elimination of the classic "M-curve" and to the female graph being similar in shape to the male one but at a lower level. Successive cohorts of American women demonstrate increasing periods of involvement in paid work; the more recent the cohort the greater the proportionate time spent in the paid labour force. At the turn of the century women spent 13 per cent of their life-time in the labour force; by 1980 the figure was 38 per cent. Since the 1960s women have been increasingly likely to stay on in employment once they have commenced paid work. These trends mean that women's labour market attachment has become increasingly like men's. Women's working life expectancy compared to men's was 32 per cent in 1940, 59 per cent in 1970 and 76 per cent in 1980 (Bianchi & Spain 1986).

Patterns of change in women's life-time involvement in paid work in Great Britain have been following the American trends but with a substantial lag. The "M-curve" has become less and less pronounced in recent decades. The initial decline in participation following the first peak in the early twenties has become less steep and increasing proportions of women in their thirties and forties have been remaining in the labour force. Each succeeding cohort has been experiencing higher levels of participation. The proportions of women who leave paid work upon marriage have been reducing, from 37 per cent of those with a first birth in the 1940s to 12 per cent of those with a first birth in the 1970s. The proportions who had returned to paid work within one year of their first birth rose from 13 per cent for births in 1950–54 to 25 per cent in 1975–9. It was ten years after the first birth before half the mothers in the earlier of these two groups were in paid work, while it took only four years for an equivalent proportion of the latter group to reach this level of participation (Martin & Roberts 1984). In the SCELI sample for 1986, 27 per cent of mothers with children aged 1 or under were in paid work. If those unemployed and looking for work are included the figure rises to 35 per cent. The cumulative effect of these processes has led to the near disappearance of the British "M-curve" and its replacement by an almost flattened mid-life curve.

Japan is unusual, not only in the strength of the "M-curve" in the 1980s and 1990s, but also in its intensification in the 1980s. This is related to the process of urbanization and the accompanying decline of agricultural employment with its high female employment levels and its replacement by urban lifestyles, which encourage the withdrawal of many wives from paid work while children are young. The "M-curve" of an initial withdrawal from work and a return when children have grown up is particularly noticeable among employees (Brinton 1993). Whether this marked "M-curve" will be subject to patterns of change similar to those observed in the USA and Great Britain remains a moot point given the strong patterns of institutionalization of existing gender roles in the country. This marks Japan out as a case which may well not conform to the general trend in advanced industrial nations towards the gradual diminution of gender role differentials in labour force participation.

Occupations

International comparisons of occupational structures are often complicated by varying classification systems. This is a particular problem for the present study. The following section tries to make the best sense of the available data on this issue bearing in mind some of the major classification problems involved.

Women in China legally and constitutionally have formal equality with men in every aspect of social life, such as politics, education and employment, although actual opportunities sometimes do not correspond to this ideal. Table 3.2 outlines the basic occupational distribution by gender in contemporary urban China and Japan. The greatest disparity between male and female occupational patterns in China is in the sphere of government employment where only one in five employees is female. Women also tend to be under-represented in manufacturing and transportation. They are over-represented in specialist and technician occupations, the service industries and agriculture. For some historical and traditional reasons, there is still a shortage of women participating in governmental organizations, although the Chinese Women's Association Committee, with the support of party and government, has in the past few decades continually kept up its efforts to enable more and more women to join in political affairs.

Table 3.2 Distribution of occupation by gender in China and Japan (percentages).

Occupational group	China			Japan		
	Female	Male	All	Female	Male	All
Specialists and technicians	13.31	9.29	11.09	14.2	10.6	11.8
Government officers	1.87	7.61	5.04			
Administrative personnel				1.2	7.2	5.2
Office workers	3.52	5.13	4.41	33.7	16.6	22.7
Commercial workers	6.94	4.89	5.81	11.1	13.2	12.5
Service industry workers	8.85	4.64	6.53	11.1	3.5	6.2
Agricultural workers	31.72	26.60	28.89	0.5	1.1	1.0
Manufacture and transportation workers	33.66	41.72	38.11	28.1	44.9	38.7
Others	0.13	0.12	0.12	0.1	2.9	1.9
Total	100.00	100.00	100.00	100.00	100.00	100.00

Sources: State Statistical Bureau [*Guojia tongji ju*] (1988, calculated from Table 6.6); Japan Ministry of Labour (1986, Table 15).

As might be expected given the comparative levels of economic development of the two Asian countries, women in China are more likely than those in Japan to be employed in agriculture and manufacturing. According to these national statistics, just under one-third of Chinese women living in urban areas were engaged in agriculture, forestry and fishing (State Statistical Bureau 1988), figures which are very much higher than in the other three countries. However, it must be borne in mind that the "urban areas" concerned included large rural hinterlands surrounding the cities (for a discussion of definitions of urban areas in China see Chan 1994). By contrast, the areas from which the Chinese sample was selected did not include these rural hinterlands, and the level of agricultural employment among the respondents was insignificant. In Japan, rapid economic development in the post-war era led to a dramatic run-down in agricultural employment. Whereas in 1950 60 per cent of female workers in Japan were employed in agriculture, by 1980 60 per cent were employed in the tertiary or services sector. The shift of employment out of agriculture also led to a doubling of the percentage of female workers in the secondary or manufacturing sector from 13 per cent to 26 per cent in the same period (Brinton 1993).The classification system in Table 3.2 suggests that a similar proportion, 28 per cent, of female workers were in manufacturing in Japan in 1985, compared to 34 per cent in China. In both China and Japan males are more concentrated in manufacturing with the discrepancy between women and men proportionally greater in Japan. In Japan women are more likely to be employed in lower blue-collar than higher blue-collar occupations. While they constituted 13 per cent of precision, production, craft and repair occupations, they were 42 per cent of lower blue-collar operators and labourers in 1980. This latter group is less sex segregated than the equivalent American occupational category (Brinton 1993) and the British equivalents.

If manufacturing is a more important source of female employment in China than in Japan, it is in turn more significant in the latter than it is in Great Britain. Saso (1990) demonstrates that whereas in the mid 1980s only 10 per cent to 15 per cent of British female full-timers were in processing and assembly work, in Japan the comparable figure was 27 per cent. The greater overall relative importance of manufacturing in the Japanese economy makes it a more common source of employment for women than in the two Western countries. As Table 3.3 shows, in 1991 only 4 per cent of female workers in Great

Table 3.3 Distribution of occupation by gender in Great Britain (people aged 16 and over in employment 1991).

Occupational group	Men %	Women %	All persons in employment %
Managers and administrators	18	10	14
Professional occupations	10	8	9
Associate professional and technical	8	10	9
Clerical and secretarial occupations	7	27	16
Craft and related occupations	24	4	15
Personal and protective service occupations	6	14	9
Sales occupations	5	11	8
Plant and machine operatives	14	5	10
Other occupations	8	11	9
All occupations	100	100	100
All persons in employment (thousands)	14,407	11,194	25,601

Source: OPCS (1992).

Table 3.4 Occupations of civilian population by gender in United States, 1983 and 1989.

Occupational group	1983 Number (millions)	1983 % of each group female	1989 Number (millions)	1989 % of each group female
Managerial and professional speciality	23.5	41	30.4	45
Technical, sales and administrative support	31.3	64	36.1	65
Service occupations	13.8	60	15.6	60
Precision production/ craft and repair	12.3	8	13.8	9
Operators, fabricators and labourers	16.0	27	18.0	26
Farming, forestry and fishing	3.7	16	3.4	14

Source: US Bureau of the Census (1991, Table 652).

Britain, compared to 24 per cent of men, were in craft and related occupations, while 5 per cent of female workers, compared to 14 per cent of males, were in plant and machine operative positions.

Similar though less marked differences between male and female occupational patterns in manufacturing-related employment are evident in American data. Table 3.4 shows that just over one-quarter of operators, fabricators and labourers in the USA were female as were

Table 3.5 Occupational distribution of women and men in UK and USA (percentages).

Occupational group	UK		USA	
	Men	Women	Men	Women
Professional, technical and related	15.2	17.0	17.9	21.7
Administrative and managerial	8.4	2.4	14.2	11.0
Clerical and related	9.5	30.6	7.6	36.5
Sales	9.3	12.9	8.0	5.1
Service	6.1	23.7	9.3	13.8
Agricultural etc.	4.0	1.0	5.2	0.2
Production and related, transport and labourers	47.5	12.3	37.8	11.7
Proportion of total	58.8	41.2	50.6	49.4

Source: Dale & Glover (1990: 15).

just under one-tenth of precision, production and repair workers. Along with farming, forestry and fishing these were the occupational sectors with the lowest proportional representation of female workers.

Table 3.5 presents data from surveys using internationally consistent definitions that compare and contrast the occupational distributions of men and women in the UK and the USA. In both countries women are under-represented in production, transport and labouring, which are major areas of male employment, and the disparity is greater in the UK. Women in the UK are especially concentrated in services and in clerical and related occupations, but not to the same extent as in the USA with respect to the latter category. Women in the USA also seem to be far better represented in the top two categories of professional, technical and related and administrative and managerial staffs which together include almost 32 per cent of employed American women and 19 per cent of employed female Britons. Overall women seem to have achieved a higher position in the American occupational structure than in Great Britain. A similar conclusion was reached by an earlier analysis by Dex and Shaw (1986). Brinton (1993) has also shown that women have a considerably higher share of higher status occupations in the USA than they do in Japan.

A consistent picture emerges from these several sources. Manufacturing is more important for female employment in the Asian countries than in the Western ones and is proportionately more important in China than in Japan. It is an important source of employment for males in all the four societies but in China women seem to have achieved a greater foothold in this sector relative to men than is the case in the other countries. This is again a further indication of the lower degree of gender inequality in that country, especially given the significance of manufacturing in the country's political economy. Conversely, manufacturing is the least common sector for female employment in Great Britain and, although problems of comparability of occupational and industrial classification hinder the exercise, it can be stated with some confidence that women have a greater role in manufacturing in Japan than they do in the USA and Great Britain. In both Britain and the USA, women are particularly under-represented in the more skilled manual, heavy labouring and routine production occupations. In Japan, the USA and Great Britain the more skilled manual occupations are dominated by men.

The converse of these differences in patterns of occupational distribution between the four countries is the relative importance of service occupations for male and female employment in each country. This sector is least important in China where just over one-quarter (27 per cent) of female employment was in this sector in 1987, compared to 69 per cent in Japan and 82 per cent in Great Britain (Sheng 1991). The different classification system in Table 3.2 shows a smaller services sector in China but, if commercial and office workers are added to that category, the combined group comes to 20 per cent. Service employment covers, of course, a wide range of activities, but in each country women are more concentrated in this sector than men.

Routine office employment in Japan is a major source of female employment but seems to be less an exclusive female enclave in Japan than in the two Western countries. Table 3.2 indicates that one-third of female workers were office workers. Brinton (1993) reports that 55 per cent of clerical workers were female in Japan in 1980 and that the category of administrative support occupations was 53 per cent female, the second highest figure among seven categories of occupational groups. In Great Britain 33 per cent of all working women and only 6 per cent of men were in clerical jobs in 1980 (Martin & Roberts 1984). On the basis of these figures women correspondingly constituted 70 per cent of clerical workers. Lockwood (1989) estimated the relevant figure in 1981 to be 75 per cent. In 1990 the British Labour Force Survey estimated 78 per cent of incumbents of clerical and related occupations to be female (OPCS 1992). In the USA 80 per cent to 90 per cent of routine office jobs are filled by females

70

(US Bureau of the Census 1991), and clerical and related work provides employment for 36.5 per cent of all employed women (Table
3.5). Dale and Glover (1990) present data which suggest that in both
the USA and the UK women were statistically over-represented in
clerical and related occupations by 70 per cent compared to men in
1983 and 1984. Definitional differences prevent precise comparisons,
but some tentative conclusions can be offered for the four societies as
a whole. Office employment lags in development in China where it
seems least gender segregated. In Japan, too, there is still a substantial male clerical workforce; 16.6 per cent of male workers were office
workers in Japan in 1985 compared to the 9.5 per cent of British male
workers and the 8 per cent of American male workers indicated in
Table 3.5. Just as Japan's patterns of female labour participation are
different from the West, so too the process of the feminization of
clerical labour, which has been such a feature of Western development in the twentieth century (Lockwood 1989, Goldin 1990), has not
proceeded as far. Possibly clerical positions in Japan play different
roles for female and male employees (as has been suggested for Great
Britain), in that for young men they are a first step up the occupational ladder whereas for women they are more likely to be the first
and last career steps. This is very likely to be the case in Japan given
the previously described pressures for women to leave paid employment after marriage or childbirth.

Sales employment, where nearly one-quarter of female employees
are concentrated, seems most heavily female in Great Britain, and the
disparity with males is considerable especially compared with the
USA (see Table 3.5). An index of occupational segregation by sex indicates that women in Great Britain are statistically over-represented in
sales occupations by 20 per cent, whereas in the USA they are under-
represented to the same degree (Dale & Glover 1990). In both the USA
and Japan men still predominate in these areas but they are important areas of female employment (Table 3.5 and Brinton 1993).

While in each society examined here women lag behind men in
employment in the manufacturing sector and are heavily concentrated in routine lower status white-collar employment, a significant
sector of female employment is also to be found in higher level
white-collar occupations. Generally women seem to have difficulty
penetrating the top levels of public administration and production
management but they are found in substantial numbers in higher
status professional occupations, especially those in the personal and

social services. In urban China and Japan they are statistically over-represented compared to men in specialist and technician roles (13 per cent compared to 9 per cent in urban China and 14 per cent compared to 11 per cent in Japan, see Table 3.2). In both China and Japan educational occupations are a major source of higher level female employment, and women are disproportionately represented in such occupations. In the Chinese survey 10 per cent of respondents compared to 5 per cent of husbands fell in these categories. In Japan the respective figures were 23 per cent compared to 12 per cent. In both countries, however, similar proportions are employed in the "free" professions, such as doctors, lawyers, artists and religious specialists.

There are some similarities too with the position of women in the higher reaches of the British occupational structure, which can be seen from Table 3.3. Furthermore, the category of "professionals and related in education, welfare and health" comprised 14 per cent of women working in Great Britain in 1990, compared to only 5 per cent of men. The combined other higher status occupational categories of "professionals and related supporting management and administration" and "professionals and related in science, engineering, technology and similar fields" and of managers comprised 12 per cent of female workers and 30 per cent of male workers. Women are thus less likely to be in these higher status occupational groups (26 per cent of female workers compared to 35 per cent of male workers) but are much more concentrated in health, welfare and education professions (OPCS 1992).

In the USA, women similarly constitute 54 per cent of workers in professional and related services, a category which includes the education, health and welfare services (Dale & Glover 1990). This compares with the 67 per cent of British workers in the (not exactly coincident) category of professionals and related in education, welfare and health (calculated from OPCS 1992, Table 5.10). A measure of the greater occupational achievement of women in the USA compared to Great Britain is the much higher representation of American women in the category of "administrative and managerial employment", which lies between "professional, technical and related" and "clerical and related". The index of occupational segregation by sex (where unity means equality between the sexes, values higher than 1.0 mean statistical over-representation and values lower than 1.0 mean under-representation) yields values for the administrative and managerial category of 0.9 for the USA and 0.4 for the UK. Thus, in the

USA women are considerably better represented in higher status non-professional occupations than are their counterparts in the UK.

In summary, the occupational patterns of women in each country are a product of the occupational structure of each society and of gendered processes of allocation to positions. Reflecting these processes, women in China are most likely to be in manufacturing and agriculture and have an occupational distribution that is the least divergent from the male pattern. Women in Japan are more frequently found in manufacturing than is the case in the Western countries. Skilled blue-collar employment tends to be dominated by men in each society, although this is less the case in China. Concentrations of female employment in each society are found in professional employment in education and social services, in clerical and office work and in sales. British women are particularly concentrated in services and clerical employment and have not penetrated the higher level white-collar jobs to the same extent as American women. While it is not possible to propose a definitive order, the evidence presented is consistent with the view that while marked differences are to be found in each society examined in this chapter, China has the least occupational gender segregation and the USA is more egalitarian in this respect than the UK. Although Japan is less egalitarian than China, the different patterns of occupational distributions make it difficult to reach a conclusion as to where it might fit along this scale (Brinton 1993).

Occupational earnings

Having examined gender differentials in labour market participation and occupational distributions in each country we now turn to differences in occupational earnings. In so far as the differential opportunities for labour force involvement for women compared to men reflect the differential valorization of women's paid employment compared to men's in each society, it should be expected that these differences will be reflected in earnings as well as these other characteristics. Following our proposed continuum, gender differentials in earnings should be lowest in China, second lowest in the USA, second highest in Great Britain and the greatest in Japan.

In China, due to the policy of a high rate of employment, of low income and low consumption, incomes are usually quite low.

Although, since the economic reforms of the post-Mao era, some people who run private businesses have become richer, Chinese personal incomes still range around 100 to 200 yuan per month. Even so, there remain some considerable differences between men's and women's incomes. Among the respondents to the Sino-Japanese survey, only 17.9 per cent of wives had an income higher than their husbands', whereas over half of the husbands had incomes higher than their wives'. The average annual income for men was 1,348 yuan compared to 1,255 for women. Women's annual income was thus 93.1 per cent of men's. But what is remarkable on a comparative international basis is that 29.2 per cent of the sample had annual incomes within 100 yuan of their partner's.

Despite these gender differences in China, it seems that Chinese women enjoy a higher degree of income equality than Japanese or British women. Only 5.5 per cent of Japanese women had a yearly income equal to or slightly higher than their husbands', whereas husbands' income was usually much higher than their own. The average annual income for men was 3,716,280 yen, but for women it was 1,768,260 yen, only 47.58 per cent of men's income. Because the Sino-Japanese survey concentrates on parents of young children, it does not provide a general picture of gender differentials in earnings. Data from other national surveys accumulated by Saso (1990) and Eccleston (1989) suggest that female earnings are in the order of 50 to 60 per cent of male earnings, a finding which is not inconsistent with the previously reported data since the earnings of mothers of young children are more likely to be based on lower status and lower paying occupations.

For British women, the situation is somewhat better than in Japan. The median weekly earnings for female workers was £132.90 in 1987, compared with £198.40 for male workers. So women's weekly earnings were just 67 per cent of men's, which breaks down into 57 per cent for part-time and 74 per cent for full-time working women. Long-term studies show that women's earnings as a percentage of men's were stable for a long period from the early decades of this century, in the range of 56 to 60 per cent of male earnings, until a sharp increase resulted from the Equal Pay Act of 1970. A new stable differential emerged thereafter, with women's hourly earnings being just under three-quarters of men's, and women's weekly earnings being approximately two-thirds that of men (Reid & Stratta 1989).

Webb (1993) has also demonstrated that increases in women's labour market participation have increased women's share of household earnings from 21.8 per cent in 1971 to 32.8 per cent in 1991.

Elias calculated that, in 1980, 9 per cent of wives in dual full-time earning partnerships earned more than their husbands and 5.5 per cent earned the same as their husbands (Reid & Stratta 1989). In the SCELI data collected seven years later, among similar couples with young children, only 3.4 per cent of employed female respondents had net earnings equal to or greater than their male partners'. Even among respondents who worked full-time, this proportion only reached 10.5 per cent.

The available evidence for the USA suggests that women's pay rates are closer to those of males than is the case in Great Britain. For full-time workers over age 24, female weekly and hourly earnings are 70 per cent of male earnings (US Bureau of the Census 1991). Bianchi and Spain (1986) report that, among the full-time year-round workers aged 25–34, a group of importance for our international comparisons, women's annual income and earnings in 1982 were 72 per cent and 71 per cent respectively of comparable male figures. Fuchs (1988) reports that women's hourly earnings in the 1980s were 67 per cent of men's and that this ratio had grown from 0.45 in 1890 to 0.60 in 1930. Blanchflower and Oswald (1989) also confirm that the inequality in earnings between women and men is slightly greater in Great Britain than the USA.

Corresponding to these gender differences in earnings in the USA, the earnings of wives in paid work have been reported in 1991 to be 69 per cent of their working husbands' earnings. Amongst all families, including those with non-working spouses, wives' contributions to family income rose from 27 per cent to 31 per cent during the period 1970–91, largely reflecting the rise in female full-time participation rates in the 1980s. Where wives work full-time they contribute 41 per cent of family income. In families with the youngest dependent child under age 6 or between ages 6 and 17 they contribute 30 per cent of family income. In 1991, 29 per cent of wives in dual earner couples earned more than their spouses (Hayghe 1993).

From these several sources, we may reasonably conclude that the differences in earnings between male and female workers are most markedly low in China, followed by the USA, then Great Britain, and at their greatest in Japan.

Part-time and full-time work

The distinction between part-time and full-time work is an aspect of employment that is vital for understanding the labour market and occupational position of women compared to men, and which has especial significance during the phase of the life course when there are young children in the family. It is, however, a distinction that is institutionalized in the three capitalist societies but has little meaning in China. Male employment in each of the societies is generally based upon the concept of the standard job of full-time paid employment for a full working week over an extended period from early adulthood to retirement in early old age. The earlier cited data on female labour market participation rates are organized around contrasts with this male model. For various reasons, among which is their greater individual responsibility for domestic work and child care, women diverge from this model. Again China is the case where this divergence is minimal. The introduction of state socialism after Liberation in 1949 entailed the development of a system of production, distribution and exchange which, as well as reconstructing employment relations, also minimized the extent to which women diverged from the male model. In a sense the standard model for employment became de-gendered as female and male workers were employed on the same basis regardless of their parental and domestic situation. The sample for the Sino-Japanese survey in China may have over-emphasized the official and formal structure of employment and neglected unofficial types of employment, but nonetheless it tells much about the patterns of employment in this very significant area of the economy. In the official employment sector the eight hour working day was the norm for all workers; 83 per cent of both female respondents and their spouses worked an eight hour day and only 1.5 per cent worked less than five hours. Eighty-nine per cent of the respondents and 93 per cent of their spouses worked eight or more hours a day. There was thus a slight tendency for women to work fewer hours than men but the overall distribution of hours of paid work between the sexes was very similar. The six day working week was also the norm for these workers. Judged by this data China has achieved a substantial de-gendering of the employment experience. Differences between men and women in labour market participation rates over the central years of the life course, in hours of paid work and the length of the working week are small or non-existent. This situation is all the more remarkable when compared to the other three countries where substantial and significant gender differences are apparent in each of these characteristics.

As we described earlier, Japan provides the most dramatic contrast with China in the life-time patterns of involvement in paid labour. Differences are also apparent in daily hours of paid work. Saso (1990) reports that 31 per cent of employed Japanese mothers work part-time (less than 35 hours per week by Japanese definitions). The median daily hours of paid work of our Japanese sample was seven and a half hours, compared to eight hours and fifty minutes for the spouses. Thus, there is an important differentiation between male and female Japanese workers in their hours of paid work, but the female workers also tended to work long daily hours even if they were considered to be part-time employees. The greater incidence of part-time work among female workers in Japan, and the disparity between hours of work of men and women, is associated with a change in women's employment status in Japan associated with marriage and childbirth. Almost all the Chinese respondents, and their husbands, had regular work status, with full employment rights. Women may take maternity leave for up to two years while retaining their employment position and seniority rights, though in the sample three-quarters took six months' leave or less. Women's employment position in China is thus relatively unaffected by maternity. In Japan, however, most women interrupt their employment careers when they have children, and consequently suffer an employment downgrading when they resume paid work. The Sino-Japanese survey covers only that minority of women in Japan who engage in paid work while they have young children, but in this sample only 39 per cent had worked continuously since leaving school, compared to 84 per cent in China. Corresponding to this only 37.5 per cent of the Japanese sample had regular worker status; 41 per cent had temporary worker status and 21.5 per cent were working in private family enterprises. Most women, 57 per cent, had left off work at marriage or pregnancy. Those who remained in full-time work were much more likely to retain regular worker status. Fifty-nine per cent of part-timers, but only 21 per cent of full-timers, had experienced a work break. The full-timers had thus managed to retain their more advantaged employment position, and two-thirds of them were regular workers compared to only 4 per cent of part-timers. The latter were much more likely than the full-timers to be in temporary positions of a short-term or long-term nature or in private family enterprises. Seventy-four per cent of the part-timers had returned to paid work after a break associated with marriage or childbirth, compared to only 39 per cent of the full-timers. The small minority of Japanese mothers who maintain their full-time employment position while having children continue to occupy relatively advantaged employment positions, but the majority of women who work during this phase of their life course experience a break in their employment careers and return later to paid employment of a part-time and less well-protected and rewarded character. Compared to the Western countries, as we shall see, the Japanese part-timers worked relatively long hours, not all that short of a full-time job in many cases, for as Saso (1990) has emphasized the part-time job in Japan marks a less protected and rewarded status in the workplace rather than a reduced load at work. Their low status is reflected in their low pay rate; among survey respondents, part-timers earned 562 yen per hour compared to 1,215 yen for full-timers. Part-timers are also much more likely to be in industrial, service, commercial employment or transport whereas full-timers are much more likely to be in professional employment and education. The findings from the Japanese survey are then in conformity with the observations of other research and the summary statement of Ueno (1988: 180) that

part-time workers work just one or two hours less a day than full-time workers. Though they are often asked to work nearly as long as full-time employees, they are paid less only because they are categorized as part-time employees. Thus, part-time employment is now used as an excuse to utilize women's labour at low cost.

The experience of part-time female workers in Great Britain, and its contrast to full-time work, bears many analogies to the Japanese situation we have just depicted, but one major contrast requires emphasis at this point – the much shorter hours of paid work undertaken by British women, especially part-timers. Table 3.6 shows hours of work for males and married and unmarried women in Great Britain in 1990–91. Non-married women work a median of 37 hours per week compared to 43 hours for men. Married women, by contrast, work a median of 31 hours. Part-time work is heavily concentrated among married women, particularly those with young children. Amongst such women in the SCELI sample, 35 per cent worked less than 15

Table 3.6 Usual hours worked per week by sex and marital status (of women) in Great Britain (people aged 16 and over, Spring 1991) (percentages).

Usual hours worked per week*	Men	Married women	Non-married women	All persons
0–8	2	7	9	4
9–16	2	15	8	7
17–24	1	17	7	7
25–30	2	10	6	5
31–34	1	4	3	2
35–40	34	30	45	34
41–44	14	7	9	11
45–50	23	6	8	15
51–60	13	2	3	9
61 and over	7	2	1	5
Not stated	1	0	1	1
	(100)	(100)	(100)	(100)
All persons in employment (thousands)	14,407	7,825	3,369	25,601

Note: *including paid and unpaid overtime but excluding meal breaks.
Source: OPCS (1992, Table A6.18).

hours per week and 74 per cent were part-time (30 or less hours per week). The median length of working hours among mothers of young children in the British sample was 21 hours, compared to 34 hours in the Japanese sample. Part-time work for the mothers of young children in Japan is thus a much more onerous commitment in terms of time required at work than is the case in Great Britain.

Alongside this major difference, there are a number of similarities between the position of part-timers compared to full-timers in the labour markets of Great Britain and Japan. Having a young child is particularly associated with part-time work. When working mothers of young children are in paid work, they are more than twice as likely to be in part-time as full-time work, whereas women with no dependent children are more likely to be in full-time work than part-time work. There are also differences among the typical labour market experiences of women during this phase of the life course. Those women who continue in full-time paid employment while they have young children tend to be of disproportionately higher occupational status. In 1989–91 34 per cent of women in professional, employer or managerial occupations who had young children under age 5 were in full-time work, compared to 13 per cent of all such mothers and

2 per cent of unskilled manual women workers. The professional and managerial group is the only one amongst which full-time jobs are more common than part-time ones. Part-time employment is more evenly spread among all socio-economic groups apart from a heavy concentration among unskilled manual workers (OPCS 1993).

The tendency of British women who are in part-time employment when they have young children to have a considerably lower occupational status than those who continue in full-time employment was evident in SCELI data. Two-thirds of the employed mothers of young children were in part-time work and well over half of them (57 per cent) were in routine non-manual – largely clerical – employment in administration and commerce and in rank and file sales and services occupations. Semi-skilled and unskilled manual work were the second most common types of employment for these workers. In contrast, those in full-time work were far less likely to be in routine non-manual office, sales and services jobs, although at 30 per cent it was still the second most common category. The most common occupations for full-timers are those in the second highest ranked category of the Goldthorpe class schema: lower professionals, administrators and officials, higher technicians, managers in small business, industries and services and supervisors of non-manual employees. In practice they are probably concentrated in occupations such as teaching, nursing and social work, the human welfare services (Dex 1987). Just as in Japan, there were also clear differences in the pay levels available to women in the two types of employment. The median gross hourly pay rate for all the relevant samples in Great Britain was £2.40, but 73 per cent of the full-timers and only 37 per cent of the part-timers earned more than this. The median hourly rate of pay for full-timers was £4.30, but for part-timers it was £2.25. The median hourly rates of part-timers compared to full-timers was 0.52 in Great Britain compared to 0.46 in Japan. Part-timers in Great Britain thus not only worked fewer hours than their equivalents in Japan but also were less disadvantaged in terms of the relative hourly earnings compared to full-timers.

The growth of female employment in Great Britain in recent decades is particularly associated with the growth of part-time employment. The incidence of full-time paid work has remained almost static, at 41 per cent of the non full-time student female population, while the proportion in part-time paid work has risen from 19 per cent to 32 per cent in the period 1971–91. This rise has largely been concentrated among women with dependent children. Among comparable men the rate has risen from 1 per cent in 1971 to 5 per cent in 1991 (Webb 1993). Labour supply considerations have played a major role in the rise of part-time paid work among women. It is the type of paid employment that is most compatible with the major responsibility for undertaking domestic labour and the care of young children, and we will go further into this in the next chapter. But there are other institutional, policy and labour demand factors as well. Individuals earning less than £3000 pay no income tax, so many women, including perhaps a majority of part-timers, avoid this liability. There are also considerable incentives for employers to recruit part-time workers. First, there is a ready pool of potential recruits who do not wish to undertake full-time paid work because of their existing commitments. Secondly, employers find part-time workers cheaper to employ, since many of them are not covered by various occupational benefits such as sick pay or pensions and they are not required to pay employer contributions under the National Insurance scheme. Thirdly, many part-time workers do not qualify for various forms of employment protection. To qualify for redundancy pay, maternity pay and protection against unfair dismissal they have to work at least 16 hours a week for the same employer for at least two years. They are also far less likely to be in trade unions than other employees and are thus perhaps more amenable to management control (Beechey & Perkins 1987). For a variety of reasons, then, the part-time paid work option is exceptionally common in Great Britain among mothers of young children.

In the USA, too, women work fewer hours of paid work per week than men. In 1980 the male median was 39 hours and the female median was 37 (Bianchi & Spain 1986). Dale & Glover (1990), comparing Great Britain and the USA on the basis of 1983 and 1984 social survey data, argued that while American women's hours of paid work per week bunched around 40, those in the UK were bi-modal with a major peak between 36 and 40 hours and a minor peak below 20 hours. Another study based on 1985–6 data demonstrated a much greater differential in median weekly hours of paid work in Great Britain compared to the USA. While male workers in both countries averaged about 44.5 hours per week, women workers in Great Britain worked 31 hours, compared to the 38 hours of female American workers (Blanchflower & Oswald 1989). Although the basis upon which these different calculations were made varies, the overall data do not challenge the conclusion that gross gender differences in hours of paid work are smaller in the USA than in Great Britain. As in Great Britain and Japan, American women were more likely to be in part-time paid work than men; 32 per cent of employed women and 13 per cent of equivalent men worked fewer than 35 hours per week in 1980, using one common American definition of part-time work (Bianchi & Spain 1986). According to Dale & Glover (1990), and in conformity with the previous source, 24 per cent of employed women and 10 per cent of employed American men worked part-time. The comparable British figures were 42 per cent and 2 per cent respectively. As in the other two capitalist countries, part-time work in the USA is also more likely to be undertaken by married women and women with young children. In 1986 25 per cent of married women in paid work, compared to 13 per cent of the non-married, were in part-time jobs of less than 30 hours per week, and 29 per cent of employed women with children less than 6 years old were in part-time work, compared with 19 per cent of women without children under that age (Fuchs 1988). Fox and Beller (1993) provide similar figures on the basis of a 1987 national survey. In Great Britain by contrast, 70 per cent of employed mothers with the youngest child 0–4 and 5–9 were in part-time work by this definition. Employed mothers of young children in the USA are thus much more likely to be in full-time paid work than is the case in Great Britain.

The relative unimportance of part-time employment for women in general and mothers of young children in particular in the USA may account for the general lack of attention given to it. Holden and Hansen (1987) make a similar observation but note that studies of labour supply are an exception. Hochschild's important and influential *The second shift* (1990) is based upon the assumption that women's paid work is in full-time paid employment, and major surveys such as Bergmann's *The economic emergence of women* (1986) and Andersen's *Thinking about women* (1988) do not explore part-time work in any depth.

Table 3.7 compares the full-time and part-time occupational distributions of female workers in the USA and the UK according to internationally standardized classification schemes. Female part-time employment in the USA is of a lower occupational status than full-time employment, in particular with a higher concentration in service employment. In Great Britain the differences in the occupational distributions suggest a wider gap in occupational status between the

Table 3.7 Occupational distribution of full-time and part-time employed women, UK and USA (percentages).

Occupational group	UK Full-time	UK Part-time	USA Full-time	USA Part-time
Professional, technical and related	20	13	22	18
Administrative and managerial	3	1	13	6
Clerical and related	38	21	37	35
Sales	10	16	5	6
Services	13	38	11	23
Agricultural etc.	1	1	0	1
Production and related, transport and labourers	15	9	12	11
Total employed	(100)	(100)	(100)	(100)

Source: Dale & Glover (1990: 22).

two types of employment with an even higher concentration of part-time employment in services and lower representation of part-timers in the top two occupational categories.

As in the two other capitalist countries the American hourly rates of pay for part-time workers are considerably lower than those of full-time workers. The median rates for those on hourly earnings, regardless of gender, were $4.83 for the former and $7.83 for the latter, a ratio of 0.61 (US Bureau of the Census 1991). Another source (Mishel & Bernstein 1993) gives a ratio of 0.76 for the hourly earnings of part-time female workers compared to full-time ones. This ratio is not as unequal as Great Britain and is even less so than Japan.

One reason why the full-time paid work option is more common in the USA among the mothers of young children may relate not only to the higher status and pay available in these jobs, but also to the associated benefits, in particular health insurance. In Great Britain health care is mainly available as a social welfare benefit through the National Health Service, and is not primarily occupationally based. Americans seeking medical insurance mainly obtain it through employment-related schemes; 59 per cent of the population receive their health insurance in this manner. Part-time workers are far less likely to have such benefits. Only a quarter of part-time employed female family heads are included in employer health plans, compared to three-quarters of full-time female family heads, and even the part-timers who are enrolled are more likely to be paying their own contributions than having them paid by their employer (Mishel &

Bernstein 1993). Health benefits are thus a further major incentive to full-time paid employment amongst American workers.

Part-time work is thus a common feature of women's employment, but not of men's, in the three capitalist countries, and is particularly common among mothers of young children. However, there are important differences between them. In Japan part-time employment usually involves close to full-time hours but has low occupational status, security and pay. Great Britain is distinctive in that part-time employment with low average hours (21 hours per week) is the typical form of employment for such women, whereas in the United States, as in Japan, near full-time hours are the norm for such women. In China, part-time work is not an option though, as we will see later, there is a potential demand for it among mothers of young children.

Patterns of child care

It is evident from the discussion so far that patterns of child care in each society are major influences upon the life-time course of labour market participation and patterns of involvement in paid work during the phase of the life course when workers are parents of young children. Men, however, seem far less affected by such factors than women. In each society being a father to a young child has less impact on labour force patterns and careers than does being a mother. The impact of maternity differs however by degrees in each society, being at its minimum in urban China, its second lowest in the USA, its second greatest in Great Britain and its greatest in Japan.

The national differences in female labour force patterns that have been identified derive in large part from the differing institutional arrangements into which women and men are socialized and in which they make decisions as to partnership, having children, continuing or interrupting labour force participation, and making arrangements for the care of their children within the range of facilities available. The contrasting institutional arrangements that provide the structure within which these decisions are made result from varying patterns of purposive policy and non-decisions at national governmental, company, local community, enterprise and family levels. Understanding these various structures and the factors influencing their development is essential for understanding the differential gendered patterns of labour force involvement that have been outlined above.

In China, women's advances to workplace and labour force equality with men are associated with the rights that they enjoy in the workplace and their relation to the phase of the life course when they are pregnant or mothers of a young child. Prior to the reform period which began in 1978, women were entitled to 56 days maternity leave during which they received full pay and retained their employment position and seniority. The reforms have created greater diversity and it is no longer so easy to generalize about all urban areas in China. Regions and work-units now have the flexibility to extend the maternity leave period for up to two years, with 75 per cent pay in the first year and 50 per cent pay in the second year, though much will depend on the relative affluence of the city or work-unit. Beneficiaries of more extended leave schemes retain their employment position but may lose out on seniority rights. The one-child policy also has the effect of minimizing the influence of such work breaks on employment careers (Croll et al. 1985). In the Sino-Japanese survey, almost three-quarters of the Chinese respondents took six months' maternity leave or less, 21 per cent took six months to one year and only 5 per cent took more than one year. These data suggest that there has been a move towards longer periods of maternity leave compared to the practice of Chinese women before reform, when only 56 days of maternity leave was allowed.

After the period of maternity leave, Chinese women normally go back to work and the social child care facilities or grandparents then take over the responsibility of caring for the children. The facilities for child care, such as kindergartens and child care centres are well developed in China, especially in the urban areas. They have been developed for essentially two sets of reasons: the practical economic one of relieving parents from child care responsibilities to concentrate on their work, and the political and ideological one of increasing the state's influence on the socialization of the younger generation (Sidel 1972, Broyelle 1977). There are three main sources of pre-school child care services: first, they may be provided by the state (city government) on a formal basis and with well-qualified staff; secondly, they may be provided by the woman's work-unit, in which case they will be considered as part of the worker's benefits and thus be relatively cheap because subsidized by the work-unit; thirdly, they can be provided by the street residents' committee, and although these are usually very small and with poorly qualified staff, they are often more convenient because they are closer to the woman's home. They may also provide both weekly and daily baby-sitting services in order to meet the needs of two-career parents. It was recently reported by the *Chinese Daily* that over 60 per cent of Chinese children below 6 years of age are cared for in these above-mentioned forms of child care facilities. The rate is considerably higher in urban centres. In urban Beijing 74 per cent of the age group attended pre-school in 1983 (Tobin et al. 1989). In urban China, then, there is a much more extensive network of pre-school child care than is found in the other societies examined in this book. The system is also unique in providing extensive nursery facilities for very young infants (*tuo'ersuo*), administered under the Ministry of Health for children from 2 months old to age 3. Kindergartens (*you'eryuan*) are preparatory pre-primary schools with a more educational orientation. About 5 per cent of Chinese pre-schoolers are boarders in child care centres, where they lodge through the week, going home at weekends. Full day care or weekly boarding is necessary in these cases to allow both parents to work full-time (Tobin et al. 1989).

In Japan, the nursery and kindergarten education movement has an extended history of concern with the welfare and development of children, and pre-school provision does not necessarily relate to the issue of women's employment. Despite the great emphasis upon maternal caring for children and the extensive discouragement of mothers from paid work (which we will consider further in Chapter 5), an 80-year-old system of nationally structured pre-schools provides at least one year's service to the vast majority of pre-schoolers. Forty per cent of 3 year olds and over 90 per cent of 4 and 5 year olds attend some form of pre-school. Two-thirds of the children are in kindergartens (*yochien*) which are open five hours a day and which generally cater for better-off non-employed mothers. They are regulated by the government Department of Education and are private operations, which may have student/staff ratios as high as 40:1. The other third, usually the children of working mothers, attend full-time day care facilities or nurseries (*hoikuen*) which are open eight hours a day, which are regulated by the Department of Health and Welfare and which accept children from infancy (Hendry 1986, Tobin et al. 1989, Simmons 1990). Part of the rationale for nurseries is that they allow both parents to be in paid work if it is necessary in their circumstances. The government sets the curriculum, licenses teachers and subsidizes the pre-schools, while parents pay means-tested fees. Government financial assistance is available to low income parents towards fees in either sector and government grants contribute towards teachers' salaries. Attempts to produce a comprehensive and uniform system have met resistance from interest groups, including the separate pre-schools themselves, and conflicts between the sponsoring government departments and the Department of Finance seeking to control public expenditure. Local government administrations are not required to provide these services (Schoppa 1991). *Yochien* and *hoikuen* are not regarded as forms of educational preparation although there is pressure from some parents for the *yochien* to move in this direction. Pre-schools provide a way of influencing mothers in the bringing up of their children, for example through the encouragement of learning at home, as well as influencing the development of the children themselves more directly. The classes are large with average student/teacher ratios of 30 or 40 to 1. There is little academic instruction. The main educational purposes are to encourage social values of co-operation, group solidarity and empathy with, and concern for, others and to develop pre-academic skills such as perseverance, concentration, ability to function as a group member and a positive attitude to learning. Pre-schools are regarded as places of fun and play to be enjoyed before the rigours of the formal educational system commence. The *yochien* offer children and mothers a rich environment providing release from the pressures of intense face-to-face interaction in the confined space of the typical home, and help create relationships between otherwise isolated housewives and children. The *hoikuen* provide a form of child care for the children of working parents superior to what might be provided in other settings. The pre-school sector also provides considerable employment opportunities at low wages for more educated young women who often engage in this employment for a few years before marriage or childbirth after having received a training in child psychology, physical education, music and the arts (Tobin et al. 1989, Simmons 1990). The Japanese example is of considerable interest in that it demonstrates that a high level of pre-school child care need not necessarily be associated with a high level of paid employment among the mothers of young children. It can meet the needs of nonworking parents as much as those of employed parents, and may be provided for educational and welfare purposes independently of the employment obligations of parents. The existence of pre-school child care does not always lead to higher levels of paid employment amongst mothers.

In Great Britain and the USA in recent years the issue of the public provision of pre-school child care has largely revolved around the question of freeing parents, especially women, from the demands of the care of young children in order to facilitate their engagement in paid work. The provision of pre-school child care in Great Britain has a chequered history. With the development of the system of compulsory schooling from 1870 onwards substantial proportions of children under age 5 have been accommodated in the schools. By 1900, 41 per cent of 3 and 4 year olds were enrolled in school. Disquiet over the conditions of these schools led to discouragement of attendance by such young pupils in the early twentieth century. The enrolment rate had fallen to 13 per cent by 1930 (Whitbread 1972). These changes were probably also associated with the growing emphasis upon the importance of care of young children by the mother and the increasing importance of the housewife role and the male breadwinner norm in the early twentieth century (Pahl 1984). Despite formal endorsement of expanded public provision in major educational acts and reports in 1933, 1944 and 1964, this has not been a priority area for public funding (Whitbread 1972, Dex & Shaw 1986). Provision on a day care, rather than an educational basis, was expanded considerably during the Second World War, but the development of secondary education was given priority over pre-school education in subsequent decades. This in its turn made it possible for many mothers to return to paid employment in part-time jobs compatible with the school timetable.

In the 1970s and 1980s, as more women sought to continue in paid work after childbirth, pre-school child care became an increasingly significant political issue. Margaret Thatcher, as Secretary of State for Education, issued a 1972 White Paper which recommended nursery education for 50 per cent of 3 year olds and 90 per cent of 4 year olds before 1982. During her premiership from 1979 to 1990 some limited progress was made in this direction. In 1988 35–40 per cent of children aged between 3 and the school entry age of 5 were reckoned to be covered by publicly funded pre-school provision (Meulders et al. 1993). In 1991 25 per cent of families with children under the school age of 5 used school or nursery school child care. A similar percentage used unpaid family or friends. Amongst those in full-time paid work, informal arrangements such as employing childminders or nannies (38 per cent) and unpaid family or friends (36 per cent) were more common than school or nursery school (29 per cent). Only 3 per cent had a workplace facility. Part-timers were more likely (35 per cent) to use schools or nursery schools because of the part-time provision that is generally available in them and were far less likely to use paid childminders or nannies (15 per cent). Schools and nursery schools and unpaid family and friends are used roughly equally across all socio-economic groups although unskilled manual families lag in the use of unpaid family and friends. Only 18 per cent of families headed by unskilled manual workers used unpaid family and friends compared to 25 per cent of all households. Private and voluntary schemes and paid childminders and nannies are used more by white-collar socio-economic groups and this is particularly so amongst professionally headed families. While 20 per cent of families with children under 5 in households headed by professional workers used paid childminders or nannies, only 3 per cent of unskilled manual workers did (OPCS 1991). In the absence of a permanent comprehensive full-time system of day care, parents, usually the mother, have to organize their paid employment around the needs of the care of their children using whatever package of public, voluntary, family, commercial and other informal assistance can be mobilized. Pressures such as these lead to many women engaging in part-time work or not working at all, and make it very difficult for all but the most well resourced to undertake full-time employment. Thirty-six per cent of families of children under age 5 make no use of any of these facilities whereas paid childminders and nannies are largely utilized by the more prosperous households. Similar pressures operate, although perhaps less intensely, when children start regular schooling. After-school-hours care and vacation care schemes are not well developed and many women have to arrange to cater for their children in these out-of-school hours and holidays. This is one reason why many more educated women have sought employment in education, since it enables their work timetable and calendar to correspond with those of their children.

American parents are more likely than British parents to be able to take advantage of formal child care arrangements such as nurseries, kindergartens, crèches, play groups and social services facilities while they are at work, but even in the American case only 17 per cent of younger employed mothers aged 14–24 and 9 per cent of those aged 30–44 were able to use such facilities in 1978. The equivalent British percentages were 11 per cent and 6.6 per cent respectively (Dex & Shaw 1986). Tobin et al. (1989) estimate that there are about one million slots for the eight million American pre-schoolers. UNESCO (1992) data for the late 1980s indicate that 61 per cent of American children are enrolled in pre-school programmes, compared to 51 per cent of British children. The relevant figures vary because of the differing basis on which they are collected but they do not challenge the general conclusion of the greater availability of formal pre-school child care facilities in the USA compared to Great Britain.

Data from official US federal government sources for 1989 show significant proportions of pre-primary school enrolments in various types of provision. The overall enrolment rate of 45.4 per cent of 3–5 year olds had reduced by four percentage points since 1978. Among 3 and 4 year olds the percentage had risen from 36.7 per cent in 1980 to 39 per cent in 1989. The enrolment rates were 27 per cent for 3 year olds, 51 per cent for 4 year olds and 86 per cent for 5 year olds. Private nurseries and public kindergartens were the major forms of provision with the latter slightly more numerous, but only 8.5 per cent of nursery provision and 11.7 per cent of kindergarten enrolment was on a full-time basis. As in Great Britain and Japan, many of the available places are half-day ones. Black and white enrolment rates were similar, but children of Hispanic origin lagged by 13 percentage points. The highest enrolment rates of 62 per cent were found among women in part-time work, suggesting that the part-time care that these institutions provide is more suitable to their needs, or that the availability of part-time care led to part-time work. Rates of enrolment among children with mothers in full-time work (55 per cent), unemployed mothers (53 per cent) and mothers not in the labour force (52 per cent) did not vary much (US Bureau of the Census 1991). The age of the child thus seems to be by far the most important factor affecting the availability of forms of pre-school child care. Formal arrangements for the care of children below age 3 are rarely available.

Provision of child care facilities by employers is limited, with only 11.1 per cent of employment establishments providing child care benefits or services, and with larger establishments and government agencies more likely to provide them. Only 2 per cent of private sector and 9 per cent of government establishments provide sponsored day care. Similar small proportions provide assistance with child care expenses. The more common types of assistance are counselling and information. By far the most important type of assistance is in the form of flexible work scheduling, and 61 per cent of establishments provide such opportunities, with flexitime, voluntary part-time work and flexible leave being the most common arrangements. In establishments of over 100 employees, only 3 per cent of employees are entitled to paid maternity leave and 1 per cent to paid paternity leave; 37 per cent have unpaid maternity leave and 18 per cent have unpaid paternity leave arrangements (US Bureau of the Census 1991).

Given the limited employer, voluntary and government support for child care, individuals, as in Great Britain, have to organize their own packages of care for children while they are in paid work. Inevitably this means a substantial reliance on market provision, and the ability of parents to provide this assistance is heavily dependent on family income. About a quarter of mothers in their twenties who are not in paid work are prevented from doing so by child care problems. This proportion is considerably higher among the poor, minority women, the poorly educated and those with large families (Mishel & Bernstein 1993). While 67 per cent of children with family incomes over $35,000 attend pre-school, the figure is 40 per cent for family incomes in the range $11,000–35,000 and 5 per cent among those families with income less than $11,000 (Tobin et al. 1989). Family child care costs vary from $1,500 to $15,000 but the average for those who use it is $3,000 (US Merit Protection Board 1991), which may eat up one-third of the annual earnings of someone on the minimum wage (Tobin et al. 1989). This compares with child care costs amounting to 10 per cent of the earnings of employed mothers of children under age 6 with earnings over $30,000 (Mishel & Bernstein 1993). Because of limited public and voluntary provision and the cost of commercial care, informal sources of care such as other family members, friends and neighbours and childminders are used much more frequently overall (Dex & Shaw 1986, Tobin et al. 1989) and are probably relied on to an even greater extent by poorer parents. There is evidence that the use of child care centres for pre-school children has been rising considerably during recent decades, from 6 per cent of working parents in 1965 to 28 per cent in 1990. Child care by parents themselves is of equal quantitative importance, increasing from 23 per cent in 1985 to 28 per cent in 1990. Increased labour market work by mothers, increased child care by fathers and more flexible work scheduling by both parents are probably responsible for this trend (Mishel & Bernstein 1993).

Parents' use of commercial child care in the USA is facilitated by the availability of tax credits which allow them to offset child care costs against taxation liabilities. Only about half of the states allow such arrangements, but Dex & Shaw estimate that many families, especially those in the states with more generous schemes, obtain reimbursement for 20–25 per cent of their child care expenses through the combined effect of federal and state tax credit arrangements. In 1978 three million families claimed some reimbursement under these programmes (Dex & Shaw 1986). These provisions undoubtedly assist parents in higher status occupations to give their employment the priority which it usually demands and contribute towards the higher occupational status of female workers in the USA compared to Great Britain and Japan.

UNESCO data for 1990 on comparative enrolment rates for pre-primary education in the four countries suggest that the lowest rate of provision was that in China at 25 per cent of pre-school children. Like many other social services in China, these facilities are heavily concentrated in the cities where the rate would be much higher, as indicated above in relation to Beijing. Aside from this problem of uneven spread in China, the USA is recorded as having the highest level of provision of the other three countries at 61 per cent in 1989, a figure, of course, higher than that stated above from official US sources. The UK is recorded as having a rate of 51 per cent and Japan 48 per cent (UNESCO 1992). In all four societies parents have to utilize the available facilities to the full by developing individual packages of care for their children if they wish or are socially obliged to maintain themselves in paid employment while they have young children. The Chinese pattern of both parents working full-time is supported by the widest provision of formal facilities for the care of young children, but even there, as we shall see, other family relatives often play a role in supplementing these arrangements. In Japan there is a substantial network of pre-school child care, although the comparative data suggest that it is the least well provided of the four countries. Although female employment patterns are most distinctive and least well rewarded compared to men's in Japan, *hoikuen* do allow poorer blue-collar women to engage in paid work while they have young children. But as the case of the *yochien* demonstrates pre-school child care can reinforce traditional separate gender spheres of home and paid employment by supporting the housewife role rather than by encouraging paid employment. In Great Britain, the USA and Japan substantial numbers of mothers of young children do not engage in paid work while caring for them although this is most common in Japan and least common in the USA. Those parents who do engage in paid work in Great Britain and the USA use considerable resources to obtain care packages for their children during working hours. Relatives, friends and neighbours provide the most common sources of care but official provision of various types supplements these arrangements and would appear to be more available and more favourable to women pursuing higher status occupations in the USA.

Standard and non-standard employment in four countries

In an important essay, Goldthorpe (1985) examined the dualism between what he called the "industrial citizenship" found among the core employees of large-scale business organizations and the several forms of non-standard employment which then appeared to be of growing importance. On the one hand advanced industrial economies exhibited a tendency towards a standard pattern of the organization of production and employment. This model drew heavily upon the work of Clark Kerr and his colleagues (Harbison & Myers 1959, Kerr et al. 1973, Kerr 1983) and suggested that

> in order to meet requirements of reliability and predictability, production would increasingly be carried out according to one standard pattern: namely the large scale bureaucratically-organized enterprise, run by a professional management team and regulating its workforce through a complex "web of rules" that are in substantial part negotiated "constitutionally" with union representatives . . . A long term historical shift in the direction of this pattern may perhaps be recognized even if with a wide and persisting degree of cross-national variation (Goldthorpe 1985: 141).

This model of standard primary employment clearly requires revision in the light of a number of factors, particularly the lessening numerical and political importance of unions in advanced capitalist economies in the 1980s and 1990s and their lack of independent negotiating power in state socialist systems such as China. Nonetheless, the large-scale private and public sector bureaucratically administered enterprise with privileged employment conditions for a large segment of core employees remains a central and defining feature of advanced industrial economies and is to be found in each of the societies in this study. The privileges of this primary sector of employment include relative security of employment and higher pay and benefits than other types of employment. Gender was an unspoken feature of the earlier formulations of this thesis and was broached but not fully developed in Goldthorpe's version. However, as several other writers (Barron & Norris 1976, Hewitt 1993) have stressed, and as we discussed in Chapter 2, this model of primary sector employment was based upon types of permanent full-time employment of indefinite duration that have tended in the West to be dominated by men.

Goldthorpe did not spell out the employment system associated with this model in any great detail, but its features are emphasized by a contrast with the characteristics of the converse type of employment which he labels as "non-standard", and which in its extreme form corresponds to the spot market for labour which we discussed in the previous chapter. These secondary sector types of employment provide the labour market and the firm with flexibility in hiring and disengaging members of the workforce and also serve the purpose of protecting the security of employment and conditions of primary sector employees as firms confront the vagaries of market conditions. Migrants, out-workers, sub-contractors, "married women with young children, juveniles, semi-retired persons, peasant-workers and various others seeking 'second' jobs", constitute the members of this secondary labour force and

> what members of these groups have in common is that their commitment to the work they have taken on tends to be strictly limited and, in turn, their expectations of what they will be able to derive from it: typically they have other sources of identity and satisfaction, and also perhaps of economic support (Goldthorpe 1985: 143).

Of the four societies examined in this chapter, urban China is the one that has most comprehensively attempted to place all adults on a formally equal basis in primary sector bureaucratic employment, although the conditions in state enterprises were always superior to those in neighbourhood collectives, and the economic reforms are now producing greater diversity in employment characteristics. Formal gender distinctions in employment rights and opportunities have been minimized. In theory, and to a large extent in practice, especially compared with the other three societies, women have been incorporated equally with men into the standard employment relationship which is based on permanent full-time, life-long work and is enmeshed in a "web of rules". Their employment careers over the life course, their weekly hours of paid working, their earnings, their occupations and their employment status all approximate to men's much more closely than is the case in the other three societies. Widespread institutional child care facilities, combined with financial imperatives and social obligations to engage in full-time paid work are among the key reasons for this outcome. This is not to say that women have achieved full equality with men in every respect (Stockman 1994). The earlier retirement of female workers is one indication of the problems in this respect and this issue is developed further elsewhere.

Japan, a neighbouring Asian society with a significantly overlapping cultural tradition for much of its history, exhibits the greatest degree of contrast to the Chinese situation. Gender much more sharply differentiates employment patterns. The incorporation of women in paid employment is on a very different basis from that of men; they are largely a secondary labour force fitting closely to Goldthorpe's model and providing a great degree of flexibility to firms and the economy by their movements into and out of employment as their domestic situations change. Their earnings exhibit the lowest ratio compared to men of the four societies studied. Their employment careers are very episodic, still ending for many upon marriage or childbirth. Even while a reasonably extensive system of pre-school child care exists these facilities are often seen as an aid to non-employed housewives and an institution for child development rather than a means of facilitating the employment of mothers. Many women take employment breaks when they have young children, resume paid work when they are older, but are placed in lower status, considerably less well-paid jobs with poor conditions and often near full-time hours despite being designated as part-time workers. Labour market and organizational flexibility provided by the labour force exits and entrances of women contributes to the overall strength of the Japanese economy, and also enhances the security of employment of the core primary male workers in the permanent employment systems of the large corporations and organizations. For instance, after the oil shock of 1973, economies in labour costs were achieved by lower levels of female labour market participation, as firms did not re-employ women returners to the labour market (Brinton 1993). Women also disproportionately provide the labour force of small firms and family businesses which sub-contract from large organizations. These are the sectors that provide additional labour requirements in times of boom and absorb many of the cutbacks at times of recession. Primary sector employment in Japan is more male dominated than is the case in any of the other three societies in this study. At best, women are only marginally incorporated into this sector, mostly as young single employees, infrequently as older single persons and frequently as part-time workers with poor conditions and low pay.

Great Britain is close to the Japanese model but has higher levels of female labour force participation and a less accentuated "M-curve". In both countries women begin their employment careers in full-time employment but their patterns of labour force participation are subsequently interrupted by the consequences of childbirth. Limitations in child care facilities in both societies place the main burden of child care upon parents, and this usually means mothers. While more mothers of young children return to paid work in Great Britain, it is primarily to part-time jobs which have, on average, considerably shorter weekly and daily hours than their Japanese equivalents, and much shorter than men's working hours in Great Britain. Part-time workers in Great Britain provide a cheap form of labour since they are not covered by forms of social protection. They also provide a form of labour market flexibility in that many employers have sought to expand their workforces considerably over recent decades by taking on part-timers. Standard bureaucratic employment in the primary sector is largely dominated by men but women have made inroads into such positions in human service professional occupations.

The USA has moved furthest of the three capitalist societies towards equality between women and men in labour market patterns, but it still falls far short of the Chinese model. Women in the USA have higher levels of labour force participation than in Britain and Japan and their work histories are less interrupted by childbearing; they are more likely to be in paid work when they have young children and to be in full-time jobs rather than part-time ones; their rate of hourly earnings is closer to the male figure, they work longer weekly hours than British women and, on average, they have a higher occupational status relative to men than do Japanese and British women. Women in the USA have thus achieved a greater representation in primary sector standard employment than have women in Great Britain and Japan.

Chapter 4

Family life in urban societies

Introduction

The varying patterns of gendered labour force participation outlined in the previous chapter are associated with varying patterns of domestic organization. The particular mode of organization of domestic relations in each society is likely to facilitate certain patterns of labour force involvement by household members. Conversely, the commitment of labour force participants to their employment will also have major implications for their domestic roles. The articulation between the household and the economy and the obligations that are placed upon individuals with regard to domestic roles and labour force involvement are also likely to be shaped to some degree by national institutional structures and policies and by governmental and institutional assumptions and "non-decisions" about the organization of these spheres which were investigated in the previous chapter. This chapter explores the interrelationship between the domestic and labour force spheres from the domestic perspective. We do not assume a strict determination of one by the other but rather that there are patterns of reciprocal interaction. We focus on the variations in patterns of domestic organization and decision-making that are evident between the four countries and analyze them as resulting from differing national and organizational policies, social and cultural assumptions, and the efforts of individuals and partners to shape their lives within the institutional and social relationships in which they are enmeshed. We examine how households organize such essential domestic functions of reproduction and maintenance as child care, cleaning, cooking and shopping in the context of differing gendered employment regimes and household structures, and the extent to which varying patterns of labour force involvement influence the domestic division of labour and the relative domestic power of husbands and wives.

Despite the variations between societies it is important to bear in mind one important constant finding that is evident in each society – the fact that the primary burden of domestic labour falls upon wives. Even in the most egalitarian case of China, women do most of the household work. Rarely do men undertake most of the domestic work or take on the major responsibility for running the household. When they do participate it is usually by sharing duties in conjunction with their wives. While husbands tend to play the greater role in the labour force in each society, the domestic sphere tends to be centred upon the wife. There are nonetheless significant national differences in the gendered division of domestic labour and patterns of domestic decision-making. This chapter begins with some of these contrasts in relation to the roles of husband and wife in the care of children and the performance of essential household tasks. It then considers the pressures of combining paid work and domestic work among parents of young children in the four societies, and examines the roles of grandparents and parents in managing these pressures, first for the Asian cases and then for the Western societies. A final section examines the part-time employment option in Great Britain as a way of coping with these pressures and its implications for domestic labour roles and decision-making.

The division of domestic labour: cross-national contrasts

Child care

In a modern industrial society arrangements for the care of young children are essential if parents are to concentrate on their occupations. The informal patterns of pre-industrial societies when young children accompanied parents or relatives as they went about their work are less appropriate when maximum attention is required of workers to their occupational role. The continuing and increasing concern in industrial societies to maximize the productivity of the workforce requires institutional arrangements that will free parents from the need to supervise and care for their children while in employment. Presser (1988) found in an American national survey that just 6 per cent of full-time and 10 per cent of part-time employed mothers of young children cared for their children at work, a phenomenon probably restricted to small family enterprises and paid work at home. Societies have developed varying solutions to this pressure for the separation of employment and child care, relying to varying degrees upon specialized child care institutions and various types of domestic or family arrangements. Western societies, despite the constant drive to increase the productivity of the workforce, still generally attach great significance to close parental involvement in the care of children (Mason & Kulthaur 1989) and a large share of this responsibility falls on parents.

In each of the four societies, discussions and assumptions about child care while parents are in paid employment frequently reflect the association of females with the domestic sphere. Mothers are generally presumed to have greater responsibility for the care of young children. Fathers' work histories are relatively unaffected by childbirth and caring for young children, while mothers' are affected more, but to varying degrees in each society, as was shown in Chapter 3. It is the mother's rather than the father's involvement in paid work that is generally regarded as rendered problematic by the care of children. The employment patterns of men generally assume that their children are being cared for, while this is not the case for women (Finch 1983). This assumption was reflected in the construction of the Sino-Japanese survey, as it is in much of the analysis and debate of these issues in the West. Thus, the survey itself assumes that specific social problems surround women's employment and questions on care of children while parents were working related exclusively to mothers. In each of the societies the husband's employment receives priority, being relatively unencumbered by child care and domestic concerns, and the wife's employment is secondary in having to be fitted around household and child care responsibilities. Nonetheless there remain important variations in these broad patterns between societies. In the previous chapter we explored differing national patterns in the provision of formal and community child care services. In this section the focus is upon the varying arrangements for the care of children during the times they are within the family home.

Among the respondents to the Sino-Japanese survey, formal institutional means of child care were the major way in which pre-school children were looked after while the mother was in employment. We know from the previous chapter that institutions play a much greater role in urban China and that most Japanese employed mothers work long hours that are facilitated through the use of child care facilities. This predominance of formal child care arrangements in our samples is also an artefact of the sources of the data, since the Chinese and Japanese respondents were recruited at child care centres. Despite this, there was some variation in the ages of the respondents' children. In China, 7.1 per cent of the children were below 3 years old, 87.4 per cent between 3 and the age of starting school (normally 6) and 5.5 per cent were attending school; in Japan, the corresponding figures were 23.1 per cent, 45.2 per cent, and 31.7 per cent. The school-age children were predominantly older siblings of the child who brought the respondent into the sample. This age variation allows us to identify certain differences in patterns of child care according to the age of the child. About two-thirds of children under age 3 in both societies were cared for in kindergartens, child care centres or nurseries. Forms of family care provided a subsidiary source of assistance. Other adults in the family (13 per cent of cases in China, 7 per cent in Japan) and grandparents who resided apart from the respondents (8 per cent in China and 7 per cent in Japan) were also alternative sources of care for these young children. Among older pre-schoolers institutional care was overwhelmingly dominant in both countries while the mother was working (97 per cent of cases in China and 86 per cent in Japan).

The use of formal child care arrangements for pre-school children is much higher in these findings than is the case for employed mothers in Great Britain and the USA where relatives, particularly husbands in Great Britain, play by far the most numerically significant role. In addition, it is amply documented that most employed mothers of pre-school children in the USA and Great Britain use informal care arrangements (Dex & Shaw 1986). A more recent survey found that formal child care centres were used by only 18 per cent of employed mothers of young children in the USA and that fathers (11 per cent) and other family relatives (29 per cent) were the most common type of carer (Veurn & Gleason 1991). Another source estimates that 28 per cent of American pre-school child care is provided in child care centres and almost half is provided by parents (28 per cent) and relatives (19 per cent) (Mishel & Bernstein 1993). These authors attribute the recent rise in parental care (from 23 per cent in 1985) to the increasing role of fathers as more mothers engage in paid work.

Fox and Beller (1993) provide similar figures for the relative importance of different types of employment-related child care. Mason and Kulthaur (1989) also note the deeply entrenched cultural preference in the USA for employment-related child care to be entrusted to parents or close relatives.

Data from the British SCELI Household and Community Survey showed that just over half of employed mothers of pre-school children relied upon relatives to look after their children while another half utilized forms of institutional day care, of which the most common (just under 20 per cent of cases) was a state nursery school. (Because some respondents used more than one source of care these forms of care can total more than 100 per cent.) Of the relatives, husbands were the most important. Two-thirds of the relatives in Aberdeen were male partners or husbands. Dex & Shaw (1986) also demonstrate that the husband is the relative most frequently providing child care in Great Britain, although this is less common in the USA. The husband's role in childminding while the mother is in paid work is particularly associated with part-time work performed while the husband is at home outside of his working hours. While the evidence is not definitive it supports a view that employed mothers of young children in the Asian countries are more able to utilize formal child care provision than is the case in the Western countries where they have to (or prefer to) rely more heavily upon informal family-based care.

Respondents in the Sino-Japanese survey were also asked questions that give revealing insight into how responsibilities for children were handled in the two societies. These reveal a pattern of greater sharing between parents in China and a sharper segregation of gender spheres in Japan, a pattern evident in many other aspects of family life. Japanese mothers were much more likely than Chinese mothers to care for young children at home alone; 63 per cent of the former and only 20 per cent of the latter undertook this task alone. This responsibility was undertaken jointly by husband and wife in China much more frequently than in Japan (43 per cent compared to 12 per cent). Exclusive husband responsibility was very rare. Similar patterns were evident in relation to the bringing up, disciplining and education of children, with joint responsibility being the most common form in China (44 per cent compared to 9 per cent in Japan) and mother's responsibility being the most common in Japan (37 per cent in Japan compared to 24 per cent of Chinese cases).

In the British SCELI data there is evidence about how responsibilities for children's education and care are allocated between parents. Respondents were asked how children were helped with their homework: 61 per cent replied that both partners helped equally, 26 per cent said that the female partner was mainly or entirely responsible, and 12 per cent said the male partner did it. When asked who has ultimate responsibility for looking after the children, 57 per cent said both parents equally and 43 per cent said the female partner. Research on national US samples (Goldscheider & Waite 1991) indicates that husbands shoulder 45 per cent of household child care time. Other work demonstrates, however, that the major responsibility for organizing this falls upon the mother (Peterson & Gerson 1992).

In summary, in each society mothers have the major responsibility for the domestic labour of caring for and bringing up children. Japan has the most extreme degree of exclusive female responsibility in this respect. In the other three societies there is evidence of substantial involvement of husbands in child care. Exclusive responsibility rarely falls upon the male in any of the societies, but the limited evidence does support the view that the husband's role in domestic-based child care is greatest in China, least in Japan and in intermediate positions in the two Western countries.

Housework

Similar national patterns and contrasts are evident in the distribution of other household labour. These can be clearly demonstrated first for the polar cases of China and Japan. The Chinese and Japanese respondents were asked about their husband's role in household work (see Table 4.1). In 9 per cent of the Chinese households, but only 0.5 per cent of the Japanese, husbands did most of the household work and, whereas 67 per cent of the Chinese wives reported that husband did the housework "together with" the respondent or "shared" it (compared to 4 per cent of the Japanese), 30 per cent of the Japanese men did "almost no housework" and a further 56 per cent "helped wife out when she was busy" or "when there was no alternative". More evidence about the details of husbands' and wives' roles in the division of domestic labour tasks in three of the countries is displayed in Table 4.2 which indicates the degree to which various domestic labour tasks are shared between husband and wife or

Table 4.1 Husband's role in household work in China and Japan.

Husband's role	China F	%	Japan F	%
Undertakes most household work	175	8.5	9	0.5
Does housework together with wife	868	42.0	52	3.0
Shares housework with wife	513	24.8	11	0.6
Shares less housework than wife	153	7.4	80	4.6
Might help wife when busy	204	9.9	539	31.2
Does a little when no alternative	94	4.5	433	25.2
Does almost no housework	58	2.8	510	29.5
No husband	3	0.1	93	5.4
Missing	4		138	
Total	2,072	100.0	1,865	100.0

Source: Sino-Japanese Working Women's Family Life Survey.

Table 4.2 The division of domestic labour tasks in China (C), Japan (J) and Great Britain (B) (percentages of each country).

Task	Female, entirely or mainly C	J	B	Both C	J	B	Male, entirely or mainly C	J	B	Other C	J	B
Washing-up	36	91	53	36	3	36	20	1	5	8	5	6
Cleaning the house	47	89	77	39	6	17	10	2	3	4	3	3
Washing clothes	43	92	94	44	4	5	9	2	1	4	2	0
Cooking	35	94	77	37	2	19	13	1	4	15	3	0
Shopping	38	92	77	39	3	18	15	1	4	8	5	1

Note: The data on shopping for Great Britain come from the Aberdeen survey only. *Sources:* Sino-Japanese Working Women's Family Life Survey; SCELI.

undertaken mainly by one or the other. The patterns are clearly much more egalitarian in China than in Britain, and are most gender-differentiated in Japan. There is a common tendency in each country for women to undertake these tasks, and in no case are husbands more likely to take the entire or main responsibility for the task than are the wives. The differentiation is at its most extreme in Japan where women are entirely or mainly responsible for washing-up, cleaning the house, washing clothes, cooking and shopping in nine out of ten cases. China is the most egalitarian, having the lowest proportions of wives exclusively or mainly responsible for these tasks and the most substantial degree of sharing. Britain occupies an intermediate position but is somewhat closer to the Japanese case.

It might be suggested that the greater degree of sharing of domestic labour in China is due to the obligation upon both partners to engage in full-time paid employment. This might require both partners to engage fully in domestic labour in order to accomplish the essential duties. This suggestion is only partly borne out by comparison with data from Japan and Great Britain. The effects of dual full-time employment upon the division of domestic labour between the partners in those two countries is presented in Table 4.3. In both countries where the female partner is in full-time employment, defined as more than 30 hours per week, there is a slightly greater degree of male participation in domestic tasks than is the case where the female partner is engaged in part-time paid work. In Japan dual full-time paid employment only very slightly increases the proportion of households where males have the major responsibility for domestic tasks and those where both are responsible. Even in such households in Japan, however, domestic tasks are undertaken exclusively by nine out of ten women. There is a more marked shift towards male participation when the wife is in full-time paid employment in Great Britain, but even here women are responsible for the bulk of domestic tasks and the shift is towards both partners undertaking the task rather than them being done exclusively by the male. Even when their wives are in full-time work, British men continue to be particularly averse to washing clothes.

Table 4.3 The division of labour tasks in Japan (J) and Great Britain (B) by hours per week employed of female partner (percentages).

Task	Female, entirely or mainly		Both		Male, entirely or mainly		Other	
	J	B	J	B	J	B	J	B
Female partner employed more than 30 hours per week								
Washing-up	90	40	4	40	1	10	5	10
Cleaning the house	86	65	7	27	2	4	5	4
Washing clothes	90	91	5	9	2	0	3	0
Cooking	93	70	3	21	1	7	3	2
Female partner employed less than 30 hours per week								
Washing-up	96	62	1	33	0	2	3	3
Cleaning the house	98	87	1	10	0	2	1	1
Washing clothes	98	97	1	2	0	1	1	0
Cooking	99	82	0	16	0	2	1	0

Sources: Sino-Japanese Working Women's Family Life Survey; SCELI.

Table 4.4 Division of domestic labour tasks in China, USA, Great Britain and Japan (female partner employed full-time only).

| Task | Who undertakes the task? (percentages) | | | |
	Female partner	Both equally	Male partner	Other
Cleaning the house				
China	47	39	10	4
USA	62	36	3	0
Great Britain	65	27	4	4
Japan	86	7	2	5
Washing clothes				
China	43	45	9	3
USA	69	22	9	0
Great Britain	91	9	0	0
Japan	90	5	2	3
Cooking				
China	35	37	13	15
USA	74	20	7	0
Great Britain	70	21	7	2
Japan	93	3	1	3

Sources: Sino-Japanese Working Women's Family Life Survey; SCELI; Mederer (1993).

To bring America, where a higher proportion of wives in dual-earner households work full-time, into the comparison, Table 4.4 presents evidence from surveys from all four countries on households where both partners are in full-time paid work. In relation to cooking the American pattern is remarkably close to the British one. American men take a greater responsibility for the laundry and for cleaning the house than do the British although again this is more in terms of sharing the duties than taking on exclusive responsibility for them. Their roles in these respects are, though, still comparatively far less than those undertaken by Chinese men, and far greater than Japanese. If dual full-time employment work patterns were the main factor behind a greater role for male partners in domestic labour tasks, it would be difficult to explain such wide variations between societies. This suggests that deeper institutional and cultural forces are at play.

From this initial discussion of the domestic division of labour as it relates to child care and the undertaking of household tasks it is proposed that China and Japan represent polar cases among the four societies under analysis. Just as China had the least differences of the four between husbands and wives with respect to labour force patterns, so it has the least differentiation between them with respect to household roles; and just as Japan had the greatest differences in the former, so it had the greatest differences in the latter. While there was the greatest overlap of male and female spheres in paid employment and the household in China, there was the least in Japan. Further, the USA with its closer approximation to the dual full-time employment model among husbands and wives seems closer to the Chinese example, while the British case lies somewhere between the US and Japanese examples with respect to female opportunities in the labour force and male involvement in the household. The analysis now moves to a closer examination of household labour and decision-making in each case, beginning with the polar Asian cases.

Dual burdens: Asian contrasts

Even though the Chinese wives report considerable assistance from their husbands, they still face a major dual burden of domestic and social labour. Daily time budgets obtained from the Chinese and Japanese respondents reveal notable differences. The average Chinese woman worked for her unit for almost eight hours. Travel to work accounted for a further 72 minutes and housework for two and three quarter hours. Around 12 hours of the day was thus consumed by employment and domestic work. After just over seven and a half hours of sleep and just over an hour spent eating at home, the Chinese women were left with two hours of "leisure". While these data were collected by not particularly rigorous methods (they were obtained by asking respondents how much time they were involved in these activities on a working day), they nonetheless give a reasonable estimate of the allocation of their daily time. The use of the same method also allows contrasts to be made with Japan. The Japanese respondents were, on average, employed for just over one hour less a day and the time taken to travel to work was half that of the Chinese. The Japanese respondents spent almost 30 minutes longer a day on housework, perhaps because of their shorter employment time and because they had less male assistance. The hard-pressed daily round of the Chinese respondents is evident in the fact that the daily leisure time of the Japanese respondents was nearly double that of the Chinese, almost four hours. The data also suggest that the Chinese respondents slept longer, as much as 45 minutes per day more than the Japanese respondents. This might also be taken as an indication that they were more tired by their daily labours.

The greater pressure on the Chinese women is suggested by several other responses: 32 per cent of the Chinese, but only 13 per cent of the Japanese, found their employment very tiring and 40 per cent of the Chinese, compared to 16 per cent of the Japanese, stated that their hours of work were too long; 36 per cent of the Chinese and 29 per cent of the Japanese claimed that they did not get enough sleep; 63 per cent of the Chinese, compared to 38 per cent of the Japanese, felt that housework was a very heavy or heavy burden. When asked which aspect of their life they would want to spend more time on if they could, 20 per cent of the Chinese, but only 3 per cent of the Japanese, mentioned housework and child care; 25 per cent of the Chinese and 20 per cent of the Japanese said that they would want more time on their own at home. The Chinese sought more time for basic personal and family functions while the Japanese wished to spend any available extra time on discretionary and recreational activities outside the home; 36 per cent of the Japanese gave this response, compared to 12 per cent of the Chinese. When asked about the bad points of married women working, 54 per cent of the Chinese respondents and 33 per cent of the Japanese believed that it made too much overall work and restricted married women's spare time; 50 per cent of the Chinese respondents and 38 per cent of the Japanese also believed that their work left them with too little time to properly attend to their children's upbringing. When asked their views on how the problems of married women combining family duties and paid employment could be solved, 97 per cent of the Chinese sample and 84 per cent of the Japanese said that shorter working hours and increased leisure time were needed. Overall these various responses support the interpretation that the Chinese respondents experience a greater degree of daily stress than the Japanese in combining their employment and domestic obligations. It might be surmised that this international contrast is in part due to the greater likelihood of the Chinese respondents being in full-time employment. Supporting this view is the fact that Japanese full-timers are more likely than part-timers to experience the stresses reported by the Chinese respondents. For instance, 48 per cent of Japanese full-timers, but only 30 per cent of part-timers, find housework a heavy or very heavy burden, and 17 per cent of the former compared to 9 per cent of the latter find their work too tiring. (Similarly the British Women and Employment Survey (Martin & Roberts 1984) found that full-time employed married mothers with children under age 16 exhibited greater difficulty coping with the demands of paid and domestic work than those in part-time employment.) It is plausible to conclude that the indications of greater workload and stress among the Chinese sample derive in part from the pattern of combining full-time paid employment with domestic responsibilities, despite the considerable availability of child care facilities.

To what extent does the greater part played in the home by Chinese husbands help relieve wives of the double burden of domestic labour and paid employment? There is indeed a direct relationship between the husband's role in household labour and the extent to which respondents experienced housework as a heavy burden. Only 38 per cent of those whose husbands undertook most of the household work experienced housework as a very heavy or heavy burden, compared to 61 per cent of those who shared it or did it together with their husband and 79 per cent of those whose husbands played an even smaller role in housework. Thus, when husbands made a substantial contribution to household work they considerably reduced the burden of household work for their wives. Since far fewer Japanese respondents experienced housework as burdensome and Japanese husbands contributed far less to household work, a comparable effect was not found in Japan.

Longer journeys to work, for both respondents and husbands in China, also led more respondents to experience housework as a very heavy burden; 67 per cent of respondents with travel-to-work times of over one hour gave this response, compared to 54 per cent of those with shorter travel times. There were similar differences with respect to husbands' travel-to-work times. The journey to work emerges as an important addition to the daily demands of labour-related activities for Chinese workers. The main forms of transportation for people travelling to work in Chinese cities are the bus and the bicycle. Because the buses are usually quite crowded and slow in the rush hours, a considerable number of people travel to work by bicycle. Cycling involves strenuous effort, but is sometimes more efficient than the bus. Among the Chinese respondents, only one-third travelled less than 30 minutes, another one-third took from 30 to 60 minutes, and the remaining third took over one hour, with more than one in ten people spending over two hours travelling to and from work each day.

The problems that travel to work causes Chinese workers are emphasized by comparison with Japanese and British data. The lengthy commuting journeys of Japanese male workers are well known but the survey evidence suggests that urban Chinese workers spend longer than their Japanese equivalents in travelling to and from work. And because of the means of transport available they also probably travel more slowly. The median travel-to-work time is 33 minutes for the Japanese husbands, and 23 minutes for their wives, compared to 45 minutes for both wives and husbands in China. Forty per cent of Japanese women had journeys of 15 minutes or less, and only 32 per cent travelled for more than half an hour, 11 per cent of whom journeyed for more than one hour. According to SCELI data for Aberdeen, over half of comparable British women had journeys to and from work of less than 30 minutes, and only 15 per cent took over an hour. Two-thirds of the Chinese women, by contrast, take more than half an hour to get to and from work, and one-third over a hour, of whom 10 per cent need over two hours. It seems that more women in Japan and Britain, especially those who have children and work part-time, are able to find jobs close to their homes and thus reduce the pressures on their time. By contrast, Chinese women are more fixed in their jobs and, if they want to reduce travelling times, have to find somewhere to live near their workplace rather than find a job close to their homes. Otherwise, they just have to put up with a long and hard journey to their work every day.

The role of grandparents

The burden on parents of domestic labour might potentially be lessened by the assistance of other adult relatives, particularly grandparents. Both Chinese and Japanese cultures have historically placed great cultural emphasis upon three or four generations of the patrilineal family of fathers, sons and their families all living together in the home of the patriarch. This Confucian ideal has, however, usually only been realized by the elite. Chinese census studies over the dynasties show that the typical domestic unit has been the nuclear family. This is the case too in contemporary Chinese and Japanese cities. Table 4.5 shows the family patterns of the respondents' households in the Sino-Japanese survey. Nuclear families of parents and their children form the majority in both samples; 62 per cent of the

Table 4.5 Household types in China and Japan.

Household type	China		Japan	
	F	%	F	%
Single person	10	0.5	214	11.5
Nuclear family	1,279	61.7	1,266	67.9
Paternal stem family	520	25.2	191	10.2
Maternal stem family	177	8.5	101	5.4
Four generations	36	1.7	17	0.9
Combined type	19	0.9	4	0.2
Other	31	1.5	72	3.9
Total	2,072	100.0	1,865	100.0

Source: Sino-Japanese Working Women's Family Life Survey.

Chinese and 68 per cent of the Japanese respondents live in households of this type. Household types corresponding more to the traditional ideal are, however, found in proportions high by Western standards. A quarter of the Chinese respondents live in paternal stem families, compared to 10 per cent of the Japanese sample. Maternal stem families, where the respondent lives with her parents, are not uncommon. Four-generation households are rather scarce. Thus, despite the cultural emphasis in China and Japan on the patriarchal and patrilineal family, the nuclear-family household is the most common among these urban respondents. There is still some substantial evidence of the historical and cultural ideal in the greater prevalence of the paternal stem family over the maternal stem family, and the fact that one in three households are non-nuclear in China. Wolf (1987) has shown that many young couples in China begin their married life in such households. The prevalence of three-generation households in China is also partially attributable to the greater poverty and housing shortages to be found in that society, factors that produce pressures for the different generations to share housing space.

The existence of these multi-generation households raises important issues of family life. Historically, in both China and Japan, many a daughter-in-law entered her husband's household as a domestic drudge under the mother-in-law's supervision (Baker 1979, Masuda 1975). However, our survey represents modern wives who, especially in China, are earning an average or near average salary, and who thus might be thought to be in a very different situation. Does having parents or in-laws co-resident add to the daily burden by increasing the numbers of people to be cared for, or do these older members of the household share in the necessary daily tasks, thus easing the workload of the employed parents? And what power does the older generation exercise in the household? Here we take up the first of these questions, leaving the second to the next section.

In modern China, the older generation usually provides much help with their married children's family life, especially with their household tasks. Some help comes in a direct form, for instance grandparents may do the housework for the young couple's family when they live together. Other assistance may be more indirect, for instance by paying the child care bill for the grandchild, so that the young couple can send their child to a kindergarten or even employ a maid. The reasons for the elderly assisting their married children are, first, that they want the younger generation to have a comfortable life and advance in their careers as a sign of the prosperity of the whole family, and secondly, that they expect a potential repayment from the young generation later on in life, possibly in the form of care and support in the event of illness and disability.

Looking after the grandchild is one of the household tasks that the elderly most like to do for the younger generation, especially the elderly on the paternal side. This help is not entirely dependent on co-residence: when the elderly live together with the young couple, they may be more likely to care for the child, but even the elderly who are not living with their married children can provide help with child care, by coming to the young couple's home or inviting the young couple to send the grandchild to their own home if help is needed. In fact where parents-in-law co-reside with respondents in China they are twice as likely to play the major role in domestic child care than is the case in the sample as a whole. In Japan this is less the case, since there are fewer multi-generation households, and even in those the grandparents play a comparatively less important role. Only 6 per cent of co-resident mothers-in-law play the major role in domestic child care in Japan, compared to 20 per cent in China.

Cooking for the family is another task that the elderly take on, though this pattern is mostly found among families where the elderly live together with the younger generation. The proportion of Chinese families in which the elderly are the main cooks is 12 per cent (3 per cent in Japan) but among those households where the respondent's mother-in-law co-resides the figure is 33 per cent (but only 12 per cent in Japan). Similarly, the cases where housework is mainly done by the elderly are largely to be found among stem families. And although the percentage of cases where the housework is mainly done by the older generation is small and only reaches 35 per cent among stem families, this does not mean that other grandparents do little. The survey question's use of the word "mainly" may have concealed the extent to which the elderly assist in various ways with household tasks. Especially in China, the elderly usually render considerable assistance when they live together with married children, even if they are not "mainly" responsible for any specific tasks; they may give the young parents a hand with looking after the young children when required, prepare ingredients for cooking, do some light shopping, and so on. The elderly who have already retired from paid work and stay at home often play an important role in assisting with household tasks.

Despite this, and perhaps in some cases because the grandparents may actually increase the load of work falling upon the respondents, the majority (55 per cent) of Chinese respondents with mothers-in-law co-resident still find housework a heavy or very heavy burden. This is a reduction on the figure of 64 per cent for the whole sample. In those cases where the parents or parents-in-law actually take a major role in the family domestic labour, e.g. by taking on the main responsibility for cooking, then this reduces the burden of housework on the respondent even further. Only 36 per cent of the respondents who received this assistance said that they found housework to be a heavy or very heavy burden. A similar effect is found in Japan, though with far fewer cases: while 38 per cent of all Japanese respondents experienced housework as burdensome, only 24 per cent of those living with their mother-in-law did, and only 14 per cent when mother-in-law took over the main responsibility for cooking. Thus, in that minority of households in which the older generation do take on these domestic responsibilities, they help ease the burden of domestic labour on working women, but the most common involvement of the older generation is as ancillary helpers to husbands and wives who as well as maintaining full-time employment still have the major responsibility for domestic tasks.

Multi-generation households are far less common in the UK and the USA than in China or Japan. Fewer than 3 per cent of married British and American women live with their parents or in-laws (Martin & Roberts 1984, Davis & Smith 1991). Compared with British and American parents, who rarely live together with the older generation, their Chinese and Japanese counterparts have a significant advantage in getting more help from the elderly with domestic tasks.

Grandparents in the West do assist in their children's domestic tasks, particularly with respect to child care while the parents are in employment, but they do so while based in their own residence. Presser (1988) in a 1984 national American survey of young dual-earner couples aged 19–26 found that grandmothers cared for the grandchildren while mothers were working in 23 per cent of cases where the latter was in full-time employment and 22 per cent of cases where she was in part-time employment. Fathers were the main carers when they were in part-time employment (26 per cent) but were of lesser importance (13 per cent) when they were in full-time employment. Given the younger age of these parents and their greater likelihood of being on shift work this data probably over-emphasizes the overall incidence of this type of assistance. Veurn and Gleason (1991) estimate that 29 per cent of employment-related child care for mothers aged 23–31 in 1988 was provided by non-nuclear family relatives and 18 per cent for women in their thirties. Other researchers have noted a long-run fall in the overall importance of non-parental relatives in this role. From 1965 to 1990 the proportion of employed mothers of children under age 5 using this form of care fell from 33 per cent to 19 per cent (Mishel & Bernstein 1993). In Great Britain the 1980 survey showed grandmothers caring for the children for 34 per cent of employed mothers of pre-school children and for 25 per cent of similar parents of school-age children. In each case their role was slightly greater among full-timers (Martin & Roberts 1984). Fathers and grandparents thus form an important element of the child care package that mothers have to put together in both East and West in order to undertake paid employment, and on the basis of the evidence available these informal family arrangements are of greater relative significance in the Western countries since more official schemes of care are available in the Eastern countries.

Given that in reality Chinese women have husbands who more often share the housework, receive more assistance from the older generation and spend less time on household tasks than Japanese women, why do they find their level of housework so burdensome and why do they display greater signs of pressure in relation to the double burden of employment and domestic labour? The answer to this question has to do with the varying composition of daily work schedules in the two countries. When we compare the average level of work time between Chinese women and Japanese women, we find

115

that, even though their housework hours are lower, Chinese women's total daily labour hours are considerably higher than their Japanese counterparts, due to the longer working hours and travel time. Employment times in China are fixed at just over eight hours a day. Hours of paid work vary little within the sample and they are not associated with feelings that housework is burdensome. In Japan those who do feel it burdensome have longer employment times than those who do not. Longer travel-to-work times add to the length of time of daily employment obligations in China compared to Japan. Women in China spend less time on housework than the Japanese respondents but as was shown earlier they find it a greater burden. In Japan it is the total combined load of domestic and employment labour that has the strongest influence on the experience that housework is burdensome, whereas in China, since there is less variation in daily employment times, it is the actual variation in the level of housework time that exerts the greatest influence on these feelings.

Family decision-making in China and Japan

Another vital aspect of the family process, which can be affected by the employment of the spouses, is domestic decision-making and the relative influence of partners in matters affecting the household. From research using "resources" theories of marital and household relations and related empirical investigations in Western societies, there are good grounds to expect that where a wife possesses greater economic resources she will also have greater influence in the affairs of the household (Blood & Wolfe 1960, England & Farkas 1986, Spitze 1988). This theory of marital power has, however, been subject to considerable criticism. The major charge levelled against it is that any variation associated with spouses' relative economic resources is minor compared to the strength of differences resulting from more fundamental gendered role formations (Allan 1985, Morris 1990). Most of the relevant work has focused discussion within one country or assumed a generalized Western industrial model. The present study can broaden this discussion through the comparative analysis of Eastern and Western societies where gender roles are structured differently. Not only are data available about cross-national differences in gender roles in the labour force and the household, but we are able to explore differences within each society as well.

Resources theory might lead us to expect that the polar cases of China and Japan would exhibit the greatest differences in domestic power patterns. The greater equivalence of economic resources within marriages in China should lead to greater female power and egalitarianism within marital decision-making in that country compared to Japan. Table 4.6 reports the replies of respondents to a question as to who ultimately makes decisions on a number of aspects of family life. Several conclusions are worth drawing from this table. First, with regard to the final item, "Overall, who has real power?", it is clear that Japanese women are much more likely than Chinese to report that their husband has real power; over half of them say this compared to only a fifth of the Chinese respondents. Further, on all but one item (and that is only marginally contrary), Japanese respondents are much more likely than their Chinese counterparts to report that their husbands make the ultimate decisions. Correspondingly, joint decisions are considerably more common in China than they are in Japan on every item, including the one relating to overall power, and are in every case the most common response in China. In Japan, too, joint decisions are often the most common response, but never to the same degree as in China. In Japan, decision-making powers in financial matters are most likely to be divided. In relation to buying a house, it is the man's influence that is greatest. In other matters of family finance, family spending and investment and saving, women are more likely to make the decisions. In every case, except the summary item of who has real power overall, the incidence of women alone making the respective decision is greater in Japan. In China there is a much greater sphere of joint household decision-making and less likelihood of exclusive male dominance.

In Japan wives have less overall acknowledged power in the family, but they do appear to have exclusive control of major areas of domestic life, especially in relation to family financial matters. These findings are congruent with the general observations of other writers such as Hunter (1989) and Eccleston (1989). It is striking that, although 56 per cent of Japanese respondents report that the husband has overall domestic power, far fewer reply that he makes decisions about specific aspects of family life. This might well indicate that respondents recognize that ultimately husbands have formal domestic authority and the greatest influence in the most important decisions, but that in practice wives exercise considerable discretion in administering family affairs. This greater degree of autonomy in

117

Table 4.6 Household decision-making in China and Japan.

						Who ultimately decides these matters? (percentages)									
	Husband		Wife		Couple together		Husband's parents		Wife's parents		Whole family		Other people		All	
Issue	Chi	Jap	Chi	Jap	Chi	Jap	Chi	Jap	Chi	Jap	Chi	Jap	Chi	Jap	Chi	Jap
Buying house	13.6	44.0	4.3	5.9	67.6	40.0	2.8	3.1	0.5	1.9	4.7	4.3	6.5	0.8	100.0	100.0
Consumer durables	15.5	25.5	4.1	21.5	77.0	47.6	0.6	1.4	0.2	1.0	2.5	2.9	0.0	0.2	100.0	100.0
Children's education	11.5	15.8	12.6	21.4	71.9	60.8	0.2	0.1	0.2	0.2	3.2	1.6	0.4	0.2	100.0	100.0
How many children	6.7	15.9	6.8	17.9	69.3	64.2	0.1	0.2	0.1	0.1	1.2	1.0	15.9	0.8	100.0	100.0
Where to take holiday	9.1	21.7	7.1	18.7	75.5	48.1	0.4	0.4	0.1	0.5	6.7	10.2	0.9	0.4	100.0	100.0
Family expenditure	9.4	7.6	29.4	73.0	57.4	16.3	2.0	1.4	0.5	0.9	1.3	0.6	0.0	0.2	100.0	100.0
Spouse's employment	12.1	26.8	5.0	10.5	60.3	59.0	0.5	0.5	0.3	0.1	2.2	2.1	19.7	1.0	100.0	100.0
Investment and saving	8.5	18.1	17.2	42.8	71.7	36.5	0.4	0.3	0.1	0.8	1.8	1.1	0.4	0.4	100.0	100.0
Who has real power overall?	19.2	55.7	28.1	19.2	48.6	20.8	2.0	2.3	0.4	1.4	1.5	0.3	0.1	0.2	100.0	100.0

Source: Sino-Japanese Working Women's Family Life Survey.

domestic decision-making experienced by Japanese wives found further expression in another item: 73 per cent of the Japanese sample compared to 51 per cent of the Chinese sample were "definitely not dissatisfied" with the degree to which husbands handed over the running of the family economy to them. Managing the household is a much more segregated and autonomous sphere for Japanese wives than it is for the Chinese.

Despite the greater degree of exclusive female control of the domestic sphere, evidence of marital conflict, and particularly of resentment against superior or arbitrary male power was more common among the Japanese women. The latter were much more likely to report that the husband "did not respect his wife's personal independence" (25.6 per cent compared to 5.3 per cent in China) and that he "obstructed her contacts, interests and social activities" (19.3 per cent compared to 6.5 per cent in China). In the extreme exercise of male power, "abuse of his wife", this was again more common as a source of dissatisfaction with male partners in Japan (6.9 per cent compared to 2.7 per cent). Japanese women are also more likely to express dissatisfaction about their relations with their husbands than are the Chinese respondents (18.1 per cent compared to 3.8 per cent). Given that it is commonly maintained that Japanese people are reluctant to express publicly disagreement about relations with close social colleagues, these expressions of resentment against their spouses is an indication of a marked degree of tension in marital relationships and of the way in which husbands are able to prevail over their wives' interests. The greater segregation of husbands' and wives' roles and the existence of a more marked separate female domestic sphere in Japan may be associated with these tensions, in that Japanese wives may have higher levels of expectation of autonomy in managing household affairs and thus be more readily offended by husbands' attempts at influence in these areas.

The gendered segregation of domestic roles in Japan does, however, raise problems for comparative cross-national studies of domestic power relations. How should we interpret the contrast in the Japanese data between attribution of overall domestic power and decision-making in specific areas? The husband's concession, the wife's taking, or the jointly negotiated outcome of a substantial sphere of control over the household and financial affairs, results in a very different configuration of power than when there is considerable overlapping of domestic and employment roles as in China.

Wives in Japan take over effective executive control of much of the domestic sphere while nominally acknowledging the husband's conventional authority. Whether or not they are more "powerful" than their Chinese equivalents thus becomes a moot point, depending on the definitions of power used and the value attached to domestic roles and paid employment. Some writers, for instance, recognize the separation of spheres but also maintain that Japanese wives are dominant in the domestic sphere (Eccleston 1989, Reischauer 1988).

The differences between China and Japan in patterns of domestic decision-making are of great significance. It might be argued that segregated and joint spheres of domestic and employment life are alternative ways of organizing the division of labour in the household and the economy. Especially from a Western perspective, it might be expected that the trend of macro-societal change in advanced industrial countries is from the former, which represents the "breadwinner–housewife" model, to the latter. Interestingly, if the direction of change is along lines evident in Chinese households, the effect is not to create separate spheres of female domestic power but to create more joint spheres of sharing among couples. Cases of exclusive female power are, in every specific aspect of decision-making, less common in China than joint decision-making and considerably less common than is the case in Japan. Women's advances in the labour force may thus not lead to female dominance in the household but to more egalitarian and sharing domestic relations.

The Sino-Japanese survey also makes it possible to analyze comparatively the relationship between husbands' and wives' economic resources and their influence in family decision-making within two very different societal contexts and to contribute further to the extensive debate about the "resources" theory of marital power. We have available two possible measures of spouses' resources, namely the women's reports of their (and their husbands') income and their educational level, and we are therefore able to explore variations in the distribution of family decision-making and power in relation to variation in resources.

We have suggested that the greater economic resources of women relative to men in terms of employment and earning power in China may be the major factor accounting for their relatively greater influence in domestic decision-making compared to Japan. It is instructive to apply the "resources hypothesis" to each national sample separately, and then compare the results. If the argument is valid, it should be expected that in each society women who have greater earning power in employment would have greater relative influence in the family in terms of domestic decision-taking. This hypothesis was examined by comparing the responses of the top and bottom income halves in both countries. In Japan, the resources hypothesis stood up quite well. In relation to overall domestic power, women with higher incomes were markedly less likely to report exclusive male power (46.5 per cent) and more likely to report joint decision-making (28.2 per cent) than respondents with lower incomes (62.0 per cent and 16.6 per cent respectively). A similar pattern to the overall question on power is evident with respect to each particular aspect of decision-making. In each case, in the Japanese responses, the relationship between the respondent's income and the pattern of decision-making is highly statistically significant. The main effect of the respondent's higher income is to shift the locus of decision-making from the husband to joint decisions rather than further increasing the like-lihood of the wife making the decision. However, even among the higher income respondents the pattern still falls considerably short of the Chinese one with a much greater orientation in Japan to exclusive male power and a reduced joint sphere of decision-making.

This relationship between the wife's income and the pattern of family decision-making was, however, entirely absent from the Chinese data. In the Chinese sample, the woman's income made vir-tually no difference to the general pattern of decision-making power reported, and this impression was borne out by the tests of statistical significance. The Chinese data thus reveal two distinct levels of egali-tarianism: first, that in comparison with the Japanese families there is a far higher likelihood of joint decision-making and shared power *within* families; secondly, that *between* the Chinese families income makes no difference to the likelihood of any pattern of family power. At least from the evidence of these data, the balance of family power in China is just not sensitive to the level of economic resources brought into the family by the wife.

It might be thought that, rather than the *absolute* level of the wife's income, it might be the *relative* income of husband and wife that would affect the balance of power in the family. Precisely this sug-gestion has been made in a recent book on women's status in society published in China (Kuang et al. 1992). However, analysis of our data reveals no relationship between family power and decision-making and the relative incomes of husbands and wives, in either the Chinese or the Japanese responses.

A similar contrast between China and Japan appears when we turn to our second indicator of the wife's resources that might be thought to have an effect on the balance of family power, namely the level of the wife's education. Once again, the suggestion has been made in China that more highly educated women are likely to enjoy the most democratic and egalitarian marriages (Kuang et al. 1992), a theory that accords well with the resources approach of Blood and Wolfe and others. However, according to our data, it is in Japan and not in China that this relationship between the wife's educational level and the power structure of the family obtains. There was no clear or statistically significant relationship among the Chinese families, whereas in Japan the expected relationship emerged clearly and was statistically highly significant. Among the Chinese families, there was indeed a small but steady decline in the incidence of male overall power as the level of the wives' education increases, but this was as nothing in comparison with the sharp drop in the proportion of dominant husbands in the families of Japanese female graduates, and the steady and marked rise in the sharing of family power at each successively higher educational level.

It appears as if egalitarian norms have had such a strong impact on the family lives of young married women in China that not only are they much more likely in general to participate in democratic and egalitarian marriages than are their Japanese counterparts, but also that such relative equality is also to be found at many different levels of society, among low earning women as well as high earning ones, among the lesser educated as well as among the highly educated. It is a mark of the continuing hierarchical and inegalitarian culture of Japan that the more "modern" egalitarian family patterns are much more likely to be found in families where the wife is highly educated and economically successful (Bonney et al. 1994).

"Resources" theories of marital power receive considerable support from these findings in the two Asian countries cross-nationally and intra-societally. The findings support it by suggesting that in China, where gender relations are relatively egalitarian in the labour force they are relatively egalitarian in the household. Gender relations in employment and in the household have in China been so profoundly restructured on an egalitarian basis and the economic resources of spouses are so equal that comparatively little variation is found within and between households with respect to the relative resources and the power of spouses over domestic decisions. Societal reconstruction has thus dramatically diminished the intra-societal variation that is assumed by resources theories. In the case of Japan in a situation where gender differences are deeply entrenched in the labour force and the household, there is a strong association between higher female resources and more shared domestic decision-making, providing confirmation for the thesis in a context where there are wide variations in spouses' labour force roles. Further, cases of high female economic resources are rare in Japan and do little to alter the overall picture of contrast between the two societies at the national level.

Having examined in some detail the major contrasts in the patterns of the domestic division of labour and decision-making in China and Japan we now turn to further analysis of the Western societies which, as we established earlier, have characteristics intermediate between the polar Asian cases.

USA: the double shift

The division of domestic labour in American households has been the subject of numerous studies. The general picture is that the greater part of domestic labour is still primarily undertaken by wives and female partners even when they are in paid employment which, as we have seen, is usually full-time. Gender is a decisive factor in the allocation of household work, but other influences are also of importance. A major determinant of variations in time consumed in household labour by either spouse is the other's paid work hours. The more the hours in paid employment of the one, the greater the housework time of the other. The effect of paid employment by wives in dual-earner or dual-career couples is to reduce the total amount of housework that is undertaken in the household and to increase the share of household labour time taken by the male partner. This general pattern is revealed by a number of studies, despite considerable variations in the estimates of time spent on housework, which result from differences in methods and samples. Berardo et al. (1987), using 1976 data, calculated that housework time in single-earner households averaged 43 hours per week compared with 33 hours in dual-earner households; 83 per cent of American housework time was undertaken by wives in single-earner households and 70 per cent in dual-earner households. This represented a small difference in the husband's household labour time of just under two hours per week more in the dual-earner case. Among dual-career couples, husbands contributed a quarter of household labour time. Ross et al. (1986) estimated that 20 per cent of dual-earner couples shared domestic labour equally compared to 7 per cent of single-earner couples. Data for 1986 indicate that when both partners are employed the wife's weekly domestic labour of 31 hours is just over double the husband's 15 hours. This represents 9 hours less for the wife and 3 hours more for the husband compared to single-earner couples (Blair & Johnston 1992). Shelton (1992) reckons the weekly housework time of employed men to be 21 hours compared to 35 hours for employed women.

The continuing rise in women's labour force participation has contributed towards a gradual increase in men's percentage share of housework time. Shelton (1992) found that men's housework time as a proportion of their wives' rose from 46 per cent in 1975 to 58 per cent in 1987 and that this trend was most evident among the younger adult population. These findings concur with other evidence of a steady diminution of gender differences in housework time between spouses. Menaghen and Parcel (1990) also point to a slow increase in male participation in housework, a trend also supported by the international studies of Gershuny and Robinson (Gershuny 1992, Gershuny & Robinson 1991). Blair and Johnston suggest that 10 per cent of husbands in dual-earner couples do as much housework as the average wife. There is thus considerable evidence for the emergence of a minority of dual-earner couples where domestic work is relatively equally shared.

The most egalitarian phase of marriage in terms of the sharing of domestic labour is what Goldscheider & Waite (1991) call the early pre-children "honeymoon" phase where most couples are both in full-time paid work and where the male share of the limited housework time is maximized. Young children increase the overall load of housework and the absolute time men spend on household tasks but it increases women's time on such tasks even more. Each additional child increases a husband's domestic work by one hour and his wife's by five hours per week. There is also evidence in trend data from 1975 to 1987 that men are increasing the time they spend with children. The diminishing difference in husband and wife domestic labour hours is, however, not found among couples where the wife is in part-time work (less than 30 hours of paid work per week). The male's domestic labour time as a proportion of the female's, among couples where the wife was employed part-time, only rose from 55 per cent to 57 per cent from 1975 to 1987, but from 53 per cent to 67 per cent among couples where she was employed full-time. Men's absolute hours in household work are also higher in the latter case. The increasing overall male share of household labour is thus attributable to increased female employment times and, in line with the general argument, the domestic division of labour is more equal among dual full-time working partners than in cases where the wife is employed part-time (Shelton 1992). Similarly Goldscheider & Waite (1991) demonstrate that wives being employed full-time is the most powerful factor, apart from the husband being unemployed, in raising men's share of the household work.

Husbands tend to contribute more to household labour tasks when young children are present. They do 25 per cent more clearing and cleaning the dishes, house-cleaning and paperwork than when there are no children under age 5 present (Goldscheider & Waite 1991). This increased role is often associated with split shift employment when the wife, for instance, transfers domestic responsibility to the husband while she is in paid work in the evening (England & Farkas 1986). The effect is more pronounced where childbirth is delayed into the mother's late twenties and the husband's role is also enhanced according to the wife's contribution to family income. Women are however overwhelmingly responsible (in nine out of ten cases) for making arrangements for the care of pre-schoolers and for school-age children (Peterson & Gerson 1992). Summarizing some of these findings these latter authors argue that husbands' contributions to household labour increase as the burden increases and the wife is not available to perform it. While husbands' contributions to domestic labour have been rising in recent years this has not prevented wives from continuing to have the major share of domestic labour. For most employed American wives labour market participation combined with the major share of domestic tasks means a greater daily workload. Even amongst those couples where both are in paid employment for 40 or more hours a week wives average over one hour more per day of labour time compared to their husbands (Shelton 1992).

There is pronounced gender segregation in the division of domestic labour tasks. Meal preparation, laundry, cleaning the house and washing dishes tend to be disproportionately undertaken by wives, while outdoor tasks and automobile maintenance tend to be undertaken by husbands (Blair & Johnston 1992). Goldscheider & Waite

(1991) estimate that husbands do 25 per cent of grocery shopping and 20 per cent of dishwashing, cooking and house-cleaning. The major areas of men's domestic work are family based child care, of which they do 45 per cent, and yard and home maintenance of which they do a similar proportion. There is some marginal reduction of task segregation when wives are in paid work, largely through men spending more time doing the dishes and laundry and cleaning the house (Blair & Johnston 1992). These are also the tasks, along with meal preparation, that have become less gender segregated in recent years (Goldscheider & Waite 1991).

Contrary to general impressions the average amount of leisure time of women and men is not very different. This is because of their different patterns of involvement in paid and domestic labour. It is, of course, the employed who experience the greatest pressure on their time. The greater combined work pressures of paid employment and domestic labour are evident in the leisure patterns of employed women who generally have less leisure time than employed men. Shelton (1992) estimates this leisure gap at 1.6 hours per week. Children reduce parents' leisure times as men increase their paid and domestic labour times and women reduce their paid labour time and increase their housework. These tendencies lead men with one child to experience three hours less leisure per week than comparable women. Further children shift the advantage in leisure time back to the male. Employment and children thus increase the overall workload pressures on men as well as women. Although gender differences in leisure time are not found overall, there are differences in the use of leisure time. The leisure of men is more passive and discretionary (e.g. watching television) while that of women is more active and related to the maintenance of the household (e.g. sewing) (Shelton 1992).

While change has been occurring in recent decades it has not been on a sufficient scale to erode the widespread prevalence of a greater female workload and responsibility in the domestic sphere and a greater male responsibility and workload in the sphere of paid employment. It is as if the male role continues to be more centred in the sphere of paid employment and the female one in the home. In seeking to explain these gendered patterns analysts have put forward similar formulations. Shelton (1992) suggests, like Finch (1983), that women and men face different assumptions at home and in paid work as to their obligations between the two spheres time constraints are gender specific. Thus, having children or a spouse has a different effect on time use for women and men. In some sense, it is our gender-specific conceptions of appropriate behaviour that lead to differences in paid labour time and household labour time (Shelton 1992: 150).

England and Farkas (1986) see an implicit gender contract element in marriage which is "deep, sticky and enduring", and which is based upon informal understandings regarding obligations of partners. These are moulded by sex role socialization and labour market discrimination and only marginally influenced by variations in spouses' labour market participation. Such profound role identities and assumptions influence wives and husbands in their relationships and patterns of behaviour and are underpinned by numerous institutional and societal influences. However, as has been shown, they are also subject to secular and incremental change and may vary cross-nationally in significant ways.

The weight of the evidence of recent research in the USA is that gender differentials between spouses in participation in the labour force and in domestic labour roles remain significant but are subject to a perceptible trend of diminution. The relative equality of the early marriage years is eroded with the arrival of children and typically, while male involvement in domestic work and hours increases with the arrival of young children, it does not do so to the same degree as that of their wives who are also typically in full-time employment. As in the Chinese case the situation where both parents are in full-time paid work leads to greater sharing of domestic labour by husband and wife. Much American discussion assumes the dual full-timer worker model. Arlie Hochschild's influential *The second shift* (1990) is a case in point. The implications of part-time employment have been less systematically explored, perhaps because full-time employment is the norm for employed American mothers of young children. As we have seen, 71 per cent of those in paid work are in full-time employment in the USA. For the remainder, however, a different pattern of labour market roles and domestic duties prevails, with lesser involvement in paid work and a greater share of domestic labour. We now turn to consider the significance of the part-time employment option in the British case where it is proportionately much more common.

Part-time employment and domestic roles

As was demonstrated in the previous chapter, part-time work is the most common type of paid employment for mothers of young children in Great Britain. Despite the growth of women's labour force participation and equal opportunities legislation, it remains the case that motherhood, for the majority of women, involves a break in the continuity of employment. In 1989–91 only 13 per cent of mothers of children aged 4 or less were in full-time employment. Part-time employment is much more common amongst mothers of dependent children than is full-time employment: 52 per cent of mothers with a youngest child of age 4 or under were not in paid work or seeking it; of the remainder 30 per cent were employed part-time, 13 per cent full-time and 5 per cent were unemployed but seeking paid work. Amongst mothers with youngest children aged 5–9, 48 per cent were employed part-time and 21 per cent full-time. Amongst all women aged 16–59 the corresponding figures were 29 per cent and 40 per cent (OPCS 1993). It was also shown in Chapter 3 that it was women in professional and higher status occupations who tended more frequently to remain in full-time employment during this phase of the life course and that part-time work tended to have a considerably lower status and low levels of pay.

While the pioneering work on women's employment in Great Britain by Myrdal and Klein (1956) and Klein (1965) tended to endorse the growth of part-time employment as a way of extending women's employment experience and combining the two roles of homemaker and paid worker, more recent British studies have been more critical of it. Part-time employment has been seen as deriving from differential gendered models of the division of domestic work and paid employment among couples, as indicative of the interruptions of women's employment careers occasioned by having children, as resulting in downward occupational mobility, low pay and low status, as a second class type of employment to which female workers are relegated by male exclusionary work practices and as an under-utilization of valuable potential workers (Beechey & Perkins 1987, Dex 1992, Hunt 1988, Walby 1986, 1990). This perspective has also been strengthened by Gallie's demonstration (1991), on the basis of SCELI data, that women's deficit in occupational skill enhancement compared to men is largely accounted for by the experience of women in part-time work. Women in full-time employment have as much opportunity as men for skill enrichment.

National surveys that question women about their actual experiences, and some other investigations of part-time employment, have produced results that paint a rather different picture. As we have seen, women, particularly mothers of young children, have been seeking out part-time employment in large numbers. Those engaged in it prefer it to full-time employment. Mothers of young children not in paid employment would also prefer it to full-time employment. And a third of full-time female workers would prefer to work fewer hours in paid employment if it were possible (Martin & Roberts 1984).

The popularity of part-time work derives from the possibility of combining it with family housework and child care obligations. Such work diversifies the daily round compared to that of women not in paid employment, gives work experience and at the same time enables mothers to meet essential daily domestic demands. It depends, in particular, upon the intermeshing of responsibilities of both parents, particularly with respect to the care of children in the split shift system, and with the school timetable. Marital status, combined with parenthood, is the major household factor that affects the likelihood of being in part-time work. The British rise in part-time work in the post-war period has often been attributed to the increasing tendency of married women to engage in paid work. In fact it is more attributable to married mothers of dependent children, rather than wives per se, engaging in paid work. Marriage as such does not diminish women's hours of paid employment. Rather, the availability of husbands or male partners to substitute for mothers as child carers in the evenings increases the ability of many mothers of young children to engage in part-time work. The 1980 Women and Employment Survey found that 38 per cent of employed mothers of children under age 5 worked in the evening when their partners cared for the children (Martin & Roberts 1984). The importance of marital status is apparent when the labour market patterns of married mothers are compared to those of lone parents. The participation rates of married mothers with dependent children are much higher than those of lone parents (66 per cent compared to 47 per cent) and the former are twice as likely to be in part-time work as the latter (42 per cent compared to 22 per cent) (OPCS 1990). It is essentially the lack of suitable child care arrangements that prevents British single mothers from seeking employment (Morris 1994).

It is thus the flexibility of combining paid work with domestic roles that makes part-time work so attractive to many women. It might be thought on the basis of the poor objective work conditions that part-time workers are more likely to be dissatisfied with their work compared to full-timers. But this is not the case. Although the full-timers have higher occupational status and earnings than their part-time peers they are slightly more dissatisfied with their job, and markedly more dissatisfied with their pay level and their promotion opportunities than the part-timers. Among the SCELI pooled sample of mothers of young children, 30 per cent of the full-timers were dissatisfied with their pay (compared to 15 per cent of the part-timers) and 34 per cent of the former and 25 per cent of the latter were dissatisfied with promotion opportunities. This apparently paradoxical combination of lower objective rewards and higher expressed satisfaction levels may arise from part-timers' lower personal investment in paid work and their correspondingly lower expectations of it, while the greater expressed dissatisfaction of full-timers with their job opportunities may reflect higher investment and greater frustrated expectations through a deeper incorporation into the norms of the world of paid work.

A further indication of the attractions of part-time employment in Great Britain comes from measures of satisfaction with various areas of respondent's lives. In analysis of SCELI survey data, there were no statistically significant differences between full-time and part-time workers with respect to their satisfaction with family life or with life in general, but 54 per cent of part-timers, compared to 42 per cent of full-timers, expressed satisfaction with the amount of their leisure time. Further indications of time pressures and limitations on leisure among full-timers compared to part-timers came from questions that asked respondents to say how they would use extra time off work were it available. Full-timers were more likely than part-timers to mention housework and odd jobs around the house and to suggest various modes of relaxation and leisure. Amongst those with children under age 5, more time with the children was the major response of both groups of workers (60 per cent in each case).

These findings are complementary to Hewitt's (1993) observations from women's discussion groups that mothers of young children in professional and managerial employment were much less satisfied with their lives than the lower paid women. The former found themselves under great pressure "as they tried to juggle the demands of children, job, partner and home" (Hewitt 1993: 69). The latter did not want to work longer hours, even if child care was available, because

PART-TIME EMPLOYMENT AND DOMESTIC ROLES

part-time work gave them flexibility and the opportunity to give what they regarded as appropriate priority to their children.

Given the widespread popularity of part-time employment among British mothers, what are the implications of these patterns for the division of domestic labour and the pattern of domestic decision-making? Earlier in this chapter we showed that the domestic labour of part-time female workers in both Great Britain and Japan was more gender segregated than that of full-time female workers. Husbands undertook a lesser share of a range of domestic tasks in the households of part-timers than of full-timers. In line with the perspectives of resources theory, we might expect that part-time work would also be associated with wives' lesser influence in domestic decision-making, compared to cases where the wife is in full-time paid work. These issues can be analyzed with data from both Great Britain and Japan.

Table 4.7 shows patterns of domestic power relations for Japanese respondents in paid work, full-time and part-time (defined for this purpose as less than 30 hours a week). The responses on overall power demonstrate that wives who work full-time are more likely than part-timers to perceive family power as shared (30 per cent compared with 16 per cent), although the majority still see power as residing in the hands of husbands. In relation to the question as to who ultimately controls family expenditure, a matter commonly within the wife's sphere of operations, the effect of full-time working is to increase somewhat the likelihood of joint decision-making, from 13 per cent to 23 per cent of cases, and slightly to diminish decision-making by either spouse alone, though more than two-thirds of wives who work full-time still manage the family budget.

Table 4.7 Domestic power by hours of work of female partner in Japan (percentages).

	Husband	Wife	Couple	Other	N
Who has overall power?					
Wife works part-time	66	15	16	3	601
Wife works full-time	53	15	30	2	718
Who decides family expenditure?					
Wife works part-time	10	75	13	2	605
Wife works full-time	6	69	23	2	730

Source: Sino-Japanese Working Women's Family Life Survey.

Table 4.8   Domestic power by hours of work of female partner in Great Britain (percentages).

	Husband	Wife	Both	Other	N
Who has final say in big financial decisions?					
Wife works part-time	27	10	63	0	104
Wife works full-time	12	1	83	4	69
Who has ultimate responsibility for organizing household money and paying bills?					
Wife works part-time	25	44	31	0	68
Wife works full-time	22	38	40	0	105

Source: SCELI.

Similar effects are evident in Table 4.8 which reports analogous British data. Full-time employment by the female partner is associated with fewer cases of exclusive male and female control of family finance and a greater likelihood of joint decision-making. In the case of the first question, "Who has the final say in big financial decisions?", the "both equally" response reaches 83 per cent, indicating a high incidence of joint decision-making. In relation to the responsibility for organizing the household money and paying the bills, the direction of effects is similar, with a greater chance of joint financial control in couples where the wife works full-time, but there is still a diversity of patterns of family financial management. The SCELI data has recently been subjected to further detailed analysis by Vogler and Pahl (1994), though without as yet an emphasis on the difference between full-time and part-time employment of female partners; the Japanese material from the Sino-Japanese survey is, however, not sufficiently detailed to allow us to pursue this topic further here. It is clear from a comparison of Tables 4.7 and 4.8, however, that family financial control is subject to quite different norms in Britain and Japan.

From various sources of evidence presented in this section it can now be convincingly demonstrated that in the cases of Great Britain and Japan, full-time employment by wives is associated with a greater degree of sharing by spouses in domestic labour tasks and a wider joint sphere of decision-making about household affairs. This is found both within the highly gender segregated Japanese family system and in the somewhat less segregated British system. Thus, while part-time employment is the most common employment option for mothers of young children in Great Britain, it is not one that produces major changes in domestic organization or relative employment opportunities between spouses. Full-time employment is more likely to be associated with a greater joint sphere of domestic decision-making and a relatively greater role by husbands in domestic labour tasks.

Conclusion: employment roles and family life

The great majority of studies of the gendered divisions of domestic labour and family decision-making have focused upon individual societies. Comparative studies have been relatively rare. In this chapter we have tried to demonstrate the value of a comparative approach. While there are common features among the four societies examined here, in particular the primary responsibility of mothers for the care of young children and for domestic work and the more marginal role of fathers in these spheres, nonetheless there are substantial variations resulting from the contrasting historical backgrounds and the contemporary institutional structures and values of the societies.

China and Japan represent the most distinctive and extreme cases. In urban China there is a prevalence of dual full-time working among spouses and parents of young children. This is associated with a widespread joint conjugal sphere, with spouses sharing the domestic tasks of housework and caring for children and with greater equality in domestic decision-making. In Japan, in contrast, gender roles in the employment and the household spheres are much more differentiated. Men play a very small role in the domestic sphere and there is little overlap between husbands' and wives' lives. Employed women have to combine their jobs with the great bulk of the responsibility for domestic tasks and child care with only minimal involvement of their husbands. However, Japan is distinctive in the wide degree to which wives exercise exclusive control of domestic finance and areas of routine decision-making. While husbands are in general terms acknowledged by wives to have overall power in the family, in practice wives exercise considerable influence on many domestic matters. If the Chinese model is characterized by overlapping and joint conjugal domestic and employment spheres, the Japanese situation is depicted by sharply segregated male and female spheres.

Summarizing the various studies that have been undertaken in the USA, it has been suggested that they demonstrate that domestic

133

labour among couples remains anchored in terms of management and function upon the wife, regardless of whether she is employed or not, and that the contribution of husbands increases only marginally when the total workload increases through the presence of young children and when the wife is unavailable to undertake domestic tasks, usually because of her own employment (England & Farkas 1986, Peterson & Gerson 1992). Much the same type of process seems to operate in other societies. Wives are generally more rooted in the domestic sphere and husbands in the employment sphere. Domestic work falls primarily upon wives and husbands step in as supplementary domestic workers only when wives are not available. But there are important variations in the degree to which this process operates. The Chinese system where both husband and wife are in full-time paid work leads to the greatest likelihood among the four societies that wives will not have time to take exclusive responsibility for domestic work and hence encourages the greatest likelihood of male participation in domestic labour. It also places the greatest load upon the two, even when there is assistance available from grandparents, to accomplish necessary domestic tasks within a full and busy daily and weekly timetable. The American system is the nearest of the three other societies to this pattern. And as Kalleberg and Rosenfield (1990) confirm when comparing the USA, Norway and Sweden, the greater role of men in domestic labour in the USA compared to these other two countries results from the relative lack of the part-time employment option for wives. The extensive resort to part-time employment in Great Britain means that most working wives continue to be available to perform domestic tasks and thus limit the call upon husbands' participation in domestic work. In Japan employed wives work long hours at home and in paid work but cultural norms and husband's employment commitments limit male involvement in household labour to an extreme degree. There is a double shift for employed wives but there is less involvement by husbands in domestic labour than in any of the four societies. The Japanese situation is not, however, unacceptable to many Japanese wives, for they also achieve a large measure of effective control in the domestic sphere, over the disposition of the family budget and over their children's upbringing.

Many earlier investigations of the impact of women's increased labour force participation upon domestic roles in the USA and UK have generally argued that the net effects of women's increased paid

work and continuing if reduced domestic roles, combined with husbands' still small but marginally increased domestic roles, has been
to maintain or increase the gender workload differentials within marriage. Core gender roles at home and in paid work are seen as so
entrenched that increases in women's workloads have small effects
on the overall shape of gendered work patterns (England & Farkas
1986, Hochschild 1990, Morris 1990). However, Gershuny (1992), on
the basis of wide cross-national comparative studies of time-budget
data up to the early 1980s, has demonstrated general tendencies for
men's labour force time to fall, women's labour force time to rise,
men's domestic labour time to increase and women's unpaid work
time to decrease. Interestingly the one capitalist industrial nation
where women's paid work time did not increase (during the period
1961–84) was the United Kingdom. We might surmise that this is due
to the importance of part-time work as the main vehicle of employment growth for women (Hakim 1993). Gershuny argues that this
convergence of conjugal work roles comes about as husbands accommodate to the growing labour force participation of wives and he
demonstrates, on the basis of SCELI time-budget diaries for Great Britain, that the greater the wife's experience of paid employment, the
greater the husband's proportion of the couple's total work. Increases
in husbands' unpaid domestic work are seen from this perspective as
lagged responses to wives' increased labour market involvement.

Gershuny's argument can be tested for China and Japan using the
Sino-Japanese survey data. In Japan wives with continuous work
histories uninterrupted by maternity-associated or other breaks (who
make up 39 per cent of the sample) were less likely to have husbands
who did no housework than those who had interrupted work histories (22 per cent compared to 36 per cent). Similarly 11 per cent of
those with uninterrupted work histories, compared to 2 per cent
of those with interrupted work histories, had husbands who shared
the housework, but did less than their wife. Because the Chinese
respondents overwhelmingly have full-time and continuous work
histories, age was used as a surrogate for continuity of employment
experience and no relationship was found between age and the husband's role in household work. We may conclude that the causal relationship between wives' labour force participation and husbands'
domestic work proposed by Gershuny is supported by the case of
Japan, but not that of China. Indeed, his model generally appears to
be more relevant to capitalist industrial countries where people have

135

somewhat greater freedom in their choice of household work strategies and the deployment especially of women's labour at any one
time, and over time, between paid work and unpaid domestic labour.
But it is less helpful for analyzing state-socialist societies where full-
time paid work is expected of all adults.

In the capitalist industrial countries secular change occurs as individuals and couples adjust themselves over time and the life course
to changing personal circumstances and labour force opportunities.
Under state socialism abrupt revolutionary change introduced and
subsequently sustained a very different gender order. In urban China
this change has been so profound that the great degree of substantive
equality between spouses, and among the mass of workers, has
eroded the variations in resources and status which in the West and
Japan result in variations in employment patterns and the organization of the household. Resources theories of marital relationships
have been shown in this chapter to be supported in contexts where
there are general substantive differences in economic and power
resources between households and spouses as in the three capitalist
societies. Urban China also provides support for the theory, but
through its contrasting conditions. Where change in social and gender roles has been so profound so as to generally equalize many
social relationships, so too has domestic life become more egalitarian.

Although gender roles at home and in paid work in the capitalist
societies demonstrate considerable stability, they are not as static as
alleged by some critics of resources theories. There is substantial evidence of secular and incremental change in line with the perspective
of Gershuny (Goldscheider & Waite 1991, Peterson & Gerson 1992,
Shelton 1992). Male contributions to domestic work have been shown
by the first-named authors to be related to wives' labour market participation and earnings. They demonstrate that the higher the wife's
earnings, the greater the husband's contribution to domestic work
and the higher his earnings, the less is his domestic labour activity.
But they also show that these effects are small and that the latter
effect is stronger. They also emphasize the importance of the qualita-
tive jump into full-time paid employment:

> These results clarify that the effects of the wife's employment
> on her husband's sharing of household tasks depend on the
> number of hours she works outside the home. If she works out-
> side the home only on a part-time basis, her spouse increases

his contribution relatively little; if she works more, most husbands increase their sharing (Goldscheider & Waite 1991: 132f).

Shelton (1992) also demonstrates husbands' greater participation in household work where wives are employed in full-time jobs. This stress on the importance of women's full-time paid employment as leading to a qualitatively different type of relationship with spouses is important and meshes with the findings of this study.

This chapter gives an international perspective to this argument. Full-time paid employment by wives is generally associated with higher involvement of husbands in domestic labour and greater female influence in domestic decision-making. Lesser degrees of wives' involvement in paid work, such as in part-time employment, mean less sharing of household tasks by husbands and less female influence in decision-making. These differences are evident in comparison between nations, especially in the distinct pattern found in China, and within the other individual societies when part-time and full-time cases are contrasted. Of the other three cases, the USA seems closest to urban China in that the typical dual-worker marriage is one involving two full-time workers, with correspondingly more frequent involvement of the husband in domestic roles. In Great Britain the frequency of part-time employment in such marriages means that the husband's involvement in domestic labour is less common and domestic decision-making is often less egalitarian. In Japan part-time employment is a less common option, and dual full-time worker partnerships display a greater likelihood that domestic labour tasks and decision-making will be shared, but the overall situation is one where husbands play the smallest role in domestic life. Finally in all of the countries the typical outcome in the dual full-time employment pattern is not a move towards more exclusive female power but towards the spouses sharing domestic labour and decision-taking. But even in those circumstances wives generally have the greater role in domestic labour and the greater overall combined burden of domestic and paid work.

If the general pattern of change in the capitalist societies is towards decreasing gender inequality in paid employment, it can be seen to be accompanied by a shift towards more sharing of housework and domestic decision-taking, but not to a degree which approaches equality in the near future. As the Chinese case indicates, fundamental change of the gender order would appear to require a fundamental and abrupt social reconstruction. Further, in so far as the increase in female employment opportunities involves an increase in part-time employment, the patterns of domestic change are likely to be less dramatic. However, the diversity of women's experience in the four societies, even when they are in full-time employment, suggests that there are no simple and direct relationships between women's increased labour force participation and change in domestic relationships. Entrenched gender ideologies must also be taken into account and, as the Japanese case indicates, may be a considerable obstacle to change. It is the ideological aspects of these issues to which we now turn in the following chapter.

Chapter 5

Ideologies of family and women's work

Introduction

Excellent intro

The roles and activities of married women tend to be matters of controversy and concern in industrializing and industrial societies. In agrarian civilizations, with much productive work centred on the household, married women could usually combine their productive tasks and their family responsibilities, if not without friction, then at least without causing moral disquiet. Industrial production, and the expansion of employment opportunities for married women outside the household, brings with it a new set of worries about how that combination can be managed in new circumstances, worries concerning in particular how women can continue to carry out those responsibilities to husband, children and other kin while being at the same time subject to the demands of employers outside the home. A frequently expressed concern is the possible harm that might be done to the young child by being deprived of the attention of the mother while the latter is out at work. The employment of married women has also been judged, by some, as harmful to the quality of family life and the proper upkeep of the home. Friction over the employment of men in industrializing and industrial societies, by contrast, relates more to the conditions of wage labour, with disputes over pay and especially over the new forms of industrial control, discipline and hierarchy very much to the fore. The absence of fathers from the home does not seem to have been identified as a major issue in industrial societies until feminist criticism of perceived double standards raised the question in the late twentieth century, although critical psychoanalysts had already feared that proletarianized fathers could no longer contribute adequately to their children's development by playing their part in the Oedipal drama (Horkheimer & Adorno 1973).

The doctrine of "separate spheres", which we have mentioned a number of times previously, is the most clear-cut attempt to resolve these new problems by means of a normative injunction on married women to refrain altogether from employment outside the home, thus building on pre-industrial gendered divisions of labour in the household-as-enterprise. However, this doctrine on the one hand made impossible demands on some poor families who could not do without the earnings of the wife, and on the other came to be seen by many women as imposing improper restrictions on them and preventing them from enjoying the benefits of the new industrial order. Industrial societies thus tend, at some point in their development, to see the growth of highly controversial campaigns promoting the right of married women to employment.

Such campaigns form part of a series of movements to loosen the bonds of patriarchal control over married women which are institutionalized in most if not all agrarian civilizations (Mann 1986). The right of a woman to choose her own spouse and to initiate divorce proceedings if the choice turns out bad, the right of a married woman to own property and to make contracts in her own name, to engage in the life of her community without the permission of her husband, and to participate in the political process of decision-making as a voter or as a member of legislative and other councils, have all been the subject of campaigns in industrial societies. The outcomes of these have varied from one society to another, depending on prevailing cultural and political circumstances, and become part of the political and administrative environment within which individual married women and their families live their lives. This environment is often characterized by tension and argument, as the roles of married women continue to be debated and transformed. Individual women will themselves form views on the moral and practical aspects of their lives, and these beliefs will combine with situational constraints and opportunities to determine their own responses. Most women work out these problems in the sphere of their own family life, but some also become actively engaged in movements in the public sphere to reshape the social conditions of women's lives in general. All are aware, through conversation or through exposure to mass media, of some aspects of public debate on these issues.

To provide a comprehensive account of the normative and political debates surrounding women's work in our four societies would be an enormous undertaking. The issue cannot be ignored, however, if for no other reason than that it is addressed by the convergence theorists whose writings we discussed in the introductory chapter. Cultural beliefs concerning the roles of women have been recognized to be a source of variation in industrial societies, and one that will continue to be at the root of continuing diversity within the general tendency towards uniformity (Kerr 1983). The dimensions of that diversity require, however, to be understood through comparative study. This chapter is an attempt to begin that study. In the sections that follow, we will outline briefly the cultural and institutional contexts in the four societies within which married women with young children now make their decisions about their work, and present data from our surveys on their beliefs and attitudes to the relationship between family life and labour force involvement.

China: Confucianism and communism

Cultural background

Traditional Chinese values strongly supported an essentialist conception of the difference between the sexes and sharply segregated roles for men and women. Yin–yang cosmology identified the male, yang, principle as bright, strong and active, and the female, yin, principle as dark, weak and passive (Croll 1978). The Confucian classics, which stemmed from the Warring States period 2500 years ago, and which became the basis for official dominant imperial ideology, elaborated this cosmological principle into a gender segregated social ethic, reinforced by the penal codes of successive dynasties. Men and women had different places in the cosmos and in society, and harmony and righteousness depended on all categories of people being true to the name of their category, knowing their rightful place and acting accordingly. Propriety and good government required that "the Emperor is Emperor, and the minister is minister; the father is father, and the son is son". In each basic social relationship there was an inferior and a superior, the superior was enjoined to be just and benevolent, the inferior to be loyal and obedient. The doctrine of filial piety interpreted all such relationships in familial terms, and all familial relationships were structured hierarchically according to age,

141

generation, and sex (Baker 1979). Women were always subordinate to men, and the doctrine of the "three obediences" laid out the duties of women during their life course: a woman should be obedient to her father before marriage, to her husband after marriage, and to her son after her husband's death. Women's responsibilities were essentially to be carried out within the family household. Women were responsible for the bearing and early upbringing of children, especially sons who would carry on the family name, and for the bulk of domestic work; they were explicitly excluded from participation in affairs outside the household, from the government of clan, the locality or the empire, or from the management of the economy or the family's business.

This normative foundation for gender segregation and subordination seems to have been deeply ingrained in the consciousness of the women and men of all sectors of Chinese society. The expression of these basic values in actual behaviour varied between the different social classes of imperial society. Women were most strictly constrained in the upper classes, where they were confined to the women's areas of the household, and where the practice of footbinding was most stringently enforced, which acted as a physical as well as a symbolic restriction on women's activities. But even in the lower classes, the norms that allocated affairs within the household to women and those outside it to men were still powerful, and, as we have seen in Chapter 2, Chinese women in the traditional agrarian society played a relatively limited role in work outside the home. Regional factors necessitated some variation in this general pattern; the labour of women in the rice-growing southern provinces, for example, was needed in the fields more than in the north, and such constraints as bound feet were more loosely exercised.

There is some evidence of criticism of these patriarchal values, and of resistance to them, on the part of both women and men, even before the growth of contact with other cultures and their norms. However, it was the greater intrusion of Western ideas after the opium wars that really stimulated attacks on the traditional gender order. Christian missionaries taught that men and women equally had souls that deserved salvation in the afterlife and equal treatment in this one, and the Taiping rebels of the mid nineteenth century incorporated such beliefs into their ideology and to some extent their practice. The leaders of the reform movement of the 1890s, especially Kang Youwei, launched a powerful critique of patriarchal Confucianism and the constraints that familistic culture placed on China's modernization, and this critique was developed further by writers of the New Culture and May Fourth period, whose views particularly appealed to the younger generation of urban elite and middle class families. As employment opportunities opened up for women in the factories, schools and hospitals, these "modern" attitudes began to gain ground, though they remained a minority standpoint mostly restricted to the urban young (Lang 1968). Strong reserves of traditionalism in beliefs about gender and family retained their hold in the countryside and among the older generations. The Civil Code promulgated by the government of the Republic of China in the 1930s took the first important steps towards legal equality for women and men and the right to free-choice monogamous marriage. At the same time, the communist movement adopted and adapted the teachings of Marx, Engels and Lenin on the relation between socialist revolution and women's emancipation (Croll 1978).

The Chinese women who responded to the 1987 Sino-Japanese survey were born in the years around 1955, and have therefore lived all their lives in the period since the foundation of the People's Republic under the Chinese Communist Party. Before examining the survey evidence on their attitudes and opinions concerning women's role in the family and at work, it is useful to provide some brief account of the atmosphere in which they grew up and came to adulthood and the ideology relating to women's work and family life to which they would have been exposed.

The Marriage Law of 1950 established the legal basis for new norms of family life, especially autonomy of marriage and the right to sue for divorce, and the equality of men and women in marriage and the family. The mass campaign to publicize and implement the law caused a profound revolution in family life, but it also provoked much resistance, especially in the countryside, from male peasants who saw their rights over women disappearing as wives initiated divorce proceedings (Stacey 1983, Johnson 1983). The party-government never intended to abolish marriage and the family as such, but rather to lay down norms of stable, harmonious and egalitarian marriage relationships based on free choice, with stable families as the backbone of the new society. Divorce should be a last resort, and once the backlog of claims resulting from unsatisfactory arranged marriages had been dealt with, not always to the satisfaction of the women involved, intensive attempts at reconciliation became the norm. Women growing up in the 1950s and 1960s might be expected to embrace this new normative framework for marriage, although they would also have been aware of more traditional family values from their parents and grandparents.

The "Engels strategy" of pursuing gender equality by the inclusion of women in the social labour force was adopted by the party as a basic principle. In practice, however, economic circumstances constrained its implementation. In the 1950s, the reconstruction of the urban economy only provided jobs for a small proportion of the female population, especially as many women were illiterate and had few skills to offer industry or administration, and the authorities had to temper their commitment to women joining the social labour force with assertions that domestic work was also a contribution to building a socialist society (Davin 1976). Many of the mothers of the respondents to the 1987 survey might have first been drawn into work outside the home by the campaigns of the Great Leap Forward, and many of them might have remained housewives throughout their adult lives. By the time the respondents themselves reached adulthood, however, the economy had developed considerably and the assumption that all women would be allocated to a *danwei*, and remain in work after marriage and childbirth, had become firmly established. The low-wage policy pursued by the government in any case made it necessary for all adult members of households to earn an income. At the same time, women's organizations, such as the Women's Federation and the women's committee of the party in work-units, were engaged in "woman work", which included the advancement of women in training and education, encouraging the employment of women in formerly male occupations (and to some extent of men in female ones), establishing the principle of equal pay for equal work, and promoting campaigns and public debate to raise the consciousness of both women and men on issues of women's social labour.

The Cultural Revolution, which took place while the respondents were in their early to mid teens, radicalized these ideological tendencies. While on the one hand women's concerns were ideologically subordinated to class struggle, and the Women's Federation was (temporarily) abolished, the comprehensive attack on all aspects of traditional culture included vigorous campaigns to eradicate gender difference, following Mao's pronouncement that "men and women

144

are equal, female comrades can do what male comrades can" (in Croll 1978: 312). This radical egalitarianism is now seen by some commentators as having put too much pressure on women, accentuating their double burden, and on work-unit leaderships to allocate women to inappropriate work, though such judgements remain controversial.

The "Engels strategy" for women's liberation also included the socialization of domestic labour, so that housework and child care would not prevent women from taking their full part within the social labour force. This strategy would also require a shift in the traditional norms of behaviour for wives and mothers of young children, and government policy in China encouraged such a shift. Radical attempts during the Great Leap Forward to socialize such aspects of domestic labour as cooking and cleaning did not prove either popular or practical, and economic development plans did not include the production of domestic technology such as washing machines. Instead, the authorities pursued the spirit of the Marriage Law by encouraging husbands to help their wives in the home. The division of domestic labour within the household became an issue for public debate during the campaign to criticize Lin Biao and Confucius in 1974, when our average respondent was in her late teens. An article in the party theoretical magazine *Hongqi* stated that "it is necessary to promote the practice that men and women must share household chores" (Croll 1978: 329). More recently, campaigns to promote sharing of household tasks have included competitions, publicized through the mass media, for the title of "model husband".

Finally, the authorities have worked to alter the normative assumption that childrearing is exclusively the private family concern of women. Partly to relieve women of child care responsibilities so that they could concentrate on their social labour, partly to increase state influence on the socialization of the younger generation, nurseries, crèches and kindergartens have been provided on a wide scale. Families have been encouraged to think of childrearing as a contribution to national regeneration and the building of a socialist society, rather than as a purely private family matter, and one that is appropriately placed in the hands of trained experts rather than untrained parents. The Western "maternal deprivation" theory is either unknown in China or is forcefully rejected (Sidel 1972, Broyelle 1977, Wolf 1987).

e survey evidence: diversity of opinion

the end of the 1970s, the economic reform programme
vitality to Chinese society, and greater openness to the
contributed to an emancipation of popular thought.
Many Chinese shared the view of the reformers that the "leftist" dog-
mas mechanically copied from Marxism-Leninism had hampered
China's social development. They began to review the world and
their own lives in the light of the principle of "seeking truth from
facts", as the reform leadership termed the new spirit of pragmatism.
The influence of Marxist doctrine and of party propaganda was weakened, and in its place came a strengthening of the influence of Western
ideas as well as, in some degree, a resurrection of Confucianism.

Thus, it is not surprising that the Sino-Japanese survey of working
women reveals a remarkable diversity in Chinese women's normative beliefs concerning women's work and family life. Given that
almost all of our respondents grew up under "the red flag", it might
be supposed that they were ideologically well equipped by Marxism,
Maoism and the party's doctrine, which stressed women's role in
social production and total gender equality both in social and in family affairs. Their answers to questions regarding gender issues should
conform to the party's propaganda. This might well have been the
case if the reform had never happened. However, just ten years after
the reforms began, although orthodox Marxist doctrine retains some
currency, Chinese views on all social matters including gender issues
have been gradually diversifying, compared with the time when
"every one had the same voice" (the party's voice). Evidence for this
may be found in a major debate that broke out in 1988 concerning
tendencies in both urban and rural China for women to "withdraw
from social production" (whether willingly or not was part of the
debate) as a response to the increasing pressure on the labour market
consequent on the economic reforms. This debate, referred to as
"1988 – the way of women", was raging at about the time that the
Sino-Japanese survey data was first being analyzed, and it revealed
widespread agreement with the practice of "returning women to the
home", current particularly in Daqiuzhuang, a small industrializing
rural township in Tianjin. The participants in this public discussion,
which took place in newspapers and magazines, came from different
social classes with different occupational and educational backgrounds, and their views on women's roles under the new social and

Table 5.1   Opinions on women's work and marriage, China (C) and Japan (J).

	Opinion (percentages)									
	Agree		Agree on the whole		Disagree on the whole		Disagree		Don't know	
Statement	C	J	C	J	C	J	C	J	C	J
1	9.0	10.6	10.2	27.5	21.0	24.6	56.7	28.3	3.0	9.1
2	61.8	40.9	27.2	34.9	5.4	9.1	2.4	2.2	3.3	12.9
3	6.9	16.1	17.8	30.0	29.3	26.3	42.1	20.8	3.9	6.8
4	28.7	12.4	34.4	16.7	13.6	28.0	11.2	25.4	12.1	17.6
5	18.3	39.4	25.6	22.6	12.9	6.0	19.5	5.9	23.6	26.1

Statements:
1. The husband should go out to work, the wife should look after the home.
2. Whether married or not, all women should go out to work.
3. After marriage, a woman should put her husband and children first, and not think about her own work or development.
4. After marriage, if one party is not satisfied with the other, it is better to get divorced.
5. In today's society, divorce is usually disadvantageous for women.
Source: Sino-Japanese Working Women's Family Life Survey.

economic conditions varied to a degree that departed greatly from the orthodox unanimity before the reforms.

The Sino-Japanese survey provides a window through which we can observe Chinese views about women's role after the reforms. Whereas the emphasis on women's participation in the labour force was still very strong, the diversity of views in this respect was quite clear, although perhaps not quite as diverse as the opinions that emerged in the 1988 debate. We present below the main relevant survey findings.

The traditional idea of "the man managing affairs outside the family and the woman managing the household" has become outmoded in the minds of the female respondents. Chinese women have a strong attachment to employment. However, the weight of the dual burden places them in a dilemma. Table 5.1 shows that 77.7 per cent of the respondents are opposed to the notion that "husband should work outside and wife should take care of the household". Although 62.5 per cent of them thought that household work was heavy or very heavy, they are inclined to accept both aspects of work. In our opinion, Chinese women's willingness to work under double pressures is actuated mainly by their families' need for their income, although the motive of seeking a career or economic independence may also play some part. In 1987 when reform of China's wage system had just started, most urban workers were still governed by "low pay and low consumption". Women's wages were still a major source of family income and their jobs were vital to their families. Nonetheless, about one in five of the respondents agreed with the idea of segregated spheres. Most of these had lower levels of education (below upper middle school), as is typical of the working class. Their jobs are usually very arduous as is their domestic work. So pressure for change comes more clearly from this group of women. It is also significant that, according to the female respondents, twice as many husbands as wives believed in the segregation of gendered spheres, that women should stay at home while their husbands go out to work.

From Table 5.2 we see the diversity of Chinese women's responses to the dilemma posed by the dual burden. Asked whether it was better to carry the double burden or to be a housewife, only 34.6 per cent of the women very clearly thought that the combination of tasks was "better than simply being a housewife", whereas 47.9 per cent of those surveyed believed that it "has some bad points but more good ones", 13.1 per cent of them said that it "has some good points, but more bad ones" and 4.4 per cent of them said that it is "much better to be a housewife". This is thought to be a remarkable change from people's views on this kind of question before the reforms. Furthermore, a new survey undertaken by the Institute of Sociology of CASS in Beijing at the end of 1993 showed that 23.5 per cent of the women

Table 5.2 Opinions on the double burden of combining paid work with household tasks, China and Japan.

Opinion	China		Japan	
	N	%	N	%
Much better than just being a housewife	713	34.6	335	19.5
Some bad points, but more good ones	987	47.9	936	54.5
Some good points, but more bad ones	271	13.1	238	13.9
Much better to be just a housewife	90	4.4	207	12.1
No answer	11		149	
Total	2,072	100.0	1,865	100.0

Source: Sino-Japanese Working Women's Family Life Survey.

agreed to the notion that "the ideal is that the husband works and the wife takes care of the housework", whereas in 1987 only 19.2 per cent agreed with this idea. At the same time, more married women (35.3 per cent) agreed with the statement: "If the husband can earn enough money, the wife would do better to stay at home". This demonstrates that ideas on work and family have become more diversified, though most urban women still stress employment and self-reliance.

The survey included a question about the difference of human abilities between the two genders. Only 11.5 per cent of the respondents believed that there are no differences, while the majority recognize some differences. However, they either think that it is not easy to make the comparison because "women and men have different fields of activity in which their abilities come into play" (54.4 per cent) or they think the differences are caused by acquired education and experiences (12.4 per cent). Anyway, it seems that most Chinese women are prepared to accept gender difference in respect of abilities. This may lead people to a more pragmatic view of gender role division and it differs greatly from Mao's idea that "times have changed, men and women are equal, female comrades can do what male comrades do" (in Croll 1978: 312). Furthermore, nearly one-fifth of the women endorsed the statement that "men are more capable than women". This is very different from the common sense of the generation before the reform.

Chinese people have been encouraged to see a relationship between married women working and social development. Probably because of the long history of the state's full employment policy and the party's propaganda on women's role as "holding up half the sky" in social production, Chinese women used not to see their marriage as an obstruction to their working life and have usually thought that it is natural for all people to work throughout their life. So it is understandable that the great majority of them thought that married women working was good for the society (see Table 5.3): 83.5 per cent of them supported the statement that "the increase in married women working will promote social equality and progress", while 80.1 per cent of them agreed that it "has expanded the goods and services aimed at families with both husband and wife working and promoted economic development". At the same time, one in four of the respondents accepted the idea that married women working caused tension in the labour market and increased the unemployment rate in the society. In fact, with economic policy aiming towards a free labour

Table 5.3 Opinions on the increase in married women at work, China (C) and Japan (J).

	Opinion (percentages)								
	Agree		Agree on on the whole		Disagree on the whole		Disagree		Don't know	
Statement	C	J	C	J	C	J	C	J	C	J
1	54.2	31.9	29.3	31.8	1.6	6.8	1.0	1.9	13.9	27.6
2	31.3	18.9	48.8	29.8	2.9	11.4	1.5	3.2	15.6	36.3
3	8.9	4.7	16.0	11.2	21.0	17.4	33.3	21.9	20.8	44.8
4	3.8	16.3	10.4	24.8	16.7	14.3	46.6	16.2	22.4	28.4

Statements:
1. The increase in married women working will promote social equality and progress.
2. The increase in married women working has expanded the goods and services aimed at families with both husband and wife working and promoted economic development.
3. The increase in married women working has created a surplus of labour, resulting in people having to wait for work and not being able to be fully employed.
4. The increase in married women working might damage family life and result in all sorts of social problems.
Source: Sino-Japanese Working Women's Family Life Survey.

Table 5.4 Opinions on the good points about married women working, China and Japan.

	China		Japan	
Good points	N	%	N	%
Can make family better off economically	939	45.4	648	44.5
Women can feel more independent	303	14.6	213	14.6
Can give full play to women's abilities	187	9.0	149	10.2
Strengthens link of women to society	70	3.4	249	17.1
Has a good influence on children	35	1.7	11	0.8
Can promote equality between husband and wife	409	19.8	35	2.4
Can enlarge the couple's shared world and deepen their feelings for each other	113	5.5	119	8.2
No good point	11	0.5	27	1.9
No answer	2	0.1	5	0.3
Total	2,069	100.0	1,456	100.0

Source: Sino-Japanese Working Women's Family Life Survey.

market, the unemployment rate in 1987 was increasing rapidly. However, the problem is why women impute it to their own but not to men's participation in the labour force. The potential answer might be an underlying belief that men are more suitable than women to work in social production. Moreover, 14.2 per cent of the respondents believed that married women's working "might damage family life and result in social problems". It appears that some Chinese have begun to consider possible negative influences of women's employment on social development.

Respondents were asked to consider the influences of women's work on their own life. Table 5.4 shows that the three main benefits that the Chinese women thought they got from their work are: it can make their family better off economically (45.4 per cent); it can promote equality between wife and husband (19.8 per cent); it is good for women's independence (14.6 per cent). The two major disadvantages are: the wife has no spare time due to the pressure of work (53.8 per cent); the dual burden causes the wife much anxiety (17.7 per cent). Answers to these questions indicated that, in the opinion of nearly half of the women, the most important consequence of their work is the money, which can improve their life, whereas the other half tend to stress its consequences for people and their relationships, such as equality between spouses, the wife's independence, and the full use of women's abilities in society. This diversity may be caused by women's different backgrounds such as their family income level, their education and occupation, which may lead to a different attitude towards women's work and family life. At the same time, only 15 per cent of women thought that work had no bad influences on women's lives, while the vast majority of them (85 per cent) acknowledged that the combination of paid work and domestic tasks created difficulties for themselves as well as their families.

Respondents were asked about the relationship between mother's work and child care. Table 5.5 reveals that Chinese women divide fifty/fifty on the question whether mothers should stop work to take care of children who are below 3 years old. This result may not appear so interesting until we put it in the context of the actual situation of Chinese women, who are used to only a short period of maternity leave. From this point of view, support for a longer maternity break is remarkably high. It suggests that many Chinese women have begun to reflect on their desire to stay with their child when he or she is very young. Curiously, the striking division on this important

Table 5.5 Opinions on mother working while child is less than 3 years old, China and Japan.

Opinion	China N	China %	Japan N	Japan %
Until the child is 3 years old, the mother should temporarily give up work and personally bring up the child	1,050	51.1	704	38.6
Bringing up the child and going to work are both important, and a mother should do her best to manage both	979	47.6	638	35.0
Other	26	1.3	483	26.4
Missing	17		40	
Total	2,072	100.0	1,865	100.0

Source: Sino-Japanese Working Women's Family Life Survey.

question does not appear to be related to any social variable among women, such as education, occupation or income. Asked whether any harm might be caused to the child by mother and father both working, even though they are doing their best to care for it, 71.5 per cent of the respondents rejected this formulation of a maternal deprivation thesis. This may be because all the women interviewed in this survey have placed their child in child care facilities, so they may not feel too worried about the effect of their work on the child. Yet even against this background, 23.4 per cent of the women still envisaged the possibility of such harmful consequences of their employment. The diversity of Chinese women's ideas on this question is again very clear.

The survey also shows that Chinese women have strong expectations concerning the sharing of household responsibilities, and that they often believe that their husbands are less egalitarian than they are (see Table 5.6). On the question "Who should do the housework?", 57.8 per cent of wives said that it should be "equally shared" between the spouses, while only 40.3 per cent thought that their husband shared this view. Additionally, 33.8 per cent of them believed that household tasks "should be done by whoever has time and ability", while 43.3 per cent of them considered this to be the view of their husbands. The latter view, which calls for an equitable rather than an equal division of housework between husband and wife, might be thought to embody the principle of "from each according to his or her ability", but also raises problems of the nature of equity which cannot be explored further here (Ferree 1994).

Table 5.6 Who should do the housework? Opinions of wife and husband, China and Japan.

| | China | | | | Japan | | | |
| | Wife | | Husband | | Wife | | Husband | |
Opinions	N	%	N	%	N	%	N	%
Even if the wife is working, housework and child care should mainly be done by the wife	37	1.8	197	9.8	462	29.0	989	68.9
Because both husband and wife are working, housework and child care should be shared equally between them	1,169	57.8	809	40.3	420	26.3	103	7.2
Since men are stronger than women, the husband should take on more housework and child care than the wife if they are both working	132	6.6	132	6.6	15	0.9	1	0.0
Housework and child care should be undertaken according to time and ability, no matter whether by husband or wife	683	33.8	867	43.3	697	43.8	343	23.9
Missing	51		67		271		429	
Total	2,072	100.0	2,072	100.0	1,865	100.0	1,865	100.0

Source: Sino-Japanese Working Women's Family Life Survey.

To explore the changing views of women on marriage in general, the survey also asked about their attitude towards divorce. Divorce was always a privilege of men in traditional Chinese society. In contemporary society, despite the legal stipulation of freedom of divorce, it has been rather difficult to get divorced due to the influence of a combination of traditional and "leftist" ideas. A divorced woman not only suffered the misery of the divorce itself, but was also reproached and subjected to prejudice by the family and society. Divorce is therefore a sensitive issue. Since the initiation of the reform policy and the opening up of Chinese society, Chinese women seem to have greatly changed their ideas on divorce. According to the Sino-Japanese survey, 63.1 per cent of those surveyed think that "it is better to seek divorce if one is not satisfied with one's spouse", which shows that quite a few women had dared to take a positive attitude on divorce by 1987 (see Table 5.1). This trend towards more flexible attitudes to divorce has continued. The survey at the end of 1993 showed that 84.1 per cent of the women took the view that one "can seek divorce if she has justifiable reason". Far more urban women take a positive attitude towards divorce. This shows that the hold of the traditional idea of "following one man to the end" has been weakened, and that the restrictive force of the clan on marriage is being loosened. The emotional bond between husband and wife has become a major link maintaining a marriage.

In summary, it appears that growing up in a society whose revolutionary government had undertaken to transform basic social relationships, and in particular those of employment and the family, had produced in this generation of young mothers ideas about gender roles that were sharply at variance with those of traditional China. They believed, far more than is common in other societies, in the acceptability, even the normality, of the employment of mothers while their children were still below school age, and expected their husbands to take a major share of domestic labour so as to limit the load of the double burden. However, at one highly significant point these women's beliefs diverge from this de-gendered conception of family and work roles, namely that half of them maintain that a woman should not go out to work until her child is over 3 years old. This is a marked deviation from normal practice in Chinese cities, where - maternity leave is usually very short. Whether this division of opinion over the employment of mothers of pre-school children contains the germ of a partial reversion to more "traditional" conjugal roles is a question we will take up again below.

✳ Japan: Confucianism and modernity

Cultural background

don't need this
history

Confucian ethics, with its strict gender segregation and subordination of women, was not dominant over the entire population of pre-modern Japan as it was in China. Confucianism was imported from China in the seventh century (although there are said to have been earlier contacts through Korea), and by the twelfth century had become established, in a reinterpreted form, as the code of the ruling military estate, the *samurai* (Morishima 1984, Storry 1960). The concept of filial piety was understood in terms appropriate to the life of the warrior, with the emphasis on absolute loyalty and obedience to authority. It was in this elite group that the "three obediences" were imposed on women, who were in all respects subordinate to men and excluded from the male pursuits of warfare and government. Footbinding was never accepted into Japanese society, but in other respects *samurai* women were confined and restricted to the affairs of the household.

Among the farmers and fisher folk, artisans and merchants, who made up the majority of the population in pre-industrial Japan under the Shogunate, the lives of men and women were by contrast more equal and less segregated (Dore 1958, Iwao 1993). "In the farm family . . . there was far less emphasis on absolute authority and filial piety and far more on the co-operation of family members in a common enterprise" (Smith 1983: 73). Women were expected to work in the fields, and men made their contribution to the upbringing of children (Uno 1991). Sexual relations were relatively lax (compared with the strict code of the *samurai*), marriages often followed trial cohabitation, and women could initiate divorce. The religious basis of the life of commoners was Buddhism and Shinto rather than Confucianism.

The men who overthrew the Tokugawa shogunate and established a new form of government in the name of the emperor themselves came overwhelmingly from the old warrior class. It is not surprising, therefore, that their reconstruction of Japanese society as a project of modernization, despite the famed borrowing of institutions from more advanced Western nations, drew on the social ethics of their own social estate. This was particularly so in questions of women and the family (Hendry 1981). The Civil Code of 1898, the outcome of a political tussle between traditionalist adherents of *samurai*

Confucianism and more liberal thinkers (Isono 1988), placed the institution of the household (*ie*) at the basis of Japanese society, with the male head exercising legal and absolute authority over all other members of the household, including his wife. The household head had the right to administer all household property, including that brought by the wife into marriage, and could determine the place of residence. Divorce could be initiated by both parties, but the grounds on which wives could sue for divorce were more restricted. In addition, women were excluded from the suffrage and denied participation in political activities. Girls were excluded from the more rigorous forms of post-elementary education offered to boys (Smith 1983).

It was at this time that the ideal of "good wife and wise mother" (*ryoosai kenbo*), specifying the appropriate behaviour of married women, was promoted by politicians and educators (Nolte & Hastings 1991, Uno 1993). The contribution of married women to the modernization of Japan was to be as support to the men in factories and offices, but even more so as mothers of the future loyal, obedient and diligent imperial subjects. The relative freedom and, as former *samurai* saw it, immorality and uncouthness of rural women was to be contained by a civilizing process. There is evidence that this educational project had considerable success: when the American anthropologist John Embree lived in a Japanese village in the 1930s, the older generation remembered their relatively liberated youth with satisfaction, and saw the younger generation as more conservative. The young people were correspondingly embarrassed and annoyed by the free-and-easy attitude of their elders towards sex, marriage and divorce, and the behaviour of women (Smith 1983).

Not all Japanese women were content to fulfil the expected obligations of wives and mothers, however. There were prominent feminists who campaigned against the restrictions imposed on women and acted as role models for others (Rodd 1991). Many middle class women managed to gain an education and strove to achieve careers in the professions and the civil service (Nagy 1991). Working class women whose families could not survive without their wages sometimes became active in struggles for improvements in pay and working conditions, though the female labour force in industries such as cotton remained predominantly unmarried (Molony 1991). However, pressure from the authorities to conform to expected patterns of life remained strong, and intensified during the Second World War, when married women were subjected to the dual demands of replacing male labour in the factories while simultaneously breeding to replace male soldiers killed in action (Miyake 1991).

The legal and constitutional changes imposed on Japan by the American occupation established the legal equality of men and women (thus going further than the constitution of the United States, where the Equal Rights Amendment has never been ratified) and removed the legal basis for the patriarchal household system in such matters as property ownership, inheritance, choice of spouse without parental consent, and divorce. Traditional beliefs remain strong, however, and "there are formidable barriers to a woman's full exercise of those rights in the face of familial opposition" (Smith 1987). Education was, according to the Fundamental Law on Education, supposed to be free of all discrimination by sex, and the language of "filial piety" and "good wife, wise mother" was to be removed from the curriculum, but the actual situation in the post-war period continues to reveal gender divisions, especially at the post-secondary stage (Buckley 1993).

Unlike in China, this legal and constitutional recognition of gender equality was not followed up by public campaigns for the furtherance of that equality in practice, either in the sphere of paid employment or in that of family life. State employment, welfare and taxation policies, right up to the passing of the Equal Employment Opportunities Law in 1986, were premissed on the assumption that married women would at most maintain part-time employment, because of their family and especially childrearing responsibilities (Uno 1993). As the economy recovered from defeat in war, and labour shortages appeared, women were encouraged to enter the formal paid labour force, reducing their informal commitment to small family business especially in agriculture, but never reducing their responsibilities as wives and mothers.

The emphasis on women's role as mothers was if anything intensified. In the late 1950s and early 1960s (when the respondents to the Sino-Japanese survey were children), there was considerable public debate over whether women should continue to work after childbirth. Government statements expressed concern about the decline in the birth-rate and a 1963 White Paper on child welfare stated that "a deficiency in the level of nurturing is creating a risk for the children of this generation", also referring to "the decline in child welfare in the wake of women's increased penetration of the workforce" (cited in

Buckley 1993: 351). Prime Minister Sato appealed to Japanese women to have more children. The issue was also discussed in popular women's magazines, where the general tone supported women placing their priority on motherhood rather than a career. The normative pressure on women to concentrate on their obligations as mothers would often be reinforced by the expectations of mothers-in-law (Masuda 1975), child care workers (Fujita 1989, Hendry 1986), and other housewives (Imamura 1987). The highly competitive nature of the Japanese education system and the importance placed on educational credentials also encourages mothers to devote themselves to improving their child's educational chances (M. White 1987).

Again by contrast with China, Japan has until very recently been marked by an absence of a discussion of the obligations of husbands and fathers to share in the work of the household. The assumption that the home is the exclusive preserve of the wife has not been actively challenged from any official or authoritative source. Even women's groups and associations have tended predominantly to accept an ideology of gender difference, and most have not campaigned on a platform of greater, let alone equal, sharing of domestic responsibilities. The saying that "a good husband is healthy and absent" retains currency (Iwao 1993). However, it is precisely the issue of the health of husbands that has led to a greater public questioning of the traditional pattern of highly segregated roles. Publication of evidence of the increasing risks to men's health caused by overwork has resulted in discussion of whether husbands would be more healthy if they were less absent, if working practices could be reformed so that absolute commitment of energies to the company were curtailed, leaving men with more time to spend with their families.

This recent development, however, is only a small breach in a public discourse that has generally explicitly endorsed or tacitly accepted highly segregated gender roles. As Buckley (1993) and others have argued, this gender ideology is increasingly at variance with the actual behaviour and experience of many women who are committed to their careers and who attempt to reduce their family responsibilities, if by no other means than by having fewer children. It is in this context that we can now go on to examine the attitudes and opinions on women's work and family life revealed by the 1987 survey.

The survey evidence: diversity of opinion

Different conceptions of the roles of husband and wife exist side by side in contemporary Japan. According to a 1975 survey carried out in Tokyo by the Japan Leisure Development Centre, 53.5 per cent of sampled housewives rejected the traditional idea of "men working for a living while women taking care of the household" (Zhang 1984). Another survey by the Japanese cabinet showed in 1980 that only 29 per cent of the women were in favour of "men in charge of external affairs while women are responsible for the family" (Zhang 1984). This picture was confirmed by the Sino-Japanese survey in 1987, which showed 52.9 per cent of the respondents were against such a mode of division (see Table 5.1). When the Kitakyushu Forum on Asian Women conducted its survey in Japan in 1989, 49.2 per cent of female respondents were opposed to this segregation of conjugal roles (Pongsapich et al. 1993). All four surveys point to one conclusion: a significant proportion of Japanese women no longer support the "traditional" division of labour inside the family and the "traditional" roles of husband and wife. Yet we also find from the Sino-Japanese survey that a certain percentage of Japanese women do still stick to the idea of gender role division: more than one-third (38.1 per cent) of the respondents accepted the idea that "the husband should go out to work, the wife should look after the home" and almost half of them (46.1 per cent) agreed that "after marriage, a woman should put care of her husband and children first, and not think about her own work or development". This diversity is partly explained by respondents' educational backgrounds: the more educated the women, the less they tend to agree with the conventional idea. For instance: 62.5 per cent of the respondents who have primary or lower middle school education agreed with the statement that "husband should go out to work, the wife should look after the home", whereas only 12.5 per cent of the respondents who have university or postgraduate education did. Of the less educated women, 68.2 per cent agreed that "after marriage, a women should put care of her husband and children first, and not think about her own work or development", compared with only 16.9 per cent of the highly educated women. This suggests that diversity and change of gender role expectations in Japan are dependent on the educational level of women. Thus, it can probably be assumed that, as the education level of Japanese women continues to rise, they are likely to further shift their views on gender division. From the Sino-Japanese survey, we also find that the wives' opinions on gender roles differ significantly from those they report their husbands to have. It seems that Japanese husbands are more likely to support the conventional idea that women should stay at home, especially after marriage and childbirth. This conflict of ideology on gender roles between husband and wife inside the family may be an important factor influencing women's labour force participation.

There are also great variations in Japanese women's views on female participation in the labour market, as well as striking differences from China. As we showed in Chapter 3, Japanese women's participation in the labour force has increased markedly in the post-war period, which may have had a great influence on Japanese women's values concerning their family life as well as its reality. However, people may have different views on this matter, given that the ideology of separate spheres is still quite strong in Japanese society. The Sino-Japanese survey's findings suggest that Japanese women's views on the effects of the increase in married women's labour force participation are not uniformly positive, with considerable proportions of women not prepared to express a view on some of the statements presented to them (see Table 5.3). Although around two-thirds of the respondents (63.7 per cent) support the statement that "the increase in married women working will promote social equality and progress" and nearly half of them (48.7 per cent) thought that it would "promote economic development", a strong sense of disquiet still comes through in other responses. More than two in five (41.1 per cent) thought that it may "damage family life and result in all sorts of social problems", whereas 15.9 per cent thought that it may be responsible for the increase in unemployment. These responses indicate that, from one point of view, the increase in women working does cause a re-evaluation of gender divisions at the levels both of society and family. And this being the case, conflict between the "traditional" norms and "modern" ways of thinking must be inevitable. The increasing rate of divorce in Japan, which we will touch on later, may be one of its consequences.

Furthermore, Japanese women's ideas on the advantages and disadvantages of married women working are very interesting compared with those of the Chinese women. Apart from similar proportions of both who support the first three statements in Table 5.4, 17.1 per cent of Japanese women, compared with 3.4 per cent of the

Chinese, picked out as the main advantage that it "strengthens a woman's links to society". The reason for this is probably related to the long working hours of husbands, and their corporate socializing after work, which leaves a Japanese housewife isolated in her home for long periods of each day. Women who have no other "link" to the wider society are "captives" in their homes. Thus, the working women recognize that the links with society that their work provides them with add meaning and variety to their lives. As for the disadvantages of married women working, Japanese women complain less about being "too busy with work and having no spare time" (32.3 per cent compared with 53.8 per cent of Chinese women). This may be because their working hours are shorter than those of Chinese women, as we mentioned earlier. However, it is surprising to see that despite this they are more likely to complain that the dual burden makes them anxious (20.6 per cent of Japanese women compared to 17.7 per cent of Chinese women), and a much higher percentage believe that married women's work prevents them from doing housework (23.7 per cent of Japanese women compared to 0.3 per cent of Chinese women). We believe that such respondents are not suggesting that Japanese working women do no housework at all, but are rather reflecting the strength of feeling in Japan that household tasks are the wife's responsibility, so that failure to carry out any single aspect of housework could be considered as a dereliction of duty. This also reflects the conflict inside Japanese women's minds between the older idea of "good wife, wise mother" and the increasing demands of the labour market. It indicates that Japanese women are faced with a great dilemma between the roles of worker and housewife.

Tradition has it in Japan that the mother is responsible for raising children. However, according to the 1975 survey by Leisure Development Centre, 35.1 per cent of housewives did not take raising children as a natural task that must by nature be shouldered by women (Zhang 1984). A decade later the Sino-Japanese survey showed a trend towards an emphasis on the couple's sharing of responsibility for children. Only 9.7 per cent of the respondents accepted the viewpoint that "raising children is after all the mother's responsibility so, even if the mother goes out to work, caring for the children is what she should put first", while on the other hand, 87 per cent of the respondents felt that "raising children is the common responsibility of a couple and should be shared between husband and wife".

Increasing numbers of Japanese women clearly expect their husbands to share the burdens of rearing children. On the question of whether a mother should give up work while her children are below 3 years old, Japanese women, like Chinese, divide equally between affirmation and denial (38.6 per cent and 35 per cent), although 26.4 per cent of the respondents failed to give an unequivocal response (see Table 5.5). Given that most Japanese women leave their jobs once they have children, the support for this line of action among the respondents might seem quite low, while endorsement for those who combine work and child care together might appear quite strong, though one must remember that the respondents in this survey came from that minority of Japanese mothers who continued to work while having a pre-school child. Again we find a close relation between educational level and opinions on working mothers, with more educated women more likely to support the view that mothers should do their best to both work and bring up children (29.3 per cent of primary or lower middle school women compared with 56 per cent of university graduates or postgraduates), and the less educated women more likely to agree that mothers should temporarily leave off work until their child is 3 years old (40.2 per cent of primary or lower middle school women compared with 22.6 per cent of university educated). Asked whether mother and father both working might be harmful to the child, 17.1 per cent of the respondents reject this maternal deprivation thesis whereas 26.4 per cent accept it. Once more there is a close relation with educational level, with the more educated women more likely to deny that both parents working could be deleterious to their children. This suggests that well-educated Japanese women are now more committed to their careers and their development, and no longer look on childbearing as the most important aspect of their lives, unlike the older generation of Japanese women.

Japanese women are far more likely than Chinese to take on the role of housewife. Even career women tend to assume the responsibilities of household labour, as we have seen in the previous chapter. However, judging from the results of the Sino-Japanese survey (see Table 5.6), Japanese women would much prefer their husbands to take on more of the work of the household, although only 26.3 per cent advocate equal sharing. The highest proportion (43.8 per cent) seek a more equitable division of household work, while it is noteworthy that 29 per cent of the respondents still believed that household labour should be mainly assumed by the wife. According to the women's own judgement, husbands were far more traditional in their views on household labour: 68.9 per cent of the husbands (compared to 29 per cent of the wives) believe that the wife should take the main responsibility of housework and only 7.2 per cent (compared with 26.3 per cent of the wives) support wife and husband sharing housework equally. This might indicate, on the one hand, that there is still a long way to go before Japanese couples can agree on a genuine sharing of household tasks, and, on the other, that for many couples the model of segregated conjugal roles can still function in the distinctive cultural environment of Japan.

Attitudes to divorce are also changing. Since the 1970s, the divorce rate in Japan has been increasing steadily. However, it is believed that economic dependence on the husband makes Japanese women today very cautious on the issue of divorce. According to a 1973 survey by the cabinet, 70 per cent of women opposed the idea that "divorce could be pursued whenever one party finds the other unsatisfactory after marriage", 18.6 per cent found the idea somewhat understandable, and only 2.8 per cent expressed their approval (Zhang 1984). In another survey in 1979 by the Yomivli News Agency, 10.6 per cent of the respondents said divorce should never happen under any circumstances, 52.2 per cent thought divorce should be avoided and 32 per cent said divorce should be the last resort. Only 2.1 per cent agreed divorce might sometimes be a necessity (Zhang 1984). These results show that the majority of Japanese women were opposed to divorce, although their attitudes were undergoing change. In the 1980s Japanese women registered major changes in their attitudes toward divorce. In the Sino-Japanese survey, 29.1 per cent agreed with the statement that "if one party is not satisfied with the other, it is better to get divorced" (see Table 5.1). The proportion accepting the need for divorce was ten times higher than in the 1973 survey. The 1989 Kitakyushu Forum survey found that 80.2 per cent of the women respondents said that "divorce is OK if justified" (Pongsapich et al. 1993). It appears that Japanese women have been increasingly expressing open acceptance of divorce in recent years.

In general, the survey evidence adds support to Buckley's (1993) suggestion that gender ideology and the actual experience of women in Japan are increasingly coming into tension with each other. Enquiries into the values and attitudes of housewives might well reveal reservoirs of support for married women with pre-school-age children who engage in paid employment. The Sino-Japanese survey showed the converse of this, that significant proportions even of women who are employed while their children are below school age have considerable doubts as to the wisdom and morality of this combination of activities. Unlike in China, where variations in opinions on married women working are difficult to attribute to any particular aspects of social diversity, variations in Japan often follow lines of education, with less highly educated women more attached to the dominant ideology of segregated spheres. But even university graduates vary considerably in their attachment to those features of gender role ideology which might be thought of as "modern" (Bonney et al. 1994). There can be no doubt that Japanese beliefs on the appropriate activities of young mothers, as on other aspects of gendered behaviour, are in a state of flux, though conservative views still have a powerful hold over many women and, even more so, men.

Go To 171 pg for USA.

Britain: a revolution of low expectations

Cultural background

However secularized British society may now be, it would be a mistake to ignore Christian tradition as a significant component of the normative background to contemporary views on women's work and family life, especially in a book that aims to compare some of the world's major civilizations. Christian teaching on gender traditionally contained a tension between spiritual equality and social subordination (Davidoff & Hall 1987). Biblical sources have it that "there is neither male nor female for ye are all one in Christ Jesus" (Gal. 3: 28), and the Church recognized the right of all women to salvation, equally with men. Consistent with this was the canon law, drawn up in the twelfth century, which defined marriage as an indissoluble sacrament of which the matter consists of the mutual consent of husband and wife (Segalen 1986). Side by side with this doctrine of spiritual equality sat a firm belief in the natural difference of men and women and the subordination of women to men in society. By the seventeenth century in England, patriarchy had been elaborated as a complete theory of authority by Sir Robert Filmer, according to whom the authority of the absolute monarch mirrored the absolute authority of the male head of each household (Laslett 1965, Elshtain

164

1981). But the social implications of patriarchal theory were accepted no less by Puritans (Hill 1969). The stress on the patriarchal household gave religious support for any conventional division of labour, which allocated tasks to all members of the household as a common enterprise under the authority of the male head (Shorter 1977). It also justified the subordinate position of women in civil marriage seen as a contract, denying a married woman the right to own property separately from her husband or to enter into contracts without her husband's consent, or any participation in the government of the country.

Davidoff and Hall (1987) have demonstrated in convincing detail the role of evangelical Christianity in reconstructing a pre-industrial, gender-based division of labour into a doctrine of the appropriate and separate spheres of middle class men and women. In the new world of industrial capitalism, men found their calling in the impersonal and amoral world of the market economy, while a woman's vocation was to provide a spiritual and moral haven at home for her husband and children. By the late nineteenth century, this had become the dominant ideology, that the role of wife and mother was incompatible with a career, that the appropriate activities of middle class women outside the home consisted of charity and philanthropy, and that respectable working class women did not have to go out to work because their husbands earned enough, a "family wage", to keep them and their children (Lewis 1984).

There was, however, an alternative normative basis for gender roles in British society, which could also draw on religious tradition, and particularly on the belief in spiritual equality. The seventeenth century saw puritanism radicalized into a range of egalitarian revolutionary ideals, such as those of the Ranters and the Levellers, which if successfully implemented would have turned the world upside down, including the world of gender subordination (Hill 1975). The radical ideas were soon extinguished, but the liberal individualism of seventeenth-century political thought lived on, as the core of a doctrine of individual citizenship which, once established, was incapable of justifying the exclusion of women from the rights of the citizen (Stacey & Price 1981, Elshtain 1981). The feminism of Mary Wollstonecraft and John Stuart Mill was built on this basis, and it resulted in legal and constitutional moves towards gender equality, the right of married women to own property and make contracts, and eventually the suffrage. The right of a woman to enter any occupation and develop a career on equal terms with men also derives from this liberal theory. Liberal individualism had and still has many obstacles to overcome, such as the marriage bars that operated in the inter-war period in many professions, and it now forms the legal basis for gender equality in Britain, as seen in the Sex Discrimination Act, the Equal Pay Act, and the work of the Equal Opportunity Commission (Lewis 1992), and in the law of the European Union.

Liberal individualism has tended to concentrate on the rights of women in the public sphere of politics, law and employment, and to neglect the private sphere of the family. Most "first wave feminists", while challenging doctrines of the natural separation of spheres based on religion or science, accepted that homemaking and child-rearing should be the responsibility of women (Lewis 1984). This has continued to be the basic assumption underlying public policy in the era of the twentieth-century British welfare state (Wilson 1977, Lewis 1983). Right into the 1980s and 1990s, the positions on women's work taken by the major political parties and interest groups have been characterized by a tension (some might say incoherence or inconsistency) between adherence to a rhetoric of equal opportunities and a conservative conception of family life, as displayed in policies and statements on parental leave and child care. Some spokesmen for the Conservative Party, for example, while not departing from a commitment to equal opportunities, argue that "the family" is the basis of a civilized society, that mothers are the most appropriate people to look after young children, and that it is not the place of the state to provide such facilities as free child care (Coote & Hewitt 1980).

When the grandmothers of present-day young children were themselves growing up, the climate of opinion strongly reinforced the norms of segregated roles. Having taken over many of the jobs of men during the Second World War, women were encouraged to return to their families and bring up their children. The child care facilities provided during the war were dismantled. The theories of "maternal deprivation", associated particularly with John Bowlby, were well publicized. Women's magazines purveyed a cult of femininity and domesticity, portraying women predominantly in the roles of wives and mothers, and accentuating the theme that "a working wife is a bad wife" (Ferguson 1983). By the late 1960s and early 1970s, when the mothers of present-day young children were themselves growing up, a much greater diversity of voices could be heard.

"Second wave" feminism was expounded by a great variety of women's groups and associations, mostly attracting the active support of small minorities of women, but gaining publicity for many new conceptions of women's possibilities. That variety makes it difficult to generalize about the influence of the "women's movement" on the climate of opinion (Coote & Hewitt 1980; Coote & Campbell 1987). A few writers and speakers, such as Germaine Greer, became household names, though we lack evidence on which households spoke those names. Women's magazines switched to the theme of "a working wife is a good wife", and maternal deprivation theory lost the prominence it once had, though women continued to be portrayed in the roles of wife and mother more than in any other roles (Ferguson 1983). More women were seen in more visible public roles, serving as role models for others, culminating in the election of the first woman party leader, Margaret Thatcher, who became Prime Minister in 1979. Many have pointed to the irony that this most public of public women stressed her own roles as wife and mother, promoted no other woman to cabinet rank, and advocated a return to Victorian family values. Perhaps we can say that in her own person Thatcher exemplified the diversity of norms for women that has characterized public discourse in late twentieth-century Britain.

Survey evidence: diversity of opinion

According to findings of the *British Social Attitudes Survey*, which has been carried out annually since 1984, the British general public has diverse and complex attitudes to women's employment (Brook et al. 1992). There is considerable support for the general principle of sex equality. The 1984 survey found that 94 per cent of respondents favoured laws assuring women and men equal pay for equal work, and the 1984, 1987 and 1991 surveys revealed 80 per cent, 75 per cent and 85 per cent respectively supporting laws against sex discrimination. A series of more detailed questions asked in the 1987, 1989 and 1991 surveys on the relationship between employment and family roles, however, uncovered strong reservoirs of attachment to "traditional" norms of separate and gendered spheres. Presented with the statement that "a husband's job is to earn the money, the wife's job is to look after home and family", respondents in 1989 divided between 27 per cent who agreed more or less strongly, 53 per cent who disagreed, and 18 per cent who had no view either way. The

1991 sample was less likely than that of 1989 to disagree (44 per cent), and more likely to agree, with this "traditional" view of conjugal roles. Also in 1991, women were more likely than men to disagree with this homemaker–breadwinner model, but not by much. The younger and more highly educated the respondent, the more likely he or she was to reject the "traditional" model (Kiernan 1992).

In 1989, 31 per cent agreed that "a job is all right, but what most women really want is a home and children", the same proportion as those who in 1987 agreed that "women shouldn't try to combine a career with children". On the specific question of mothers working while their child is below school age, 2.3 per cent in 1989 approved of women working full-time, 26.2 per cent accepted that they might work part-time, but 64 per cent thought that such mothers should stay at home and look after their children. The 1991 survey showed a small shift towards greater acceptance of mothers of pre-school children working, with 5 per cent accepting that they might work full-time, and 33 per cent agreeing that they could work part-time. A majority of the 1989 sample (53 per cent) accepted the maternal deprivation thesis that "a pre-school child is likely to suffer if his or her mother works" (Brook et al. 1992).

Many of the questions asked in the *British Social Attitudes Survey* followed up the particularly thorough analysis of women's attitudes to paid employment in Great Britain in the report of the 1980 Women and Employment Survey by the original authors (Martin & Roberts 1984) and the subsequent secondary analysis by Dex (1988). Evidence was provided of a considerable continuing diversity of views among women on the appropriateness of the employment of mothers with young children and about the extent of women's obligations in paid employment where there might be perceived to be conflicts with domestic and child care duties. Attitudes of women and husbands have slowly become more accepting of women's involvement in paid work in recent decades and since 1965 this is related among women to their increasing experience of paid work. Martin and Roberts characterized 30 per cent of the female respondents as having "traditional" attitudes, reflecting a preference for domestic roles over paid employment and a perception of the male as the main breadwinner. For instance, 46 per cent of respondents in the 1980 survey accepted the statement that "a husband's job is to earn the money; a wife's job is to look after the home and family", while 25 per cent agreed that "a woman's place is in the home". Opinions varied systematically between working and non-working women, and 41 per cent of non-employed women were classified by Martin and Roberts as having "traditional" attitudes. Nearly twice as many non-working women as working women (37 per cent compared with 20 per cent) agreed that "a woman's place is in the home". The authors observe that "work is considered by many women to be secondary to the home and family and something to be accommodated to domestic demands". On the other hand 21 per cent of all women and 31 per cent of employed women were categorized as having "non-traditional" attitudes, agreeing with the obverse of these propositions and with a greater centrality of paid employment in the lives of women. Dex (1988) demonstrates how these attitudes vary by age, educational level and employment status, with the younger, the more highly educated and full-time workers having less traditional views. Women working in family businesses were the most traditional of all. With regard to the particular category of women with whom we are especially interested in this study, Dex also showed that having young children is associated with a higher incidence of traditional attitudes.

SCELI data also supports this general pattern, reinforcing the picture of a diversity of opinions on gender roles and the employment of women. We concentrate here on the pooled sub-sample of employed married mothers of children under age 11. Fifty-two per cent of this group of women agreed with the statement that "I'm not against women working, but men should still be the main breadwinner in the family", compared with 46 per cent agreement among all women under age 45. Asked about which partner of a couple had the responsibility for obtaining income to support the family, 43 per cent of mothers of young children say that the responsibility should be the male partner's, while 56 per cent say it should be shared equally; 26 per cent of these women assert that the female partner should be responsible for looking after children, while 70 per cent say that this responsibility should be shared equally by both partners. Fifty-nine per cent of mothers of young children say the female partner should be responsible for housework, compared with 40 per cent who say it should be shared equally.

In a number of surveys, women have been asked to relate their views on women's employment to the state of the wider economy. One statement put to women was: "In times of high unemployment, married women should stay at home". In 1980, 35 per cent of working

IDEOLOGIES OF FAMILY AND WOMEN'S WORK

age women agreed with this statement, 16 per cent had no opinion either way, and 49 per cent disagreed. The 1987 *British Social Attitudes Survey* found 21 per cent of women agreeing with this idea, 18 per cent with no definite opinion, and 60 per cent opposed to it (Witherspoon 1988). Our SCELI sub-sample of married women with young children were even more opposed to the idea that men should be given this priority when jobs were scarce: 76 per cent rejected it, 18 per cent accepted it, and a scant 6 per cent expressed no firm opinion. British women seem increasingly resistant to the suggestion that they should give way to men in the labour market though, unlike in the case of the Sino-Japanese survey, women in Britain do not seem to have been asked whether they think male unemployment might actually be caused by female employment.

There is also evidence from the various surveys that British husbands, like husbands in China, Japan and elsewhere, hold more "traditional" views on conjugal roles than their wives. Martin and Roberts (1984) classified 41 per cent of husbands as "traditional" compared to 31 per cent of wives. Younger husbands are less likely to adhere to traditional conjugal roles than older ones, but SCELI data on the partners of mothers of young children nonetheless show a clear divergence on some questions between partners' opinions. For example, whereas 43 per cent of employed mothers of young children believe that the responsibility for earning family income lies with the male, as many as 60 per cent of their male partners share this view. Similarly, while 40 per cent of the mothers thought that the housework should be shared equally by the two partners, just 31 per cent of male partners agreed with this. On the other hand, 70 per cent of both mothers and their male partners agreed that looking after children should be shared equally. More generally, husbands' opinions are noticeably influenced by the employment status of their wives, so that men whose wives are in employment are far less likely to hold to the male breadwinner–female homemaker model than men whose wives are not in paid work (Kiernan 1992).

The climate of attitudes concerning women's roles at home and in employment in Great Britain thus exhibits considerable diversity. Women in general neither completely accept nor reject women combining domestic and employment roles, and there are among them substantial reservoirs of support for both "traditional" and "non-traditional" attitudes. It is worth stressing, however, that women's stated opinions in attitude surveys do not necessarily dictate their actual courses of action: significant proportions of employed mothers of young children appear to believe that mothers of young children should in principle not be employed, and significant proportions of non-employed mothers of young children see nothing wrong in the behaviour of such mothers who do take paid work. Against the rather "pluralist" cultural background in Britain sketched out in the first part of this section, such phenomena should come as no surprise. Yet the degree of change in attitudes to women's employment can easily be exaggerated. The fifth report of the *British Social Attitudes Survey*, referring to the finding that the proportion of respondents who believed that mothers of pre-school children ought to stay at home rather than take paid work had gone down from 78 per cent in 1965 to 45 per cent in 1987, spoke of "a sea-change" (Witherspoon 1988). Yet the continued preference of mothers themselves, of their male partners, and of the weight of public opinion, that mothers of pre-school age children should seek part-time work that would enable them to accommodate their need to supplement family income or their interest in work to their responsibilities to child care, speaks of a low-key and genteel revolution, a revolution indeed of low expectations.

The United States: a "stalled revolution"

Cultural background *excellent* *onto*

Gender roles in some sections of American society have become a field of conflict and tension, some even say war (Berger & Berger 1983, Skolnick 1991). It is impossible to survey this field without considerable oversimplification, but it is useful to begin with the two major ideologies that have informed gender roles in Britain: patriarchal Christianity and liberal individualism. The Puritans who crossed the Atlantic to establish the colonies in America took with them a strict version of the former and, for the first century and a half, this doctrine set the tone for women's lives. Preached by ministers and enforced by community sanctions, Christian morality stipulated that self-sufficient farming families were ruled over by father-husbands who ran the co-operative household-as-enterprise and decided the marriages and occupations of children (Degler 1980). Within the household-as-enterprise, a clear gender division of labour was the norm, with women responsible for the homestead and children.

During the nineteenth-century phase of industrialization, the normative basis for women's roles followed the same pattern as in Britain, and the doctrine of "separate spheres" developed with the same kind of religious backing. When Tocqueville visited America in the 1830s, clergymen were writing and preaching about the importance of women's role in the home, a sphere "of peace and concord, love and devotion, in contrast to the selfishness and immorality characteristic of 'the world'" (Bellah et al. 1988). Despite the attempt of manufacturers and Hamiltonians to encourage women into the workforce, the moral code of domesticity denied legitimacy to the employment of married women outside the home, and it was predominantly young unmarried women who answered the call, apart from women forced by necessity to earn an income of their own (Kessler-Harris 1982). Male trade unions reinforced this code in their campaigns for a "family wage", which would allow working men the same kind of family life enjoyed by the middle classes, and eventually the family wage was accepted as a bargaining position by employers, though for their own reasons (May 1991). As we have seen, by the turn of the twentieth century only 4 per cent of married women were registered by the census enumerators as being in paid employment.

At the same time, however, the theories of liberal individualism were beginning to have an impact on the thinking of some women. The Declaration of Sentiments and Resolutions passed by women's rights activists at Seneca Falls in 1848 used the language and conceptual framework of the Declaration of Independence to demand equal citizenship rights for women and men, in politics, property ownership, business and employment. It also criticized the religious morality that confined women to the domestic sphere and subjected them to their husbands' will in family life (Chafe 1991). This critique of gender inequality was radicalized at the turn of the century by such writers as Charlotte Perkins Gilman (1966 [1898]) and, although this more radical version of individualism attracted few supporters, the early part of the twentieth century saw many of the Seneca Falls demands realized, most obviously the suffrage in 1918. The liberal individualist perspective continued to underlie further campaigns for the legal equality of men and women, and especially the struggle for the Equal Rights Amendment to the Constitution, which was at its height in the 1920s and again in the 1970s. The ERA has never been ratified, however, coming up against resistance not just from conservative supporters of separate spheres but also from those defending specific rights for women, such as those embodied in protective factory and employment legislation (Chafe 1991, Rosenberg 1993).

Liberal individualism as such took no more than a permissive attitude towards the employment of married women outside the home. If women wanted or needed to pursue such employment, the law should not hinder them. Yet even in its most radical version, such as that of Gilman, individualistic feminism did not challenge the association of women with childrearing and the domestic virtues. Less radical tendencies shared with conservatism a belief that a married woman's first commitment was to her family, her husband and children, and that her search for individual self-determination through a career should be subordinated to that prior responsibility. Most American women, particularly of the middle and upper classes, were committed to the idea of "separate spheres" (Chafe 1991). A brief flowering in the first quarter of the twentieth century of the idea that women had a right to greater independence from the claim of the family gave way in the 1930s and 1950s to a reassertion of the cult of domesticity (as Betty Friedan (1963) was to call it), to which the recruitment of married women into war-related jobs in the 1940s was seen as only a temporary and necessary exception.

Liberal individualism translates in America into an absence of public policy over the employment of married women, and Congress and government have generally rejected anything that might be taken as "government interference in the family". Thus, as we have seen in Chapter 3, there is no national system of child care in the United States, though public money is spent on tax credit subsidy of some private child care expenses and to support federally funded day care centres for the children of the working poor. There is no statutory maternity benefit for employed women. Rather than become involved in facilitating parents in combining work and family life, the United States "has opted for avoidance of public provision, and left the solutions to the market or to whatever personal arrangements individuals can make" (Kamerman 1980: 91).

It was not until the 1960s and 1970s that the war over gender roles and the family broke out. Public debates over the role of women came to greater prominence during the Kennedy administration, with the young and modernizing president setting up the Presidential Commission on the Status of Women, resulting in the Equal Pay Act of 1963. The inclusion of sex as a category of discrimination prohibited under Title VII of the Civil Rights Act passed in 1964 was also highly controversial, and the first head of the Equal Employment Opportunity Commission publicly refused to enforce this provision (Rosenberg 1993). The rapid absorption of married women into the labour force coincided with the appearance of the various manifestations of the women's movement, each adding impetus to the other. The association founded by Friedan, the National Organization for Women (NOW), acting as a conventional pressure group, was at the respectable end of a continuum of feminist groups whose more radical wing included SCUM, The Feminists, The Redstockings, WITCH, Cell 16 and Bread and Roses.

However small the active membership of such groups might have been, the publicity attracted by such events as the disruption of Miss America Pageants gave middle America the impression that they were facing a widespread movement to overthrow the gender order and "the family". The reaction against the women's movement took the form of a wide variety of conservative and religious organizations which saw a need to defend the "traditional family". The women's movement was branded as anti-family, anti-child, and anti-moral. Organizations such as the Moral Majority, Christian Family Renewal, and United Families of America campaigned against the ERA, against laws permitting abortion, against gay and lesbian rights, and against the provision of child care. Such media as film, television and magazines were widely used, especially by evangelical Christians, to promote an image of the family under attack and to support what they saw as moral and conventional gender roles, especially the role of married woman as wife and mother (Hunter 1987). In the 1980s, the administrations of Reagan and Bush were widely perceived as supporting this conservative agenda: for example, Reagan's appointments to the judiciary were influenced by the "pro-life" issue, and Bush vetoed a parental leave bill passed by Congress in 1990 (Rosenberg 1993).

Women who were mothers of pre-school children in the late 1980s and early 1990s have thus grown up and come to adulthood in a period when discussion over appropriate roles for men and women, their responsibilities towards each other, their children and themselves, have become highly politicized (Berger & Berger 1983, Popenoe 1988, 1993, Stacey 1990, 1993, Skolnick 1991). Widespread interest in such debates is revealed by the success of magazines such as *Ms.*, most of the readers of which were never active members of any feminist group. Nor is this a set of debates between entirely closed and entrenched positions: James Hunter (1987) shows how both faculty and students at evangelical Christian colleges and seminaries, while considerably more conservative on family and gender issues than their equivalents at public institutions, are themselves divided on such questions, many of them having been influenced by the feminist tone of much public discussion as well as by the "pro-family" doctrines of their preachers. If the generality of young mothers were themselves divided on their attitudes to the employment of married women and child care, it would not be at all surprising.

Survey evidence: diversity of opinion

In accord with these strong divisions of opinion in public discourse, survey evidence on Americans' personal attitudes to women's employment, especially during the phase of life when they are parenting young children, reveal a marked lack of consensus. Views are divided as they are in Great Britain but, in line with the greater vigour and influence of the women's movement in the USA, there is a greater acceptance of the paid employment of mothers of young children. Attitudes to women's employment have generally been becoming less "traditional" over recent decades, both through new cohorts of younger people having more liberal attitudes and older people changing their opinion. However, substantial elements of American opinion still hold conservative views. For example, according to the General Social Survey of 1988, 47 per cent of women did not disagree that "it is much better for everyone if the man is the achiever and the woman takes care of the home and family" (Scott & Dunscombe 1991).

Scott and Dunscombe (1991) have investigated whether American attitudes are less traditional than British ones, which might be expected given the greater labour force involvement of women in the USA. British respondents were overall more likely to endorse mothers being out of paid work when children were of pre-school age and to endorse part-time work when the children were of school age. The differential incidence of part-time and full-time work among mothers of young children in the two countries complicates the comparisons since employment has different characteristics in each country. These differences may help explain the fact that the British sample were "more egalitarian in their stance that role-combination *in principle* is beneficial" while they were "more traditional than Americans in their concern that *in practice* working may clash with family life, and in particular the care of pre-school children" (Scott & Dunscombe 1991).

The greater general acceptance of the practice of paid employment by mothers of young children in the USA has been found in other survey research findings. Alwin et al. (1992) demonstrated wide opposition, among both women and men in Britain and the USA, to women working while they have a pre-school child, but the American respondents, although still a small minority, were more likely to accept such women being employed full-time: 11.5 per cent of American women and 2.8 per cent of British women supported this pattern of behaviour. Fifty per cent of female respondents in the USA were opposed to any paid employment of women while they had pre-school children, compared to the even higher figure of 66 per cent in Great Britain. American opinion was also far more favourable to women working full-time once the youngest child was attending school than the British were: 38 per cent of American women, compared to 15 per cent of British women were in favour of mothers working full-time in such circumstances. In both countries, only 10 per cent of women were opposed to any employment by mothers when the children were at school. Interestingly these authors find that parents of pre-school children in the two countries do not have distinctive attitudes on these issues. Once other factors are controlled for, they share the attitudinal features and divisions of the general population.

The authors of these studies of American opinion also found that men were in general more traditional in their attitudes. Scott and Dunscombe (1991) present evidence which suggests that these differences are of a similar order of magnitude in Britain and the USA and Mason and Lu (1988) demonstrate that men tend to espouse more strongly the view that young children suffer if their mother is employed.

Americans are thoroughly and almost evenly divided over the issue of maternal deprivation. The General Social Survey of 1988 revealed that 43 per cent of all respondents agreed or strongly agreed that "a pre-school child is likely to suffer if his or her mother works", while 44 per cent disagreed. American women were somewhat more opposed to this thesis (49 per cent) than men. They were also more likely than British women to disagree that pre-school children suffer from their mother's involvement in paid work: 40 per cent of the latter held this view critical of the maternal deprivation argument (Alwin et al. 1992).

Mason and Kulthaur (1989) also found from a 1986 sample survey of mothers of pre-schoolers in Detroit that there was an overwhelming preference among them for employment-related care of children to be done exclusively by a parent or close relative, and that this preference was rooted in a broader ideology of gender and family. Those respondents with traditional attitudes preferred exclusive care by parents and close kin, while the more egalitarian minded were more open to other forms of care. As in Great Britain the younger and the more educated and employed women tend to be less traditional (Mason & Lu 1988). The married, the non-employed, regular attenders at religious services and those not committed to the work role tend to be more traditional than those with the converse of these characteristics (Mason & Kulthaur 1989).

Hakim (1991) has presented evidence that suggests that husbands' attitudes play an important role in determining whether women engage in paid work on a full-time or part-time basis or indeed whether they work at all. In Britain, Hakim argues, many women defer to their husband's preferences as to whether and how much they should work outside the home, which goes some way to explain why the British data show relatively little evidence of discrepancies in spouses' attitudes on these questions. She marshals evidence showing that women in the USA, by contrast, have from the 1970s onwards come to challenge more overtly their husbands' resistance to their being in paid employment and that this factor had become the most important variable in explaining women's labour force participation. This more assertive attitude on the part of American women is in line with our earlier discussion of the "war" over gender roles. The fact that, despite continuing diversity, women in the United States have shifted their attitudes to family and employment roles more than men have also underlies Hochschild's (1990) phrase "a stalled revolution". While British women's expectations of life tend more often to display an accommodation to the claims of the family, American women's expectations have begun, to some extent and to varying degrees, to challenge those claims. They have, Hochschild argues, started a revolution, but they have outstripped the capacity of men and of the social institutions surrounding the family to change accordingly. The revolution has therefore stalled, with problematic consequences for all involved.

Comparative discussion:
"housewives" and "working women"

In each of the three capitalist countries, though to varying degrees, paid employment by mothers of young children faces opposition from general public attitudes, both from men and women. In each society women's employment is a public issue; in each society there are many women, even those in employment, who do not approve of such behaviour, and husbands are less favourably inclined than employed wives. Official government policies may not encourage it. On the other hand each society contains specific inducements or compulsions for such women to participate in employment, and ideologies that to varying degrees provide support and justification for involvement in paid employment. In China, by contrast, participation in social labour by all competent adults, male and female, is treated as normal. Apart from the fact that the economic circumstances of most families require all adult members to bring in some income, work in the social economy has been officially encouraged as contributing to the building of a socialist society and to social equality.

In the concluding section of this chapter we want to raise two sets of questions. First, how, in the context of the three capitalist societies, do women, and specifically mothers of young children, explain and rationalize their involvement in paid work and what further insights do their explanations give into the place of mothers' paid employment in these three societies? Secondly, how consistent are the Chinese women's work orientations with the official doctrine of universal labour force participation, and do their responses to the survey questionnaire give us any indication as to the future of the employment of mothers of young children in the changing Chinese society?

We begin by examining women's responses to questions asking them about their reasons for working. Table 5.7 summarizes such responses from the Sino-Japanese survey and from SCELI (for the present we will neglect the case of the United States). Chinese and Japanese women were asked to give the two reasons, from an array of ten, which were closest to their own views. British women were presented with a list of 11 reasons, and asked to select their main reason and their second most important reason for wanting a paid job; here we just present their main reason. The table classifies the reasons into related groups: financial, work-intrinsic, independence, social contact, work as normal.

Table 5.7 Distribution of reasons for working by country, China, Japan and Great Britain.

Reasons	China		Japan		Britain	
	F	%	F	%	F	%
Financial (total)	2,089	55.3	2,004	60.8	319	67.1
Basic living needs	1273	33.7	930	28.2		
Basic essentials					155	32.6
Own pocket money	15	0.4	106	3.2		
Support myself	722	19.1	150	4.6		
Pay off loan	7	0.2	300	9.1		
Save for future use	72	2.0	518	15.7		
Buy extras					164	34.5
Work-intrinsic (total)	1,013	26.8	528	16.1	93	19.6
Use of spare time	23	0.6	171	5.2		
Use abilities fully	309	8.2	308	9.4	25	5.3
Contribute to society	681	18.0	49	1.5		
Do something worthwhile					26	5.5
Enjoy working					42	8.8
Sense of independence					26	5.5
Social contact						
To have social contact	138	3.6	309	9.4		
Get out of house/ company of others					28	5.9
Working is normal	463	12.2	294	8.9	5	1.1
Other or no reason	79	2.1	159	4.8	4	0.8
Total	3,782	100.0	3,294	100.0	475	100.0

Sources: Sino-Japanese Working Women's Family Life Survey; SCELI.

The prominence of financial motives is clear. Around 30 per cent of women in each society refer to their need for income to cover basic essentials of life. Around 30 per cent of Japanese and British women choose other financial motives, buying extras in the case of the British, saving for some future expenditure or to pay off a loan in the case of the Japanese, whereas only a little over 20 per cent of the Chinese women mention other financial reasons. It is worth pointing out that, quite apart from their genuine need for money, these respondents are also drawing on a legitimate vocabulary of motives. A series of responses to the British Social Attitudes Surveys and elsewhere shows that "only if she needs the money" is an increasingly popular answer to questions about whether mothers of pre-school children should be in employment (Witherspoon 1988).

Chinese women can draw on an additional vocabulary of motives to explain their work, namely their contribution to society, and 18 per cent of them chose this reason, compared with much smaller proportions of Japanese or British women. Around 12 per cent of Chinese and 9 per cent of Japanese women felt that working needed no further explanation other than that it was the normal thing to do. British women, on the other hand, were more likely to refer to individualistic motives, such as enjoying work or gaining a sense of independence. In all three societies the desire to make good use of her abilities attracted the attention of less than 10 per cent of respondents. The third highest Japanese response, "to have social contact", reinforces the prevalent view that Japanese housewives often feel isolated and seek wider incorporation in society through other activities.

We have seen at several points in this study that it can be instructive to distinguish between full-time and part-time work. This distinction is once again important in the present context, since full-time employment is a greater challenge to the view that mothers of preschool children should not work, while part-time work can be seen as a compromise between the need or desire to work, on the one hand, and normative opposition to the employment of mothers of young children, on the other. Part-time work is not an option in China, so we restrict this analysis to Japanese and British women. Comparing the reasons for working given by full-time and part-time employed women in these two countries, we discovered no significant difference between the two groups in Japan, but a striking difference emerged among the British women, with full-timers far more likely than part-timers to cite intrinsic reasons (31 per cent compared with 14 per cent). British part-time workers were more likely to say they worked to earn money to buy extras, or for social reasons, while Japanese part-timers shared the full-timers' financial preoccupations. Other differences between full-timers and part-timers were reversed in the two countries: whereas British full-timers were more dissatisfied with pay levels and promotion prospects than part-timers, in Japan it was the part-timers who more often voiced these complaints. These differences between Britain and Japan are consistent with a point we stressed in Chapter 3, that part-time work in Japan involves just as long hours as full-time work, but with lower pay and fewer prospects, and is therefore much more likely to be done for reasons of financial necessity. In addition, full-time female workers in Britain are more likely than part-timers to be married to higher earning husbands, and therefore less likely to be working full-time out of financial need, while in Japan no such difference appears to exist.

Despite these differences between Britain and Japan, in other respects the two societies show similarities. In particular, in both countries part-time employed mothers of young children are more "traditional" in their views on gender roles than full-timers. Part-timers are more supportive of the male breadwinner–female homemaker role division than full-timers, more likely to believe that mothers should give up work while their child is below 3 years old, more likely to put their husband and children before their own self-development.

In general, this analysis of the work motives and orientations of full-time and part-time employees in Britain and Japan suggests that mothers who continue to work while their children are below school age can be roughly divided into two categories. The first, closer to the type Hakim (1991) calls the "family-centred woman" and Hochschild (1990) calls "the housewife" (even if she works outside the home), are more likely to work part-time and to believe that their work should be accommodated to the demands of the household. They have relatively low expectations from their work, and also relatively low expectations concerning their husband's participation in family labour. They have a relatively restricted sense of their "entitlement" (Major 1993) in either of these aspects of their lives, are more likely to find the allocation of responsibilities at home and at work to be "equitable" (Ferree 1994), and are more likely to be satisfied with what some might see as objectively more restricted life chances. The others, closer to what Hochschild calls "the working woman", display what Hakim sees as greater and more male-like "commitment" to paid work, and offer greater resistance to the conventional ideology concerning the employment of mothers of young children. Having higher expectations and a stronger sense of entitlement, they are less likely to see the divisions of labour at home and at work as equitable, and are more frustrated and dissatisfied as a result. The relative proportions of women corresponding to these two ideal types varies from society to society, influenced by and in turn influencing the ideological climate of opinion. In Japan, where a lower proportion of mothers of pre-school children are in employment, the "housewife" type will be even more common than appears from our data, which selects out that minority who do take paid work. In the United States, which we have not considered in detail here, there will probably be a higher proportion of "working woman" types than in Britain, corresponding to the higher proportion of mothers of pre-school children in full-time work.

One must add a cautionary note to this typological analysis. While this duality of orientation may be discerned from the survey data available, we cannot conclude that a "working woman" or "housewife" orientation is a fixed and stable characteristic of any particular woman. Gerson (1985), using intensive interviews with relatively small numbers of American women to explore their "hard choices" between paid work and childrearing, discovered a considerable degree of shifting orientations over the course of many women's lives. Those who left school with strong orientations to domestic life did not necessarily remain housewives, and those who entered the workforce with expectations of building a career and forgoing either children or marriage or both not infrequently found that circumstances led them towards the housewife role. While comparative survey analysis may reveal relatively stable differences between societies in their culture and their members' attitudes, for individuals life may remain somewhat unpredictable and surprising.

And what of China? Since there is no established system of part-time employment in Chinese cities, we can only speculate whether variations in gender role ideologies and orientations to paid work might find expression in demand for part-time work in future. Although in our comparative framework the Chinese women appear to have departed the furthest from belief in the gendered roles of male breadwinner and female homemaker and have high expectations of gender equality both in the workplace and at home, there is always a significant minority whose responses do not fit this pattern but are closer to a "housewife" type of orientation. And on the question of the mother working while the child is below 3 years old, this minority swells into half the sample. The issue of maternity leave is, however, problematic in China. Work-units cannot afford to pay women while they are on leave, and few women can afford to take extended unpaid leave. When women were asked their opinion on various proposed "solutions" to the problems of married women combining work with the care of young children, an extended period of unpaid maternity leave attracted the lowest level of support. Very few respondents, on the other hand, rejected the idea of shorter working hours. It remains unclear whether there is potential demand for part-time work for women in Chinese cities, and whether such potential demand might reflect a continued hold of "traditional" gendered role expectations on the minds of some Chinese women. We will return to these issues in the final chapter.

Chapter 6

Patterns of stability and change

Introduction

In the previous four chapters we have examined the historical background to the development of women's work and family life in our four chosen societies, the present-day patterns of women's employment and their domestic workloads, and the frameworks of values and beliefs within which they interpret their dual burden. As is perhaps natural in a comparative study of this kind, our emphasis has been on differences and similarities between the four societies taken as a whole, although we have also, especially in the previous chapter, highlighted important variations in women's experience and attitudes within each society.

All advanced societies, however, are complex and internally diverse. None of the institutional patterns of paid work or family policy, nor any of the domestic arrangements by which parents of young children attempt to cope with often heavy workloads, are unchallenged or completely stable. They are subject to shifting economic and political forces, and they are open to reinterpretation and remodelling through the active efforts of the women and men who make and remake them. These social forces and these individual and collective projects create fields of force and tension which make for varied tendencies towards stability or change.

In this final chapter, which takes up again the question of convergence and divergence, we attempt to summarize the internal tensions within each society that might contribute to a dynamic of change, the combined result of which might be either increasing similarity or increasing difference between the societies under consideration. Finally, we draw together the varied threads of our analysis, and recognize that societies are not isolated units whose internal tendencies might bring them closer together or drive them further apart, but are themselves enmeshed in global processes, the dynamics of which link the women and men of the world together in a shared though diverse fate.

China: socialism and gender equality challenged

When the Sino-Japanese survey, which forms the basis for much of the material in the previous three chapters, was carried out in 1987, China had already experienced several years of transition to a new era. Following the death of Mao Zedong and the removal of the Gang of Four in 1976, the new leadership led by the veteran Deng Xiaoping embarked on what they and much of the rest of the world saw as a necessary programme of economic reform. Under the slogans of "the four modernizations", "the socialist commodity economy" and "the open door policy", the reformers aimed to dismantle much of the apparatus of central planning and to decentralize much economic decision-making to enterprises and households. The overall economic result of these policies can be seen in the rapid rates of growth of the Chinese economy in the last 15 years, despite repeated pessimistic claims that the surge of growth had to be temporary and that the bubble would burst. The effects on working women and their families, which must be our main concern here, have however been somewhat varied. In this section we outline some of these recent trends, in an attempt to judge whether the relative egalitarianism both at work and home, documented in the previous chapters, is firmly rooted or fragile.

The changes have been most marked in the countryside, where the People's Communes were dismantled and the majority of land redistributed or rented to individual families, which thus became once more units of production as well as consumption. Once farmers were producing crops for the market, it became apparent that the countryside contained vast reserves of workers who were not needed for efficient production. Especially after the government ceased to enforce its strict controls over internal movement, families responded by sending their excess members into towns to seek work. In some cases these would be the men, who went off in search of jobs in the urban construction boom while leaving the women and elderly to work the land. In other cases it was the women, especially young unmarried women, who were recruited into the rapidly growing light industries of the Special Economic Zones such as Shenzhen. Women also figured greatly in the growth of sideline production in rural areas, and many experienced increased opportunities for rural entrepreneurship. However, the return to household enterprise, coupled with the effects of the single-child family policy, has also been a return to patterns of patriarchal authority and discrimination against women, of which the rise in reported female infanticide has been a disturbing aspect (Davin 1988).

In the cities which are our present concern, however, the reforms in some respects have been much more limited. The reformers wanted to introduce markets for labour as well as for products (G. White 1987), but movement in this direction has been controversial and has provoked much resistance, not least because the legitimacy of the regime rests on its being the representative of the working class whose labour it was proposed to commoditize (White 1993). Despite political support for contract labour and for private enterprise, the vast majority of urban residents remained members of a state or collective *danwei*, and their households primarily units of consumption (Davis & Harrell 1993). Although the absolute numbers involved might seem, by the standards of less populous societies, rather large, the proportion of urban residents working in private business remained little more than 5 per cent, and those on labour contracts less than 10 per cent. The situation is, of course, by no means static, and the reform process continues, with another series of reforms of enterprise management and increased commodification of housing, stocks in state enterprises and labour announced in 1992 and now in the early stages of implementation, but it is too early to say how this is going to affect families, households and especially married women.

Nonetheless, the drive for greater efficiency in state and collective enterprises has already resulted in some weakening of the position of female workers (Rai 1992). The 1988 debate mentioned in the previous chapter, about whether women, especially those with young children, should "return to their family" or go "back to the wok" (Jacka 1990), was no mere theoretical exercise, but reflected the actual policies of some enterprises. Statistics on the scale of this development are scarce. One survey in Tianjin found contradictory evidence that gender discrimination in recruitment to state enterprises, although strong, was declining, while gender inequalities in bonus payments were increasing, and men experienced greater upward mobility when they changed jobs (Bian 1994). The problem is widely discussed in the Chinese literature (Kuang et al. 1992, Hu 1992). Women, it is often claimed, are less productive because they are less educated and less dynamic, because they take more time off to deal with family responsibilities, and because companies have to make special provision for their female employees. Women are transferred to jobs requiring less skill and carrying lower rewards, or even pressured into leaving state employment for the lower status and lower paid collective sector where they are already over-represented, and in some cases laid off altogether. As far as taking on new staff is concerned, many enterprises do not want to recruit women at all. Recruiters for female employees to work in the new industries in the special zones often stipulate that women must be unmarried. The implication is that women are expected to give up such employment on marriage or on childbirth.

The claim is made, for example in the case of the thriving model small industrial village Daqiuzhuang, that women themselves are keen to give up work while their children are young, and there is some evidence that this is indeed the case, but the extent to which this retirement is voluntary is also disputed (Wu & Zhang 1987, Jacka 1990). We have seen from the 1987 survey that many women do approve of a longer period of maternity leave (as long as it is paid), shorter working hours, extended systems of leave to care for family members, and other methods which, from their point of view, would help women to combine paid work and family responsibilities. In the present economic climate in China, however, such programmes of accommodating the needs of female employees will often be seen by enterprise managements, who now have more autonomy over employment policies, as an unnecessary cost. With no shortage of male labour, and a possible belief on the part of managements that men do not have conflicting family duties, the incentive to employ women with young children is likely to dwindle. Since there is no established system of part-time employment, with specific national regulations concerning employment rights, welfare benefits and pensions for part-time workers, it is also difficult to know whether there might develop a demand for part-time workers, such as might be filled by mothers of young children, as in Britain and to a lesser extent elsewhere.

It seems that the relative egalitarianism that we have found in China is thus threatened by the process of economic reform. It was the life-long membership of the *danwei* for all adults that provided the social conditions for gender equality, and it is precisely that system of life-long membership, the "iron rice-bowl", that reformers have challenged as an obstacle to labour mobility and as a disincentive to high productivity. Without a strong political will to enforce the constitutional and legal rights of women, and without a legal procedure by which women could challenge the employment policies of managements, it will be difficult to maintain the level of gender equality, which was in any case always partial, achieved in the state and collective sectors (Stockman 1994).

Although the small private business sector as yet accounts for only a small proportion of urban residents, it is worth taking a brief look at how this form of economic activity may affect women's work and family life. The growth of individual enterprise (*geti hu*) is interesting in this context, because it is evidence of what is, from the standpoint of the theory of industrial society, a reversal of the process of structural differentiation. Individual enterprise households are predominantly based on family relations, and in the ideal typical case the separation of household and enterprise vanishes. Little has yet been written on urban private family business, but Bruun's recent study of private business households in Chengdu, Sichuan Province (Bruun 1993), reveals a number of significant facets of this process. Those who launch private family businesses, he says, "are energetic and dedicated, which is evidenced in their working hours: twelve or more hours a day, seven days a week, totally eradicating any distinction between work and spare time, between business and family life" (Bruun 1993: 49). There are strains towards a unified authority structure of these "households-as-enterprises", with a reversion to patriarchal control. Men like to exert their authority as head of the household, and the running of the business reflects this, with women allocated more menial and subordinate tasks, and men taking every opportunity to avoid the manual labour associated with the business. Instead, the male head of the household-as-enterprise assumes the role of external representation of the business, whether this be in trading relations with suppliers or in bureaucratic dealings with the various officials charged with regulation of private business, such as the Tax Bureau or the Industrial and Commercial Administration Bureau. Problems and disputes can arise where there is a mismatch between household and enterprise, such as when a shop run by the wife makes higher profits than the wage income of the husband who has retained his state employment. If Bruun's findings are typical of the situation of urban private business, we have here the makings of a return to the patriarchal structures characteristic of the pre-communist period.

The future of women's work in China is also going to be influenced by demographic factors, and these may well act as a counterweight to the anti-egalitarian pressures we have just discussed. The generation of young mothers represented by the respondents to the Sino-Japanese survey were born well before the introduction of the single-child family policy, at a time when public policy if anything favoured large families (Croll et al. 1985). These mothers (and their husbands) are thus likely to have brothers and sisters, and although the survey questionnaire did not reveal any major contribution of siblings (either their own or those of their husbands) to the domestic lives of respondents, and relatively few women reported that siblings lived in their household, personal acquaintance with urban Chinese families suggests that siblings are not unimportant, and that they may share such responsibilities as care of children and of the elder generation, their own parents. Such exchange of services between family members, even if they do not live in the same household as narrowly defined, has given rise to a discussion in Chinese circles of so-called "networked families (*wangluo jiating*)" (Unger 1993). As the single-child family policy works its way through to its consequences in the next generation, young mothers (and fathers) in 15 or 20 years time will have no siblings, and sibling mutual aid will be a thing of the past. Other kinds of networks may of course take its place but, given the Chinese preference for keeping mutual aid within the family, the most likely outcome is an extension of the exchange between the generations. The current exchange between the older and the middle generation, by which retired grandparents provide child care, shopping and cooking in exchange for a commitment to future personal care when they need it (Ikels 1993), is likely to be intensified when each potential set of four grandparents only has one grandchild. Even if housing provision makes actual stem family households unnecessary, the terms of the "intergenerational contract" will bind the generations together, and the material base for this arrangement will require that married women continue to be in employment, mostly on a full-time basis. Whether jobs will be available for them depends on the future for economic growth in China which at this distance of time, despite currently fashionable talk of the twenty-first century belonging to the Pacific Rim, scarcely allows of sensible prediction.

If, however, the general prospect is a retreat from the commitment to gender equality enshrined in the slogan that "women hold up half the sky", the consequence must be a degree of tension over gender roles. The evidence from the 1987 survey, as we have seen, reveals a considerable attachment on the part of these young mothers to their participation in social labour outside the home. There is little sign of a desire of the majority of them to "return to the family". They want shorter working hours, more labour-saving machines in the home, more public services outside it, and more shouldering of domestic responsibilities by their husbands, to enable them more comfortably to combine paid work with their family life. The housewife role has lost legitimacy in their eyes, with some exceptions. This is not surprising. This generation of women grew up in times that were indeed turbulent, living as they did through the Cultural Revolution, but times when they were consistently told that women's freedom and status depended on their ability to participate, on equal terms with men, in the social labour force. This argument, whatever its faults, is not obviously misguided, and there is no reason why these women should not accept it. They know that their menfolk need continual persuasion to behave in a way that corresponds to it, and fear that any weakening of their resolve and their persuasive powers will result in a setback in the long road to emancipation. Just as there are deep reserves of support among the working masses for Maoist egalitarianism, and suspicion and resentment of the increasing inequalities between rich and poor, so there are deep reserves of support among the female working masses for Maoist gender egalitarianism. The tension between these values and the realities of life in "socialism with Chinese characteristics" will be apparent to many, with consequences that the future will reveal.

Japan: can exceptionalism continue?

A considerable literature has grown up in Japan in the second half of the twentieth century concerning the proclaimed "uniqueness" of Japanese culture, society and mentality. Known as *nihonjinron*,

191

literally "discussions of the Japanese", this discourse has been interpreted by more sceptical Japanese scholars as a form of "cultural
nationalism" (Yoshino 1992) or as a substitute for national symbols
such as the emperor or the flag, which in Japan are controversial and
divisive rather than universal and integrative (Befu 1992). One Western writer who has made a thorough study of this literature has
branded its claim to Japanese uniqueness as a "myth" (Dale 1986).
These are clearly dangerous waters, and it is prudent to be aware of
them whenever statements about the distinctiveness of some aspect
of Japanese society are advanced.

Nonetheless, much of the empirical material reported in the previous three chapters has confirmed the widespread impression that
Japanese ideas about the appropriate lives of men and women do
retain a certain distinctiveness, if not uniqueness, among industrial
societies, and continue to inform the work and family experience of
people and the organizations that shape their lives. As Coleman
(1983) puts it, on the question of sex-role division of household activities and responsibilities, Japan stands at one end of a continuum
among industrial societies (and, he suggests, the United States at the
other end). Mothers of young children are least likely to be in paid
work. If they are in paid employment, they are most likely to have
doubts about combining it with their responsibilities to their children
and homes. Their husbands are least likely to give them any help
with domestic tasks and running the house, and they are most likely
to feel the double burden. In summary, gender roles are most segregated in Japan.

There are two diametrically opposed perspectives that might be
taken towards this exceptional nature of gender roles in contemporary Japan.

The first sees the continuity, even the intensification, of traditional
segregated gender roles as an obstruction to the full modernization of
Japanese society. The gender role system is seen as oppressive of both
women and men, though in different ways. The main emphasis is on
the restrictions on opportunities for the career advancement and personal development of women (Brinton 1993, Lam 1992). Women are
denied the chance to compete in the occupational system on equal
terms with men. On the assumption that they will not be able to give
the same commitment to their careers in the company as men, but
will rather withdraw from the labour force to bring up their children
and make their home, they are channelled into tracks that lead no-

where, having already been given an education that cannot put them on an equal footing with their male contemporaries. They are also forced, by male reluctance and the pressure of peer and parental opinion, to take full responsibility for the affairs of the household, so that even those women who stay in the labour force while they have young children experience a heavy double burden, only mitigated by the possibility of finding part-time employment close to their home. Men, on the other hand, have the educational and social advantages necessary to pursue a career in the company, and so appear to win out in the distribution of life chances. However, this apparent victory may also be interpreted nowadays as another form of oppression, with men forced into a traditional breadwinner role and subjection to the super-exploitative demands of the company. From both points of view, the gender role system must increasingly come under attack from women, and even from men, and give way to a more egalitarian pattern of more equal opportunities in the occupational structure and more equal responsibilities, and even symmetrical relationships, in the family (Uno 1993). The Japanese sexual division of labour, from this perspective, will have to break down and converge, even if only partially, towards the American model.

The second perspective is quite different, in that it sees the Japanese maintenance of a traditional sexual division of labour as a culturally plausible response to industrialization, one which better fits the culturally different set of values in Japan (Usui 1993, M. White 1987). The persistence of segregated roles, both in the occupational and in the domestic spheres, is seen not so much as an unequal distribution of life chances but rather as the realization of enduring values accepted by women as much as by men. The Japanese, with a much more relational concept of the self, place value on the performance of complementary expectations in role relationships, rather than the individualistic search for self-realization (Iwao 1993). Male and female are inherently different, should be brought up differently to recognize that inherent difference, and be prepared to fulfil gender-specific social obligations. The emphasis on complementary relationships finds one of its most profound instances in the marriage relationship, in which the exchange of different obligations by the two partners is seen to bind the couple closer together in mutual dependence and mutual responsibility, to provide enduring and stable social linkages in which gender-specific social identities rooted in family and kinship can be maintained. The ideal would still, in many cases, be the complementary union of husband and wife in the *ie* form of household-as-enterprise, and this can partly explain the continuing very high level of very small family enterprises in the Japanese economy, usually owned by the husband (or his father) with the wife appearing in national statistics as a "family enterprise worker" (often incorrectly referred to as "unpaid family worker" by economists wedded to the modern wage economy (e.g. Patrick & Rohlen 1987)). But where this is not possible, the appropriate model for modern industrial society is for the husband to take the main responsibility for the economic support of the family and for the wife to take full responsibility for homemaking and childrearing, and for subsidiary income provision if required or desired.

The material on Japan presented in the previous three chapters provides support for both of these perspectives. Both the behaviour and some of the stated beliefs of young mothers reveal an attachment to the "modernized Confucianism" that underlies the latter view. Many of them, even of those who return to work when their children are still very young, appear to accept that gender is a matter of intrinsic difference and complementarity, and that their paid work is only done out of regrettable financial necessity. They accept that their primary role is as mother and housekeeper, and do not seek greater equality of opportunity in employment. However, there is also a minority of women, particularly among the regular workers and the more highly educated, who are critical of this gender segregation of spheres. They perceive unreasonable differences between men and women in their opportunities at work, and they also believe that the division of domestic responsibilities between spouses should be more even (although many think their husbands do not see eye to eye with them on that). This minority of young women appear to endorse, at least partially, the liberal individualism that is characteristic of much of the United States and underlies much American writing on Japanese women.

That the majority of Japanese women, even of the younger generation, adhere to what both Western and Japanese feminists see as an outmoded perspective on gender roles is readily understandable, though it should not be seen as a mere passive assimilation of traditional culture. In fact, as we have seen in Chapter 2, the emergence of the segregated roles of full-time housewife/mother and *sarariiman* at the complete disposal of the company is a post-war adaptation of traditional gender roles that has been actively constructed. It has been constantly reinforced by official and political statements about the obligations of Japanese women to their families and, through them, to their country, represented most starkly in Prime Minister Sato Eisaku's 1964 injunction on Japanese women to have more children. It has also been constantly propagated by discussions of women's true role conducted in mass-circulation women's magazines. The educational experience of Japanese women is also a highly gendered one, with clearly distinct curriculum choices, culminating for those who go on to post-school education in the sharp gender division between two-year junior college diplomas and four-year university degrees (Buckley 1993). At an ideological level, gender segregation has firm roots, and it takes determination and conviction to oppose strong consensual norms.

In addition, unmarried women's experience of work before marriage, and their perceptions of the work experience of men, may often be enough to convince them that the man's world of work is one they would want to join only out of necessity, and even then only as an associate member. "Office Ladies" are treated as domestic aides to male managers, and they soon get the message that they should be looking for a husband, possibly among the rising stars of the company, after which they will leave to have children (McLendon 1983, Lo 1990). Factory workers simply find full-time work too exhausting, and retreat into domesticity for a breather before returning to the labour force in a subordinate part-time capacity (Lo 1990). Both understand the sacrifices required of women who might want to pursue a male-type career in the company. They see the inordinately long hours that men have to put in to stay in the race for career advancement, a feature of over-commitment often resulting in illness and family problems which have received much publicity in recent times (Usui 1993). They know that men intent on building a career often have to accept transfers around the country and endure periods of *tanshin funin*, alone and separated from their family. Whether or not this is acceptable to a woman, it is extremely difficult for a couple with children to pursue dual careers under these conditions, short of adopting the Chinese method of boarding children with grandparents. Even for those women who break through the cultural and ideological constraints, the practical obstacles to career-building make gender segregated roles a rational choice for many.

Is it possible to see any significant change occurring in the gender segregated patterns of work in the future? The consensus on this question is well summed up by Andrew Gordon, the editor of a recent collection of essays on post-war Japan: "Women did redefine the meaning of their roles as wives and mothers to include supplementary wage labour, but any dramatic reordering of gender relations may actually have become a more distant prospect in the late postwar years" (Gordon 1993: 459). A number of other contributors to the book, while pointing to the vigour of many groups of women campaigning for such a "dramatic reordering", concede that support for such feminist groups is quite limited (Buckley 1993, Uno 1993). Much hangs, of course, on what level of change would be seen as "dramatic". Despite much change in the social role of women and in the relations between the sexes, none of the societies we have been examining, nor many others that we might have studied, has undergone any fundamental transformation of gender roles, except possibly China; and even in this case, as we have suggested in the previous section, there can be doubts as to the permanence of the changes achieved during the era of Mao.

Nonetheless, there are indications that a more significant change may be in the offing. Buckley (1993) refers repeatedly to what she calls the "reality gap" between conventional gender ideology, apparently accepted by women, and the actuality of their own experience, which does not square with that ideology. Kelly (1993) also points to the discrepancy between the standardization of conventional ideology and the diversity of actual experience (although a number of writers point out how conventionalized women's lives often are in Japan, especially in the strength of age-specific norms for life course experiences such as marriage and childbirth (Coleman 1983, Brinton 1992)). A most striking example of this kind of gap was experienced by Fujita (1989), when she found that the child care workers who were condemning her for seeking to place her child in the centre so that she could work were themselves in the same position. Some women seem to be more aware of the gap. In our own survey findings, we saw that some women whose actual division of domestic labour was conventionally asymmetrical believed that it ought to be more egalitarian, and were dissatisfied with this aspect of their lives. Iwao (1993) is also convinced that women's views on appropriate roles for women and men are changing, but more so than is apparent in their actual behaviour, since their husbands and their husbands' employing companies are reluctant to change in their turn. A related example of quite recent change is found in a study of beliefs about filial obligations to the elderly, which showed a sudden decline in support for such a value in the second half of the 1980s (Ogawa & Retherford 1993).

Yet change in orientations to life and to social relationships on the part of women, however widespread this may become, is not enough to enable actual changes in the way such women lead their lives. As we have repeatedly stressed throughout this book, the "separation" of household and enterprise does not do away with a myriad of systematic or "functional" interconnections between them. For more women to be able comfortably to combine motherhood and a career in the paid labour force they would not only have to convince more companies to take the provisions of the Equal Employment Opportunity Act seriously and accept more women on to the *sogoshoku* track of management training rather than the *ippanshoku* track for Office Ladies (Lam 1992, Lo 1990). They would also have to convince companies to restructure the sequencing of a career in a company so that parents could alternate periods of greater commitment to the family with periods of greater involvement with the company. And if this were to be more than another ghetto for women they would also have to convince husbands of the merits of less segregated roles in the family as well as at work, so that they too might be prepared to build a life course made up of alternating involvements. This would be a major restructuring of many Japanese men's conception of their life course, since it would involve a weakening of their sense of work as their central life interest and of membership of their company as all-encompassing, which Japanese socialization processes do so much to encourage. Although there are indications that a very small number of Japanese couples are thinking along these lines, movement in this direction in Japan generally is infinitesimal. As we have seen, and in the next section of this chapter will see again, movement in this direction is not very evident in Western societies such as Britain or the United States either.

Diversity and change in the West

Despite some significant differences, the basic situation of women's work in Britain and the United States can be summed up in similar terms. In both countries there is a systematic and mutually reinforcing relationship between, on the one hand, women's greater responsibility for housework and child care within the context of the private nuclear family and, on the other, women's relatively subordinate position within patterns of both private enterprise and public sector employment, which are segmented and occupationally segregated to varying degrees on lines of gender (as well as race and other ascribed characteristics). Women are more likely than men to break their work history for parenthood and later to care for elderly relatives, more likely to work part-time, more likely to be low paid, and less likely to rise through career grades. The orientations of both employers and employees are structured in accordance with those general patterns, although these vary considerably in detail from one industry and occupation to another. The main difference between Britain and the United States can be seen in the greater apparent "accommodation" (Parkin 1971) to the primacy of their family responsibilities on the part of British women. British women are thus more likely than American women to withdraw from employment while their children are young, more likely to return to part-time employment, more likely in general to believe that their employment patterns should be adapted to the claims that their roles as mothers and wives make on them. Even in the USA, however, only a quarter of married parents living together with a child under age 6, and a third of those with a youngest child between ages 6 and 17, are both employed full-time year round (Hayghe & Bianchi 1994). American institutions and values are more conducive to change towards the dual full-time worker model, but in both societies, where structural change is occurring, it comes about through the gradual accumulation of the consequences of individual and family decisions as successive generations confront the life course challenges of parenting young children, combined with the employment strategies of enterprises in their shifting economic environments, rather than as a result of rapid and deep policy changes by government as in China.

As earlier chapters have stressed, this basic situation is just the latest stage in the long historical development of industrial capitalism with its separation of the private family household from the capitalist business enterprise. The latter part of the twentieth century has witnessed the increasing incorporation of married women into the labour force, bringing more and more mothers of young children under the weight of the "dual burden". In this section we will briefly outline the main trends discernible in this development as the twentieth century nears its end and attempt to project them into the future, with the aim of identifying whether there are any prospects for any radical reshaping of this basic institutional complex shaping women's work.

The distinction between "standard" and "non-standard" jobs, which we discussed briefly in Chapter 3, is useful in charting these trends. Since the mid 1980s, many commentators in both countries have discussed what is often referred to as the "restructuring" of the workforce, a tendency for work to be polarized between a primary or "core" sector of full-time permanent positions with privileged membership rights in large organizations and an expanding secondary "periphery" of less rewarding, part-time or less stable jobs. Legislative and managerial pressures that decrease the contractual security of employment (for example proposed changes in civil service employment and contracting out of public services in Great Britain) affect, or are intended to affect, some aspects of primary sector employment as well, but there is no denying that major contrasts in rewards, status and employment stability continue to exist between the two sectors. Hakim (1987) suggested that one-third of the workforce in Britain had non-standard jobs in the mid 1980s, and the trend is rising. In the United States, Kuhn & Bluestone (1987) referred to similar tendencies with the phrase "the disappearing middle", the decline of well-paid and secure skilled blue-collar jobs, and the rise of low-wage and insecure jobs as well as growth in upper level managerial and professional employment. These processes have strong implications for gender divisions in both societies. While in both countries women have taken a slowly increasing proportion of the increasing numbers of "standard" jobs in management, administration and the professions (Marshall et al. 1988, OPCS 1992, US Bureau of the Census 1991), much of the expansion of non-standard jobs has also corresponded to the increase in the labour force participation of women. Male employees in both countries have been the major victims of the erosion of heavy industrial and manufacturing employment, with sharp declines in such predominantly male blue-collar occupations as automobile construction, coal-mining, iron and steel manufacture and ship-building.

The most striking feature of the growth of the employment of women in Britain, especially of those with young children, is that most of it has been in part-time jobs (Hakim 1993). This is a continuing trend, and has attracted considerable public comment. According to official statistics (Employment Department 1994), the nine months from March to December 1993 saw the workforce in employment grow by 104,000, made up of an expansion of 144,000 in part-time jobs and a reduction of 40,000 in full-time jobs. Although there is a growth in the numbers of men working part-time, most of this rise in part-time employment has been taken by women. The British Conservative Government sees the rise of part-time employment as consistent with its general strategy to enhance competitiveness by increasing the "flexibility" of the labour market. Critics describe the same trends as the increasing casualization of labour, as part-time workers on low wages may find themselves without national insurance cover, losing their right to a state pension, unemployment benefit, sickness and invalidity benefit. So-called "flexible contracts", even zero hours contracts, which specify that the worker will be available for work as required or not required by the employer, are a further accentuation of this casualization, and are used especially in the retail trades which primarily employ women.

Yet, as we would expect in the light of the findings reported in the previous chapter, the vast majority of women part-time workers do not respond by seeking full-time work. According to the most recent *Social Trends* (Central Statistical Office 1994) survey, only 10 per cent of women employed part-time would prefer full-time jobs. This could reflect an accommodation to the scarcity of full-time jobs, but it is in sharp contrast to the 40 per cent of the far smaller number of men employed part-time who want full-time work. Similar findings have been reported for the USA, where in 1971 and 1981 70 per cent of females in part-time employment indicated to the Current Population Survey that they did not want full-time work (Stern 1987). This is further evidence of the accommodation that women are prepared to make in both societies, whether enthusiastically or reluctantly, to the claims of the family. Other government policies in the UK, such as the shift towards the care "in the community" of the elderly and the long-term sick and handicapped, including the mentally sick, are likely to intensify these claims on women, who are the main carers in the community and the family, and thus strengthen their commitment to part-time employment.

Another aspect of British Government labour market strategy is also likely to reinforce existing patterns of gendered segmentation. The emphasis on creating an "enterprise culture" includes support for self-employment and the formation of small businesses. Such businesses are predominantly headed by men, who make up 75 per cent of all those categorized as self-employed (Employment Department 1994). Studies of small businesses have shown that their success often depends on the participation, frequently on an unpaid basis, of family members and especially wives (Finch 1983, Scase & Goffee 1987). The wife is able to combine running the household, in which she takes full responsibility for children and housework, with auxiliary work in the husband's business, doing the accounts, serving behind the counter, acting as telephonist and receptionist, and thus avoiding the need for additional paid staff. This invisible form of double burden is not unlike the position of women in small family business in China and Japan, which we have described earlier. In addition, however, there is the attempt by many women in Britain (as in China) to join the enterprise culture by starting their own businesses. Such businesses are of many kinds, but what is typical of many of them is that they have to be run in a way that allows the female entrepreneur also to manage her family responsibilities, often without the aid of her male partner (Goffee & Scase 1985, Rees 1992). This deprives the businesswoman of the unpaid aid of family members that male-headed businesses so often enjoy, on the one hand intensifying the double burden experienced by such women, and on the other reducing the economic viability of the business. Thus, the growth of self-employment and small family business is unlikely in itself to challenge the basic patterns we have outlined.

In assessing the overall effects of labour force changes account must also be taken of the inter-relationships between labour force status and domestic circumstances. Because marital partners are not randomly selected, they tend to share similar labour force as well as other characteristics. Those married women who achieve primary sector employment status tend to be married to males of a similar status, and part-time employment tends to be more characteristic of women married to lower status men (Bonney 1988a,b; McRae 1986). The ability of couples to deploy two earners is thus structured along the lines of social class. In the USA Brown (1987) has shown that the white salaried middle class has since 1918 consistently had a higher level of dual-earning than white wage earners and that it is among the former that there has been the greatest rate of growth in dual employment. Applebaum (1981) has also demonstrated for the USA, on the basis of longitudinal data, that women with labour force careers less interrupted by maternity had husbands with higher incomes, had higher earnings and job status and were more likely to be in full-time employment than other women. Increasing rates of female labour participation are thus unevenly distributed across the population and may contribute to increasing inequalities in family incomes (Glass 1992). In Britain, McRae (1991) has found the same polarizing consequences of the noticeable increase in women's return to work within the first year after childbirth, since women who held full-time non-manual and professional positions before childbirth are least likely to experience downward mobility upon their return to work.

Nonetheless, as demonstrated in previous chapters, part-time workers are much more likely to be married than single precisely because they do not have to support the whole family from their employment. Their employment is often part of a broader household strategy of maximizing family income and undertaking family labour. The growth and widespread incidence of part-time employment among married mothers of young children in Great Britain is a result of their and their husbands' increasing desire to construct a more flexible household work strategy, just as much as it derives from the search by enterprises for more flexibility. While this trend marks the erosion of the exclusive domesticity of the housewife role (which is still followed by a bare majority of British mothers of pre-school children), it does not involve any fundamental reconstruction of gender roles at home or in paid work. It is an accommodation to the primacy of the woman's domestic role and an acceptance of a marginal role in the workplace. It does not involve major changes in the domestic division of labour nor in domestic power relations, and compared to maintaining full-time employment it offers relatively little occupational advantage (Applebaum 1981, Waldfogel 1993). In fact, as has been shown, the husband's disapproval of his wife taking a full-time job is often a factor behind her part-time employment. From this perspective the considerable growth in labour force partici-pation by women in Great Britain in the second half of the twentieth century is nowhere near as revolutionary as is often heralded, since it is largely composed of women entering part-time employment (Hakim 1993).

Nor is this accommodative strategy necessarily an unstable one. Relative insecurity in the labour force may be cushioned, or even motivated, by relative security in the household. Part-time employment thus does not necessarily correspond to labour market insecu-rity. Many part-time jobs are permanent (Hakim 1987). Part-time employment opportunities call forth labour force participants who would not otherwise be active if only full-time jobs were available and they enable many families to earn extra income than is available through one earner. Although the "traditional family" of the female housewife and the male breadwinner is still numerically the most common arrangement among parents of pre-school children, many families operate on this "one-and-a-half earner" basis throughout the period of childraising. Part-time work by mothers of young children departs least from the "traditional" model, and together with families where the wife is not employed, it covers over three-quarters of households with pre-school children in Britain. This accommodative model also has considerable potential for continuation into the future, since the majority of children growing up in such households are being exposed to role models exemplifying this pattern and may well follow them in later life.

A more radical source of change in gender roles at home and in paid work is likely to be found among the minority of mothers of young children who are continuing in full-time paid employment. These women tend, as we have seen, to be well-educated professional and managerial workers married to similar high status husbands. Their patterns of paid work are far less disturbed by maternity. Waldfogel (1993) has demonstrated that those mothers of young children who continue in full-time paid employment and who take advantage of maternity leave arrangements suffer far less wage erosion compared to those with more interrupted careers involving career breaks, changes of jobs and part-time work. The former are able largely to escape the financial loss associated with the first child and to halve the effect of a second one. This slowly growing minority of women who are creating male-like middle class careers are also the women who have more egalitarian patterns of domestic labour and decision-making at home. It is in this sector of the society that the most noticeable change is occurring but at the current rate of change it is not likely to become the dominant pattern in Great Britain for many decades. The greater incidence of full-time paid work among the mothers of young children in the USA means that American families are more likely to display the dual full-time worker pattern with its greater degree of domestic sharing of housework and decision-making, and a higher proportion of them than in Britain are found among the blue-collar working class.

Yet this challenge to deeply rooted gender assumptions has its price. It is in these families with their deeply burdened daily schedules in both countries that there is the greatest pressure for change in gender roles at home and paid work, since neither wives nor their partners in the marriage are willing to adopt the homemaker or part-time worker model. This pressure is evident, for instance, in the popularity of books such as Arlie Hochschild's *The second shift* (1990) in the USA, with its assumption of the dual full-timer model. The phenomenon of the "overworked American" (Schor 1992) is to be found particularly in this group with their peak life course combination of employment and domestic commitments and their most cramped opportunities for leisure (Shelton 1992). In Great Britain the recent work of Patricia Hewitt (1993) has highlighted the need to consider new patterns of work-time regimes to accommodate the desire of both parents to be in paid employment. The rigidity of male full-time working hours is however a great obstacle to change. While there is a trend towards men retiring earlier, for most of their working life employers and workers alike show little enthusiasm for changes in daily working schedules. Indeed, many British men would like to work longer hours for more pay (Marsh 1991) and women who are highly occupationally motivated have to conform to the long daily and weekly hours expected of men. While there are cases of job-sharing or part-time work in such positions these are very uncommon and married couples where both spouses are occupationally ambitious generally have to conform to patterns that require long weekly hours of full-time commitment by both partners. In general terms there is little sign of any diminution of pressure on the daily schedules of such couples on either side of the Atlantic. The flexibility that they seek is not likely to be yielded by employer work-time policies. It is usually only obtainable by adjustments on the domestic front such as the purchase of domestic help, child care services and ready-prepared or restaurant meals, by increased involvement of the husband in domestic work, or by one partner giving up full-time paid employment. Hewitt is right, for both Great Britain and the USA, in stressing that there is an unmet need for structural change in social and economic institutions to accommodate household work strategies, especially among parents of young children where both partners are in, or desire, full-time paid work. Such changes are slow in coming and meanwhile it is this group that must bear the greatest resultant stresses as well as reaping the rewards of their endeavours.

The increasing instability in certain aspects of employment relationships, especially in non-standard employment, is paralleled to some degree by a growing instability in family relationships. For the purposes of the present study, and in order to concentrate on British and American women who are comparable, so far as possible, with the target respondents of the Sino-Japanese survey, we have mainly described and analyzed the work and family life of married women who co-resided with their husbands and young children. A snapshot picture of such women, however, fails to capture the extent of diversity and change in the family and household relationships of women with young children in these Western societies. There is no need to rehearse well-known facts on decreasing marriage rates, the rising experience of cohabitation, the rise in the numbers of children born to unmarried (though often stably cohabiting) women, increasing rates of divorce and remarriage, and thus of reconstituted families, and increasing proportions of single-parent households which are predominantly female-headed (Kiernan & Wicks 1990, McRae 1993). We have already alluded in the previous chapter to the vigorous ideological debates that have sprung up around these trends, debates that can themselves contribute to the direction of change.

Central to our current concerns, however, are not debates over whether these tendencies signal a "decline" in family values (Popenoe 1988, 1993) or a new "postmodern" kaleidoscope of diverse family possibilities (Stacey 1990, 1993), but rather the relationship between trends in family relationships and the paid and unpaid work of women. The most important relationships appear to be these. First, the greater incorporation of women into the paid labour force is one of the factors making for family instability, since the relatively greater independence accorded to women by their own earnings makes it possible for them to escape from unsatisfactory marriages or other family circumstances. At the same time, their greater labour force participation also gives many women reasons to delay or forego both marriage and childbearing. The trend for American women (and Britain is following in the same direction but somewhat further behind) has been summed up thus:

As they enter the final decade of the twentieth century, they are entering higher levels of education, working more often, delaying marriage and childbirth, divorcing more frequently, heading households more regularly, and living longer than at any time in this century. Overall, these changes have resulted in the family exercising less power over women's lives than was true in 1900. Especially in recent years, women have come to spend more of their lives as single adults, pursuing personal and occupational objectives. They devote less time to child care and housework and more time to employment. As women's opportunities have increased, their reliance on family ties has declined. More than ever, women today are on their own (Rosenberg 1993: 245).

From this point of view, our study of the work of partnered women is of necessity only part of the story.

Secondly, however, the majority of women who do marry (or cohabit) and have children are increasingly likely to be in two-earner households. The trends in the overall workload of such women point in the same direction in both Britain and America, but the much greater prevalence of part-time work in Britain means that Britain lags considerably behind America in moving along the same path. The full-time employment of American women would, as we have seen, result in absolute work overload if they were not able to transfer some of their domestic burdens to men. Despite the problems that women in dual-earner heterosexual households still have in inducing their male partners to share domestic responsibilities equitably (Hochschild 1990), we must concur with the judgement of Judith Stacey (1990) in perceiving that there has been a major shift in America in gender norms surrounding housework, and particularly in families where both partners work full-time. In Britain, the trend in this direction is muted by part-time work, which allows more couples to preserve a greater approximation to the "traditional" division of domestic labour than is the case in America.

Conclusion: convergence or divergence?

We began this book by reminding ourselves of what Talcott Parsons had written in the 1940s – that industrial societies created a tension in the social role of women. On the one hand, he argued, the separation of home and work characteristic of industrialism generated a functional strain towards a gendered segregation of roles, with the man specializing in the instrumental roles of work in the formal economy and the woman concentrating on the expressive roles of homemaking in the family household. On the other hand, the universalistic values characteristic of industrialism generated a pressure for equal opportunities for all members of society to achieve any position consistent with their abilities and efforts, irrespective of any ascribed characteristic such as sex. This tension pushes and pulls women in two different directions, towards acceptance of the claims placed on them by their family roles as wives and mothers, and towards participation in the public world of paid work, business and citizenship. Many other sociologists since Parsons have also stressed the tension between these two life course possibilities, using such terms as "cultural contradiction", "structural ambivalence" or "structural ambiguity" (Komarovsky 1946, Epstein 1970, Oakley 1976, Gerson 1985). The failure of any society to enable full compatibility of these two sets of roles is encapsulated in the phrase "the double burden". In the language of contemporary feminist theory, one might say that Parsons saw women in modern industrial society as confronted by a dilemma of "sameness" and "difference".

What we have seen in the body of the book is that the institutions of different societies lead women to "resolve" the tensions of this dilemma in different ways. Japanese society continues to be structured around an essential "difference" between men and women, and this is manifested in family roles as well as in employment roles. There are some indications that ideas of gender equality are beginning to erode the essentialism of gender difference, more so in the minds of women than of men, but the family and work institutions do not encourage such an erosion. In Britain and the United States, as examples of Western capitalist industrial societies, the critique of gender essentialism has proceeded further, but the tensions still remain. In Britain, for reasons that are both economic and cultural, women's work and family lives still exhibit major differences from those of men, especially in the spheres of domestic responsibilities and in the prevalence of part-time employment. In the US, more women attempt to pursue a working life that is close to that of the typical male, with continuous full-time employment, and those who live with male partners often attempt to construct ways of family living that also reject gender difference, but with very variable results. It is in the US that the tensions between sameness and difference are perhaps most evident, a situation for which Hochschild (1990) coined the term "the stalled revolution". Finally, Chinese institutions are, to the greatest extent, structured around gender sameness, with a norm of permanent full-time work for all adults irrespective of sex, and a high degree of egalitarianism in family roles.

But the tensions are never completely resolved. In each society there remain dissatisfactions and uncertainties that lay the basis for instability and change. In each society there is a diversity of orientations with the possibility of continuing an internal cultural debate (Moeran 1984) over the appropriate roles of men and women in modern industrial society. These cultural debates can draw on a number of sources. They can draw on interpretations of the traditional culture of each society, its religious heritage, its family values, its understanding of the place of work in the life of people. They can draw on ideologies of revolutionary change, as in the case of the Chinese Communist Party. They can draw on the researches of academics and the reflections of intellectuals, especially those of sociologists who can uncover unrecognized structures and sub-cultural variations, and of historians who can recover forgotten pasts. Critics of established gender relationships, including feminist critics of various colours, will also continue their attempts to raise the consciousness of those whom they believe to be trapped in conventional roles and will campaign for changes in the conditions that constrain women and men in those roles and hinder their search for better lives. The outcome of these debates is open, and no abstract theory of convergence can settle the future of human thought. The basic structure of industrial society merely poses questions that need to be addressed, not the answers themselves.

Nor are the debates constricted by societal or national boundaries. Comparative research, such as we have pursued in this project, tends to treat each society as a self-contained entity and neglects the interrelationships between societies. In the closing pages of this book we move tentatively beyond the comparative framework of our research design towards a perspective that sets each national society in a wider global setting. "Globalization" is the watchword of much contemporary social science (although the phenomena of globalization themselves have a long history), and two aspects of globalization processes are especially relevant here – on the one hand the increasing internationalization of economic activity (Dicken 1992, Reich 1992), on the other the much discussed globalization of culture (Featherstone 1990, Robertson 1992).

The increasing globalization of economic life has intensified competitive pressures on many "actors" in the world economy. Companies, especially transnational corporations operating in many parts of the globe, have responded by restructuring their activities not just within nation states, but also at an international level, for example by relocating routine assembly work to parts of the world where there is a supply of cheap and unorganized labour. This has been a widespread practice in such manufacturing industries as textiles and clothing, electronics and automobile assembly. This restructuring has had numerous consequences that affect other actors on the economic stage, such as workers and governments. Workers in older industrial societies, such as Britain and America, have seen their jobs in manufacturing industry disappearing. Many new jobs have also been created and, although there has also been an expansion of work requiring high levels of scientific, technological and professional skills, a high proportion have tended to be low-paid, often part-time, jobs that have been designed to attract the kind of women who are the subject of this book, young mothers, as well as older women who have family commitments. Workers in developing countries, and China could be taken as an example of this category, though perhaps an atypical one, have seen manufacturing jobs provided on terms that, though not very generous in pay or conditions of employment, are better than anything else available in their predominantly agricultural societies. Once again, women are often the target for such jobs, though in developing countries, and export-processing zones in particular, it is often unmarried young women who are particularly sought after as a source of cheap and pliable workers (Mitter 1986). The result of these restructuring processes has been a "feminization of the labour force" (Jenson et al. 1988), though one that has taken different forms in different countries.

Governments of nation states have also come under pressure through this globalization of the economy, with the governments in older industrial societies having to deal with the related problems of increased unemployment and economic competitiveness. Most such governments have retreated from the post-war Keynesian (or socialist) commitment to full employment, though the extent to which they have followed policies designed to force down indigenous labour costs in an attempt to attract inward investment from transnational companies has varied, with Britain under Thatcher and Major being the most outstanding example. Once again, women are deeply implicated in such policy issues, since they are often seen as a major source of the "flexibility" that companies are seeking, being most prepared to work part-time, for lower wages, and in a temporary capacity, not least because it makes it possible for them to combine employment with motherhood. Governments have to decide whether, in the name of equity and equal opportunity, to attempt to counter the intensified segmentation of the labour market on lines of gender (as well as on lines of race, ethnicity, and age) that may accompany such flexibility.

The question of convergence takes on a new significance in the light of these aspects of economic globalization. It is striking that, of all the major industrialized countries, Japan has until recently best weathered the economic storms of the 1970s and 1980s, with the consistently lowest rate of unemployment and the highest rate of growth. It might be argued that Japan's particular combination of industrial, employment and family structures, which we have out-lined in this book, has facilitated its competitiveness in the global economic environment. A highly segmented labour market, with long-term employment in major companies reserved for men, with women exposed to much greater economic competition and moving in and out of relatively low-skill and low-paid employment as required, and a long flexible tail of small family businesses, comple-menting a family structure built on a powerful doctrine of separate spheres, might appear to be a recipe for "success" in the international economy, although the early 1990s has seen Japan, too, affected by the worldwide recession. At the other extreme, China's strategy of life-long full membership of a work-unit for all adults, male and female, with a relatively low degree of gendered segmentation of the labour force, complementing a relatively egalitarian family structure, could work so long as China was isolated from the pressures of inter-national competition. The open-door policy, integrating China into the capitalist world economy, has generated pressures that, as we have seen, are likely to put the trends towards egalitarianism into reverse.

If there is pressure towards convergence, the argument from economic globalization might suggest that it would be convergence towards the first pole of Parsons's dilemma, with sharper gender divisions in both the economy and the family. Whereas the theorists of industrial society originally perceived an inexorable tendency towards bureaucratization of industrial production (Kerr et al. 1973), employment might actually continue to be pulled by the opposite poles of bureaucratic inclusion and market exposure (Kreckel 1980), creating dualistic structures with shifting balances of "standard" and "non-standard" jobs, and with women identified as one of the most suitable sources of flexible and intermittent labour.

There is, however, a second aspect to globalization which casts the convergence problem in yet another light. The people of the world are increasingly interrelated, not just in terms of objective economic processes, but also in terms of their cultural understandings and self-identities. Robertson (1992: 12) has argued that this cultural globalization is an intrinsic feature of the modern world, and that processes of modernization are essentially *reflexive*: "all societies implicated in projects of modernization are also involved in processes of interactive comparison with other societies". The field of relevance for modernizing societies is global, the "international system" (Nettl & Robertson 1968) conceived as "a place in which societies – more accurately, the influential and powerful elites within societies – in different degrees and with greatly varying degrees of success construct their own and other societal identities in tandem with constructions of the whole system" (Robertson 1992: 91). The parenthetical emphasis on elites may be appropriate for certain kinds of such globalizing processes, and Robertson himself has in mind such examples as the modernizing project of the elites of Meiji Japan. But in the contemporary world, this cultural globalization affects the lives of everyone, to varying degrees and in varying ways.

Through a variety of channels, such as international travel and tourism or the communications media of television, film and so on, which owe their existence to advanced technologies, people are exposed (or are able to expose themselves) to cultural meanings originating from outside their own cultural milieu. They have greater access to representations of life in other societies than earlier generations have had (though one should not underestimate the degree of cultural interchange in less technologically developed times). Among the representations available to them are those relating to gender, to what it means to be men or women, and in particular to gender roles in the family. There is a growing literature on representations of gender and of family life, stemming from media sociology and cultural studies, but much less consideration has been given to the intercultural aspects of such representations (though the new field of inter-cultural communication may do something to remedy that). Nor has much attention been paid to the consequences of exposure to such representations for the lives of those so exposed. Anything we say about this aspect of globalization must of necessity be speculative, but a little speculation at the end of a book packed with empirical findings might perhaps be permitted.

One possibility is that this globalization of culture might reinforce what Yoshino (1992) calls "cultural nationalism". For example, Japanese women may have images, which are available in Japanese media, of the high rates of divorce in the US and Britain. They may interpret these divorce rates as associated with women's employment. In Japan, for example, women may think that what is happening in America *proves* that if women push too hard to enter the man's world of the company, divorce could be the result. This may strengthen their tendency to value the stability of family relationships more than they value the opportunity to rise in the company hierarchy. It might thus consolidate their propensity to give up paid work to look after the family, and to return to work when the children are old enough, and only in a capacity that cannot threaten their husbands and disturb the stability of their marriages. Conversely, American women may have images of passive and subservient Japanese women, who are trained to look after their husbands and children more than they look after themselves. Such images may fuel a common-sense "orientalism", and provide a conception of "the other" against which their own self-identity of self-development and achievement is contrasted. By perceiving negative models in other cultures, women in both Japan and America might gain reasons to become more like themselves, and the differences between the societies might be reinforced. To the extent that processes like this were significant in maintaining cultural diversity, one might coin the term *reflexive divergence* to describe them.

However, this intensification of cultural nationalism is only one possible outcome of cultural globalization. Another possibility might be a stimulation of inter-cultural learning, associated with what Robertson (1992) calls the "relativization of self-identities". Awareness of alternative ways in which women and men may arrange their work and family life might encourage a search for improvements, without taking any existing pattern as a model to be emulated. The search for better ways of living could widen internal cultural debate into inter-cultural debate. Admittedly, recent examples of global dialogue on gender issues are not promising. The loosely structured series of movements sometimes referred to as Women in Development appears to have run into confusion and misunderstanding, with Western feminism criticized as inappropriate to many third world contexts. And the United Nations Decade for Women (1976–85) also ran into the sands of conflicting national and regional interests (Newland 1991). However, the globalizing movement continues, and in the year in which the fourth United Nations International Women's Conference is held in Beijing, who is to say that international exchange of ideas on such questions as women's combination of work and family life cannot bear fruit?

Bibliography

All China Women's Federation Research Institute [Zhonghua quanguo funü lianhehui funü yanjiusuo] 1991. *Zhongguo funü tongji ziliao [Statistics on Chinese women] 1949–1989.* Beijing: Zhongguo tongji chubanshe [China Statistical Publishing House].

Allan, G. 1985. *Family life.* Oxford: Blackwell.

Allan G. C. 1965. *Japan's economic expansion.* Oxford: Oxford University Press.

Alwin, D. F., M. Braun, J. Scott 1992. The separation of work and the family: attitudes towards women's labour-force participation in Germany, Great Britain, and the United States. *European Sociological Review* **8**, 13–37.

Andersen, M. 1988. *Thinking about women.* New York: Macmillan.

Andors, P. 1983. *The unfinished revolution of Chinese women, 1949–1980.* Bloomington, Ind.: Indiana University Press.

Applebaum, E. 1981. *Back to work: determinants of women's successful re-entry.* Boston: Auburn House.

Bacon, A. M. 1902. *Japanese girls and women.* London: Gay & Bird.

Baker, H. D. R. 1979. *Chinese family and kinship.* London: Macmillan.

Barron, R. D. & G. M. Norris 1976. Sexual divisions and the dual labour market. In *Dependence and exploitation in work and marriage*, D. Barker & S. Allen (eds), 47–70. London: Longman.

Beechey, V. & T. Perkins 1987. *A matter of hours.* Oxford: Polity.

Befu, H. 1992. Symbols of nationalism and *nihonjinron.* In *Ideology and practice in modern Japan*, R. Goodman & K. Refsing (eds), 26–46. London: Routledge.

Bellah, R., R. Madsen, W. M. Sullivan, A. Swidler, S. M. Tipton 1988. *Habits of the heart: middle America observed.* London: Hutchinson.

Berardo, D. H., C. L. Sheehan, G. R. Leslie 1987. A residue of tradition. *Journal of Marriage and the Family* **49**, 381–90.

Berger, B. & P. L. Berger 1983. *The war over the family: capturing the middle ground.* London: Hutchinson.

Bergmann, B. R. 1986. *The economic emergence of women.* New York: Basic Books.

Bernstein, G. L. (ed.) 1991. *Recreating Japanese women, 1600–1945.* Berkeley: University of California Press.

Bian, Y. 1994. *Work and inequality in urban China.* Albany, New York: State University of New York Press.

Bianchi, S. M. & D. Spain 1986. *American women in transition.* New York: Russell Sage Foundation.

Blair, S. L. & M. P. Johnston 1992. Wives' perception of the fairness of the division of household labour. *Journal of Marriage and the Family* **54**, 570–81.

Blanchflower, D. G. & A. Oswald 1989. International patterns of work. In *British social attitudes: special international report*, R. Jowell, S. Witherspoon, L. Brook (eds), 15–34. Aldershot, England: Gower.

Blood, R. & D. Wolfe 1960. *Husbands and wives*. Glencoe: The Free Press.

Bonney, N. 1988a. Gender, household and social class. *British Journal of Sociology* **39**, 28–45.

— 1988b. Dual earning couples: trends of change in Great Britain. *Work, Employment and Society* **2**, 89–101.

Bonney, N., N. Stockman & Sheng X. 1994. Shifting spheres: the work and family life of Japanese female graduates. *Work, Employment and Society* **8**, 387–406.

Boydston, J. 1990. *Home and work: housework, wages, and the ideology of labor in the early republic*. Oxford: Oxford University Press.

Bradley, H. 1989. *Men's work, women's work*. Oxford: Polity.

Brannen, J. & P. Moss 1991. *Managing mothers: dual earner households after maternity leave*. London: Unwin Hyman.

Brinton, M. C. 1988. The social-institutional bases of gender stratification: Japan as an illustrative case. *American Journal of Sociology* **94**, 300–34.

— 1992. Christmas cakes and wedding cakes: the social organization of Japanese women's life course. In *Japanese social organization*, T. S. Lebra (ed.), 79–108. Honolulu: University of Hawaii Press.

— 1993. *Women and the economic miracle: gender and work in postwar Japan*. Berkeley: University of California Press.

Brook, L. et al. 1992. *British social attitudes: cumulative sourcebook*. Aldershot, England: Gower.

Brown, C. 1987. Consumption norms, work roles, and economic growth, 1918–80. In *Gender in the workplace*, C. Brown & J. A. Pechman (eds), 13–58. Washington, DC: The Brookings Institution.

Broyelle, C. 1977. *Women's liberation in China*. Hassocks: Harvester.

Brunner, O. 1968. *Neue Wege der Verfassungs- und Sozialgeschichte*. Göttingen: Vandenhoeck & Ruprecht.

Bruun, O. 1993. *Business and bureaucracy in a Chinese city: an ethnography of private business households in contemporary China*. China Research Monograph 43. Berkeley: University of California Institute of East Asian Studies.

Buckley, S. 1993. Altered states: the body politics of "being-woman". In *Postwar Japan as history*, A. Gordon (ed.), 347–72. Berkeley: University of California Press.

Central Statistical Office 1994. *Social Trends 24*. London: HMSO.

Chafe, W. H. 1991. *The paradox of change: American women in the twentieth century*. Oxford: Oxford University Press.

Chan, K. W. 1994. Urbanization and rural–urban migration in China since 1982. *Modern China* **20**, 243–81.

Clark, R. 1979. *The Japanese company*. New Haven, Connecticut: Yale University Press.

Coleman, S. 1983. The tempo of family formation. In *Work and lifecourse in Japan*, D. Plath (ed.), 183–214. Albany, New York: State University of New York Press.

Coote, A. & B. Campbell 1987. *Sweet freedom*. Oxford: Basil Blackwell.

Coote, A. & P. Hewitt 1980. The stance of Britain's major parties and interest groups. In *Work and the family*, P. Moss & N. Fonda (eds), 135–57. London: Temple Smith.

Corrin, C. (ed.) 1992. *Superwomen and the double burden*. London: Scarlet Press.

Coser, L. A. 1974. *Greedy institutions: patterns of undivided commitment*. New York: The Free Press.

Cowan, R. S. 1989. *More work for mother: the ironies of household technology from the open hearth to the microwave*. London: Free Association Books.

Croll, E. 1978. *Feminism and socialism in China*. London: Routledge & Kegan Paul.

— 1983. *Chinese women after Mao*. London: Zed Books.

Croll, E., D. Davin, P. Kane (eds) 1985. *China's one-child family policy*. London: Macmillan.

Dale A. & J. Glover 1990. *An analysis of women's employment patterns in the UK, France and the USA*. Research Paper 75. London: Employment Department Group.

Dale, P. N. 1986. *The myth of Japanese uniqueness*. London: Routledge.

Davidoff, L. & C. Hall 1987. *Family fortunes: men and women of the English middle class 1780–1850*. London: Hutchinson.

Davin, D. 1976. *Women-work: women and the party in revolutionary China*. Oxford: Clarendon Press.

— 1988. The implications of contract agriculture for the employment and status of Chinese peasant women. In *Transforming China's economy in the eighties, Volume 1: The rural sector, welfare and employment*, S. Feuchtwang, A. Hussain, T. Pairault (eds), 137–46. London: Zed Books.

Davis, D. 1992. "Skidding": downward mobility among children of the Maoist middle class. *Modern China* **18**, 410–37.

Davis, D. & S. Harrell 1993. Introduction: the impact of post-Mao reforms on family life. In *Chinese families in the post-Mao era*, D. Davis & S. Harrell (eds), 1–22. Berkeley: University of California Press.

Davis, J. A. & T. W. Smith 1991. *General social surveys 1972–1991: cumulative codebook*. Chicago: NORC.

Davis-Friedmann, D. 1985. Intergenerational inequalities and the Chinese revolution. *Modern China* **11**, 117–201.

Degler, C. N. 1980. *At odds: women and the family in America from the revolution to the present*. New York: Oxford University Press.

Delphy, C. 1984. *Close to home*. London: Hutchinson.

Deutschmann, C. 1987. Der "Betriebsclan": der japanische Organisationstypus als Herausforderung an die soziologische Modernisierungstheorie. *Soziale Welt* **37**, 133–47.

Dex, S. 1987. *Women's occupational mobility*. London: Macmillan.

— 1988. *Women's attitudes to work*. London: Macmillan.

— 1992. Labour force participation of women in the 1990s. In *Women's employment: Britain in the Single European Market*. London: HMSO.

Dex, S. & L. Shaw 1986. *British and American women at work*. London: Macmillan.

Dicken, P. 1992. *Global shift*. London: Paul Chapman.

Dore, R. P. 1958. *City life in Japan*. London: Routledge & Kegan Paul.

— 1973. *British factory – Japanese factory*. London: Allen & Unwin.

— 1989. Where are we now? *Work, Employment and Society* **3**, 425–40.

Eccleston, B. 1989. *State and society in post-war Japan*. Oxford: Polity.

Elshtain, J. B. 1981. *Public man, private women: women in social and political thought*. Oxford: Martin Robertson.

Employment Department 1994. *Employment Gazette*. London: HMSO.

Engels, F. 1962 [1884]. The origins of the family, private property and the state. In *Karl Marx and Frederick Engels: selected works in two volumes*. Moscow: Foreign Languages Publishing House.

England, P. & G. Farkas 1986. *Households, employment and gender*. New York: Aldine.

Epstein, C. F. 1970. *Woman's place: options and limits in professional careers*. Berkeley: University of California Press.

Featherstone, M. (ed.) 1990. *Global culture: nationalism, globalization and modernity*. London: Sage.

Ferguson, M. 1983. *Forever feminine: women's magazines and the cult of femininity*. London: Heinemann.

Ferree, M. M. 1994. Gender, earnings and the division of household labour. Paper presented at the XIII World Congress of Sociology, Bielefeld, Germany, 18–23 July.

Finch, J. 1983. *Married to the job: wives' incorporation in men's work*. London: Allen & Unwin.

— 1989. *Family obligations and social change*. Oxford: Polity.

Fox, K. & A. Beller 1993. Part-time work and child care choices for mothers of pre-school children. *Journal of Marriage and the Family* **55**, 146–57.

Friedan, B. 1963. *The feminine mystique*. London: Penguin.

Fuchs, V. R. 1988. *Women's quest for economic equality*. Cambridge, Mass.: Harvard University Press.

Fujita, M. 1989. "It's all mother's fault": childcare and the socialization of working mothers in Japan. *Journal of Japanese Studies* **15**, 67–91.

Funk, N. & M. Mueller (eds) 1993. *Gender politics and post-communism: reflections from Eastern Europe and the former Soviet Union*. London: Routledge.

Gallie, D. 1988. *The Social Change and Economic Life initiative: an overview*. Oxford: Nuffield College.

— 1991. *Technological change, gender and skill*. ESRC SCELI Working Paper 4. Oxford: Nuffield College.

Garon, S. 1987. *The state and labor in modern Japan*. Berkeley: University of California Press.

Gershuny, J. 1992. Change in the domestic division of labour in the UK, 1975–1987. In *Social change in contemporary Britain*, N. Abercrombie & A. Warde (eds), 70–94. Oxford: Polity.

Gershuny, J. & J. Robinson 1988. Historical change in the household division of labour. *Demography* **25**, 537–52.

— 1991. The household division of labour: multi-national comparisons of change. In *The changing use of time*, W. O'Conghaile & E. Kohler (eds), 153–184. Luxembourg: European Foundation for the Improvement of

Living and Working Conditions.

Gerson, K. 1985. *Hard choices: how women decide about work, career, and mother-hood*. Berkeley: University of California Press.

Gilman, C. P. 1966 [1898]. *The economic factor between men and women as a factor in social evolution*. New York: Harper & Row.

Glass, J. 1992. Housewives and employed wives: demographic and attitudinal change. *Journal of Marriage and the Family* **54**, 559–69.

Gleason, A. H. 1965. Economic growth and consumption in Japan. In *The state and economic enterprise in Japan*, W. W. Lockwood (ed.), 391–444. Princeton, N.J.: Princeton University Press.

Goffee, R. & R. Scase 1985. *Women in charge*. London: Allen & Unwin.

Goldin, C. 1990. *Understanding the gender gap: an economic history of American women*. Oxford: Oxford University Press.

Goldscheider, F. K. & L. Waite 1991. *New families, no families*. Berkeley: University of California Press.

Goldthorpe, J. 1985. The end of convergence. In *New approaches to economic life*, B. Roberts, R. Finnegan, D. Gallie (eds), 124–53. Manchester: Manchester University Press.

Gordon, A. (ed.) 1993. *Postwar Japan as history*. Berkeley: University of California Press.

Hakim, C. 1979. *Occupational segregation by sex*. Department of Employment Research Paper No. 9. London: HMSO.

— 1987. Trends in the flexible workforce. *Employment Gazette* **95**, 549–60.

— 1991. Grateful slaves and self-made women: fact and fantasy in women's work orientations. *European Sociological Review* **7**, 101–21.

— 1993. The myth of rising female employment. *Work, Employment and Society* **7**, 97–120.

Harbison, F. & C. A. Myers 1959. *Management in the industrial world: an international analysis*. New York: McGraw-Hill.

Harding, S. (ed.) 1987. *Feminism and methodology: social science issues*. Bloomington, Ind. and Milton Keynes, England: Indiana University Press and Open University Press.

Harris, C. C. 1983. *The family and industrial society*. London: Allen & Unwin.

Hayghe, H. W. 1993. Working wives' contributions to family incomes. *Monthly Labour Review* **116**, 39–43.

Hayghe, H. V. & S. Bianchi 1994. Married mothers' work patterns. *Monthly Labour Review* **117**, 24–30.

Hebel, J. 1990. Der Betrieb als kleine Gesellschaft: die Bedeutung des chinesischen Betriebtyps im Prozess der Reform. *Soziale Welt* **40**, 222–42.

Hebel, J. & G. Schucher 1991. From unit to enterprise? – the Chinese *tan-wei* in the process of reform. *Issues and Studies* **27**, 24–43.

Henderson, G. E. & M. Cohen 1984. *The Chinese hospital: a socialist work-unit*. New Haven, Conn.: Yale University Press.

Hendry, J. 1981. *Marriage in changing Japan*. London: Croom Helm.

— 1986. *Becoming Japanese: the world of the pre-school child*. Manchester: Manchester University Press.

Hershatter, G. 1986. *The workers of Tianjin, 1900–1949*. Palo Alto, Calif.: Stanford University Press.

Hewitt, M. 1958. *Wives and mothers in Victorian industry*. London: Rockliff.

Hewitt, P. 1993. *About time*. London: Institute for Public Policy Research & River Orams Press.

Hill, C. 1969. *Society and puritanism in pre-revolutionary England*. London: Panther.

— 1975. *The world turned upside down*. London: Penguin.

Hochschild, A. with A. Machung 1990. *The second shift: working parents and the revolution at home*. London: Piatkus.

Holden, K. C. & W. L. Hansen 1987. Part-time work, full-time work and occupational segregation. In *Gender in the workplace*, C. Brown & J. A Pechman (eds), 217–38. Washington, DC: The Brookings Institution.

Honig, E. 1986. *Sisters and strangers: women in the Shanghai cotton mills, 1919–1949*. Palo Alto, Calif.: Stanford University Press.

Honig, E. & G. Hershatter 1988. *Personal voices: Chinese women in the 1980's*. Palo Alto, Calif.: Stanford University Press.

Horkheimer, M. & T. Adorno 1973. *Aspects of sociology*. London: Heinemann.

Hsu, F. L. K. 1975. *Iemoto: the heart of Japan*. Cambridge, Mass.: Schenkman.

Hu, L. 1992. Lun kefu gaige dui nüxingde chongji xiaoying [On overcoming the battering which the reforms are giving women]. *Shehui Kexue Yanjiu [Social Science Research]* **79**, 67–9.

Huang, P. C. C. 1985. *The peasant economy and social change in north China*. Palo Alto, Calif.: Stanford University Press.

Hunt, A. (ed.) 1988. *Women and paid work*. London: Macmillan.

Hunter, J. 1989. *The emergence of modern Japan*. London: Longman.

Hunter, J. D. 1987. *Evangelicalism: the coming generation*. Chicago: University of Chicago Press.

Ikels, C. 1993. Settling accounts: the intergenerational contract in an age of reform. In *Chinese families in the post-Mao era*, D. Davis & S. Harrell (eds), 307–33. Berkeley: University of California Press.

Imamura, A. E. 1987. *Urban Japanese housewives: at home and in the community*. Honolulu: University of Hawaii Press.

International Labour Office 1992. *Yearbook of labour statistics*. Geneva: ILO Publications.

Isono, F. 1988. The evolution of modern family law in Japan. *International Journal of Law and the Family* **2**, 183–202.

Iwao, S. 1993. *The Japanese woman: traditional image and changing reality*. New York: The Free Press.

Jacka, T. 1990. Back to the wok: women and employment in Chinese industry in the 1980s. *Australian Journal of Chinese Affairs* **24**, 1–23.

Jankowiak, W. R. 1993. *Sex, death and hierarchy in a Chinese city: an anthropological account*. New York: Columbia University Press.

Japan Ministry of Labour 1986. *Survey of the situation of women's employment*. Tokyo: Women's Bureau, Ministry of Labour.

Jenson, J., E. Hagen, C. Reddy (eds) 1988. *Feminization of the labour force: paradoxes and promises*. Oxford: Polity.

Johnson, K. A. 1983. *Women, the family and peasant revolution in China*. Chicago: University of Chicago Press.

Joyce, P. 1980. *Work, society and politics: the culture of the factory in later Victorian England*. Brighton, England: Harvester.

Kalleberg A. & R. Rosenfield 1990. Work and family in the labour market. *Journal of Marriage and the Family* **52**, 331–46.

Kamerman, S. 1980. Managing work and family life: a comparative policy overview. In *Work and the family*, P. Moss & N. Fonda (eds), 87–109. London: Temple Smith.

Kelly, W. W. 1993. Finding a place in metropolitan Japan: ideologies, institutions, and everyday life. In *Postwar Japan as history*, A. Gordon (ed.), 189–216. Berkeley, University of California Press.

Kemeny, J. 1993. *Housing and social theory*. London: Routledge.

Kerr, C. 1983. *The future of industrial societies: convergence or continuing diversity?* Cambridge, Mass.: Harvard University Press.

Kerr, C., J. T. Dunlop, F. Harbison, C. A. Myers 1973. *Industrialism and industrial man*, 2nd edn. London: Penguin.

Kessler-Harris, A. 1982. *Out to work: a history of wage-earning women in the United States*. Oxford: Oxford University Press.

Kiernan, K. 1992. Men and women at work and at home. In *British social attitudes: the 9th report*, R. Jowell, L. Brook, G. Prior, B. Taylor (eds), 89–111. Aldershot, England: Dartmouth.

Kiernan, K. & M. Wicks 1990. *Family change and future policy*. London: Family Policy Studies Centre.

Klein, V. 1965. *Britain's married women workers*. London: Routledge & Kegan Paul.

Kobayashi, T. 1976. *Society, schools and progress in Japan*. Oxford: Pergamon.

Komarovsky, M. 1946. Cultural contradictions and sex roles. *American Journal of Sociology* **52**, 184–9.

— 1964. *Blue collar marriage*. New York: Random House.

— 1988. The new feminist scholarship. *Journal of Marriage and the Family* **50**, 585–93.

Kondo, D. K. 1990. *Crafting selves: power, gender, and discourses of identity in a Japanese workplace*. Chicago: University of Chicago Press.

Kreckel, R. 1980. Unequal opportunity structure and labour market segmentation. *Sociology* **14**, 525–50.

— 1992. *Politische Soziologie der sozialen Ungleichheit*. Frankfurt: Campus Verlag.

Kuang S., Li D., Wen X. 1992. *Dangdai Zhongguo funü diwei [The status of women in contemporary China]*. Chengdu: Northwestern University of Economics and Finance Press.

Kuhn, S. & B. Bluestone 1987. Economic restructuring and the female labour market: the impact of industrial change on women. In *Women, households and the economy*, L. Beneria & C. R. Stimpson (eds), 3–32. New Brunswick, New Jersey: Rutgers University Press.

Lam, A. 1992. *Women and Japanese management: discrimination and reform*. London: Routledge.

Land, H. 1980. The family wage. *Feminist Review* **6**, 55–78.

Lang, O. 1968. *Chinese family and society*. Hamden: Archon Books.

Laslett, P. 1965. *The world we have lost*. London: Methuen.

Lebra, T. S. 1984. *Japanese women: constraint and fulfilment*. Honolulu: University of Hawaii Press.

Lewis, J. (ed.) 1983. *Women's welfare – women's rights*. London: Croom Helm.
— 1984. *Women in England 1870–1950: sexual divisions and social change*. Brighton, Sussex: Wheatsheaf.
— 1992. *Women in Britain since 1945*. Oxford: Basil Blackwell.
Li Hanlin 1991. *Die Grundstruktur der chinesischen Gesellschaft: vom traditionellen Klansystem zur modernen Danwei-Organisation*. Opladen: Westdeutscher Verlag.
Lincoln, J. R. & A. Kalleberg 1990. *Culture, control and commitment*. New York: Cambridge University Press.
Litwak, E. 1960a. Occupational mobility and extended family cohesion. *American Sociological Review* **25**, 9–12.
— 1960b. Geographic mobility and extended family cohesion. *American Sociological Review* **25**, 385–94.
Lo, J. 1990. *Office ladies, factory women: life and work at a Japanese company*. Armonk, New York: M. E. Sharpe.
Lockwood, D. 1989. *The blackcoated worker*. Oxford: Clarendon Press.
Lown, J. 1991. *Women and industrialisation*. Oxford: Polity.
Lu Feng 1989. *Dan Wei* – a special form of social organization. *Social Sciences in China* **10**, 100–122.
Luhmann, N. 1982. *The differentiation of society*. New York: Columbia University Press.
Ma Youcai, Liu Ying, Sheng Xuewen, Meng Chen 1992. *Funü jiuye yu jiating: Zhong-Ri bijiao yanjiu diaocha baogao* [Women's employment and family: report of the Sino-Japanese comparative survey]. Beijing: Social Science Literature Press.
McLendon, J. 1983. The office: way station or blind alley? In *Work and lifecourse in Japan*, D. Plath (ed.), 156–82. Albany, New York: State University of New York Press.
McRae, S. 1986. *Cross-class families*. Oxford: Clarendon Press.
— 1991. Occupational change over childbirth: evidence from a national survey. *Sociology* **25**, 589–605.
— 1993. *Cohabiting mothers: changing marriage and motherhood?* London: Policy Studies Institute.
Major, B. 1993. Gender, entitlement, and the distribution of family labour. *Journal of Social Issues* **49**, 141–59.
Mann, M. 1986. A crisis in stratification theory? In *Gender and stratification*, R. Crompton & M. Mann (eds), 40–56. Oxford: Polity.
Marsh, C. 1982. *The survey method*. London: Allen & Unwin.
— 1991. *Hours of work of women and men*. London: HMSO.
Marshall, G., H. Newby, D. Rose, C. Vogler 1988. *Social class in modern Britain*. London: Heinemann.
Martin, J. & C. Roberts 1984. *Women and employment: a life-time perspective*. London: HMSO.
Mason, K. O. & Y. Lu 1988. Attitudes toward women's familial roles: changes in the United States 1977–85. *Gender and Society* **2**, 39–57.
Mason, K. O. & K. Kulthaur 1989. Determinants of child-care ideals among mothers of preschool aged children. *Journal of Marriage and the Family* **51**, 593–603.

Masuda, K. 1975. Bride's progress: how a *yome* becomes a *shutome*. *Journal of Asian and African Studies* **10**, 1–19.

Matthaei, J. A. 1982. *An economic history of women in America: women's work, the sexual division of labor, and the development of capitalism.* Brighton, England: Harvester.

May, M. 1991. Bread before roses: American workingmen, labor unions and the family wage. In *Women, work, and protest*, R. Milkman (ed.), 1–21. London: Routledge.

Mederer, H. J. 1993. The division of labour in two earner homes. *Journal of Marriage and the Family* **55**, 133–45.

Meisner, M. 1977. *Mao's China: a history of the People's Republic.* New York: The Free Press.

Menaghen, E. & T. Parcel 1990. Parental employment and family life. *Journal of Marriage and the Family* **52**, 1079–98.

Meulders, D., R. Plasman, V. Stricht 1993. *Position of women on the labour market in the European Community.* Aldershot, England: Dartmouth.

Mishel, L. & J. Bernstein 1993. *The state of working America 1992–93.* Armonk, New York: M. E. Sharpe.

Mitter, S. 1986. *Common fate, common bond: women in the global economy.* London: Pluto.

Miyake, Y. 1991. Doubling expectations: motherhood and women's factory work under state management in Japan in the 1930s and 1940s. See Bernstein (1991), 267–95.

Moeran, B. 1984. Individual, group and *seishin*: Japan's internal cultural debate. *Man* (N.S.) **19**, 252–66.

Molony, B. 1991. Activism among women in the Taisho cotton textile industry. See Bernstein (1991), 217–38.

Morishima, M. 1984. *Why has Japan "succeeded"? Western technology and the Japanese ethos.* Cambridge: Cambridge University Press.

Morris, L. 1990. *The workings of the household.* Oxford: Polity.

— 1994. *Dangerous classes: the underclass and social citizenship.* London: Routledge.

Murakami, Y. 1984. *Ie* society as a pattern of civilization. *Journal of Japanese Studies* **10**, 279–363.

Myrdal, A. & V. Klein 1956. *Women's two roles.* London: Routledge & Kegan Paul.

Nagy, M. 1991. Middle-class working women during the interwar years. See Bernstein (1991), 199–216.

Nakane, C. 1970. *Japanese society.* London: Weidenfeld & Nicolson.

Nettl, J. P. & R. Robertson 1968. *International systems and the modernization of societies: the formation of national goals and attitudes.* New York: Basic Books.

Newall, S. 1993. The superwoman syndrome. *Work, Employment and Society* **7**, 275–89.

Newland, K. 1991. From transnational relationships to international relations: Women in Development and the International Decade for Women. In *Gender and international relations*, R. Grant & K. Newland (eds), 122–32. Bloomington, Ind: University of Indiana Press.

Nolte, S. H. & S. A. Hastings 1991. The Meiji state's policy toward women,

1890–1910. See Bernstein (1991), 151–74.

Oakley, A. 1976. *Housewife*. London: Penguin.

Ogawa, N. & R. D. Retherford 1993. Care of the elderly in Japan: changing norms and expectations. *Journal of Marriage and the Family* **55**, 585–97.

OPCS (Office of Population Censuses and Surveys) 1990. *General household survey*. London: HMSO.

— 1992. *Labour force survey 1990 and 1991*. London: HMSO.

— 1993. *Social trends*. London: HMSO.

Osterud, N. G. 1986. Gender divisions and the organization of work in the Leicester hosiery industry. In *Unequal opportunities: women's employment in England, 1800–1918*, A. V. John (ed.), 45–70. Oxford: Basil Blackwell.

— 1991. *"Bonds of community": the lives of farm women in nineteenth-century New York*. Ithaca, New York: Cornell University Press.

Ouchi, W. G. 1980. Markets, bureaucracies, and clans. *Administrative Science Quarterly* **25**, 129–41.

Pahl, R. E. 1984. *Divisions of labour*. Oxford: Basil Blackwell.

Parish, W. L. & M. K. Whyte 1978. *Village and family in contemporary China*. Chicago: University of Chicago Press.

Parkin, F. 1971. *Class inequality and political order*. London: McGibbon & Kee.

Parsons, T. 1943. The kinship system of the United States. *American Anthropologist* **45**, 22–38.

— 1966. *Societies: evolutionary and comparative perspectives*. Englewood Cliffs, New Jersey: Prentice-Hall.

Parsons, T., R. F. Bales, J. Olds, M. Zelditch, P. E. Slater 1955. *Family, socialization, and interaction process*. New York: The Free Press.

Patrick, H. T. & T. P. Rohlen 1987. Small-scale family enterprises. In *The political economy of Japan*, K. Yamamura & Y. Yasuba (eds), 331–84. Palo Alto, Calif: Stanford University Press.

Peterson, R. R. & K. Gerson 1992. Determinants of responsibility for child care arrangements among dual earner families. *Journal of Marriage and the Family* **54**, 527–36.

Pinchbeck, I. 1969. *Women workers and the industrial revolution, 1750–1850*. London: Cass.

Pleck, E. 1976. Two worlds in one: work and family. *Journal of Social History* **10**, 178–95.

Pongsapich, A., N. Bunjongjit, S. Masami 1993. *A study of family consciousness in contemporary Thailand, with comparison among Bangkok, Seoul and Fukuoka*. Kitakyushu, Japan: Kitakyushu Forum on Asian Women.

Popenoe, D. 1988. *Disturbing the nest: family change and decline in modern societies*. New York: Aldine de Gruyter.

— 1993. American family decline, 1960–1990: a review and appraisal. *Journal of Marriage and the Family* **55**, 527–42.

Presser, H. 1988. Shift work and child care among young dual earner American parents. *Journal of Marriage and the Family* **50**, 133–48.

Rai, S. 1992. "Watering another man's garden": gender, employment and educational reforms in China. In *Women in the face of change: the Soviet Union, Eastern Europe, and China*, S. Rai, H. Pilkington, A. Phizacklea (eds), 20–40. London: Routledge.

Rees, T. 1992. *Women and the labour market*. London: Routledge.

Reich, R. B. 1992. *The work of nations*. New York: Vintage.

Reid, I. & E. Stratta 1989. *Sex differences in Britain*. Aldershot, England: Gower.

Reischauer, E. O. 1988. *The Japanese today: change and continuity*. Cambridge, Mass.: Harvard University Press.

Riskin, C. 1987. *China's political economy: the quest for development since 1949*. Oxford: Oxford University Press.

Roberts, E. A. M. 1986. "Women's strategies", 1890–1940. In *Labour and love: women's experience of home and family 1850–1940*, J. Lewis (ed.), 223–47. Oxford: Basil Blackwell.

Robertson, R. 1992. *Globalization: social theory and global culture*. London: Sage.

Rodd, L. R. 1991. Yosano Akiko and the Taisho debate over the "new woman". See Bernstein (1991), 175–98.

Rohlen, T. P. 1974. *For harmony and strength: Japanese white-collar organization in anthropological perspective*. Berkeley: University of California Press.

Rosen, S. & D. Chu 1987. *Survey research in the People's Republic of China*. Washington, DC: United States Information Agency.

Rosenberg, R. 1993. *Divided lives: American women in the twentieth century*. London: Penguin.

Ross, C., J. Morowsky, J. Huber 1986. Dividing work, sharing work and in-between. *Journal of Marriage and the Family* 48, 809–23.

Rowe, W. T. 1984. *Hankow: commerce and society in a Chinese city, 1796–1889*. Palo Alto, Calif.: Stanford University Press.

— 1989. *Hankow: conflict and community in a Chinese city, 1796–1895*. Palo Alto, Calif.: Stanford University Press.

Rubin, L. B. 1976. *Worlds of pain: life in the working class family*. New York: Basic Books.

Saso, M. 1990. *Women in the Japanese workplace*. London: Shipman.

Scase, R. & R. Goffee 1987. *The real world of the small business owner*. London: Croom Helm.

Schoppa, L. J. 1991. *Education reform in Japan*. London: Routledge.

Schor, J. 1992. *The overworked American*. New York: Basic Books.

Schurmann, F. 1968. *Ideology and organization in communist China*. Berkeley: University of California Press.

Scott, J. & J. Dunscombe 1991. A cross-national comparison of gender-role attitudes. *Working Paper 9*. ESRC Research Centre on Micro-Social Change, University of Essex.

Seccombe, W. 1986. Patriarchy stabilized: the construction of the male breadwinner norm in nineteenth-century Britain. *Social History* 2, 53–76.

Segalen, M. 1983. *Love and power in the peasant family*. Oxford: Basil Blackwell.

— 1986. *Historical anthropology of the family*. Cambridge: Cambridge University Press.

Sennett, R. & J. Cobb 1977. *The hidden injuries of class*. Cambridge University Press.

Shelton, B. A. 1992. *Women, men and time*. New York: Greenwood Press.

Sheng Xuewen 1991. *Working women's family life: a comparative study of China,*

Japan and Britain. Research report submitted to the K. C. Wong Trust and the British Academy.

Shorter, E. 1977. *The making of the modern family*. London: Fontana.

Sidel, R. 1972. *Women and child care in China*. London: Sheldon Press.

Siltanen, J. 1994. *Locating gender: occupational segregation, wages and domestic responsibilities*. London: UCL.

Simmons, C. 1990. *Growing up and going to school in Japan*. Milton Keynes, England: Open University Press.

Skinner, G. W. 1977. Urban social structure in Ch'ing China. In *The city in late imperial China*, G. W. Skinner (ed.), 521–53. Palo Alto, Calif.: Stanford University Press.

Skolnick, A. 1991. *Embattled paradise: the American family in an age of uncertainty*. New York: Basic Books.

Smelser, N. J. 1959. *Social change in the industrial revolution: an application of theory to the Lancashire cotton industry 1770–1840*. London: Routledge & Kegan Paul.

Smith, R. J. 1983. Making village women into "good wives and wise mothers" in prewar Japan. *Journal of Family History* **8**, 70–84.

— 1987. Gender inequality in contemporary Japan. *Journal of Japanese Studies* **13**, 1–25.

Solinger, D. J. (ed.) 1984. *Three visions of Chinese socialism*. Boulder, Col.: Westview Press.

Spitze, G. 1988. Women's employment and family relations. *Journal of Marriage and the Family* **50**, 595–618.

Stacey, J. 1983. *Patriarchy and socialist revolution in China*. Berkeley: University of California Press.

— 1990. *Brave new families: stories of domestic upheaval in late twentieth century America*. New York: Basic Books.

— 1993. Good riddance to "the family": a response to David Popenoe. *Journal of Marriage and the Family* **55**, 545–7.

Stacey, M. & M. Price 1981. *Women, power, and politics*. London: Tavistock.

State Statistical Bureau [Guojia tongji ju] 1988. *Zhongguo 1987 nian 1% renkou chaoyang diaocha ziliao [Chinese 1987 1% sample survey]*. Beijing: Zhongguo tongji chubanshe [China Statistical Publishing House].

Stern, D. 1987. Comments on Holden and Hansen. In *Gender in the workplace*, C. Brown & J. A. Pechman (eds), 240–46. Washington, DC: The Brookings Institution.

Stockman, N. 1992. Market, plan and structured social inequality in China. In *Contesting markets: analyses of ideology, discourse and practice*, R. Dilley (ed.), 260–76. Edinburgh: Edinburgh University Press.

— 1994. Gender inequality and social structure in urban China. *Sociology* **28**, 759–77.

Storry, R. 1960. *A history of modern Japan*. London: Penguin.

Taylor, B. 1983. *Eve and the new Jerusalem*. London: Virago.

Tilly, L. A. & J. W. Scott 1989. *Women, work, and family*. London: Routledge.

Tobin, J. J., D. Wu, D. Davidson 1989. *Pre-school in three cultures*. New Haven, Conn.: Yale University Press.

Tsurumi, E. P. 1990. *Factory girls: women in the thread mills of Meiji Japan*.

Princeton, New Jersey: Princeton University Press.

Ueno, C. 1988. The Japanese women's movement: the counter-values to industrialism. In *The Japanese trajectory: modernisation and beyond*, G. McCormack & Y. Sugimoto (eds), 167–85. Cambridge: Cambridge University Press.

UNESCO 1992. *Statistical year book 1992*. Paris.

Unger, J. 1993. Urban families in the eighties: an analysis of Chinese surveys. In *Chinese families in the post-Mao era*, D. Davis & S. Harrell (eds), 25–49. Berkeley: University of California Press.

Uno, K. S. 1991. Women and changes in the household division of labour. See Bernstein (1991), 17–41.

— 1993. The death of "good wife, wise mother". In *Postwar Japan as history*, A. Gordon (ed.), 293–322. Berkeley: University of California Press.

US Bureau of the Census 1991. *Statistical abstract of the United States: 111th edition*. Washington, DC.

US Merit Protection Board 1991. *Balancing work responsibilities and family needs*. Washington, DC.

Usui, C. 1993. Do American models of female career attainment apply to Japanese? Paper presented at the Midwest Japan Seminar, Purdue University.

Veurn, J. R. & P. M. Gleason 1991. Child-care: arrangements and costs. *Monthly Labour Review* **114**, 10–17.

Vogel, E. F. 1979. *Japan as number one*. Cambridge, Mass.: Harvard University Press.

Vogler, C. & J. Pahl 1994. Money, power and inequality within marriage. *The Sociological Review* **42**, 263–88.

Walby, S. 1986. *Patriarchy at work*. Oxford: Polity.

— 1990 *Theorising patriarchy*. Oxford: Basil Blackwell.

Walder, A. G. 1991. The urban Chinese work unit: a study in economic sociology. Paper given at the International Conference on Sociology in China, Chinese Academy of Social Sciences, Beijing, 23–7 July.

Waldfogel, J. 1993. *Women working for less*. Discussion Paper WSP/93. London: LSE Suntory-Toyota International Centre for Economics and Related Disciplines.

Webb, S. 1993. Women's incomes: past, present and prospects. *Fiscal Studies* **14**, 14–36.

Weber, M. 1978. *Economy and society*. Berkeley: University of California Press.

Whitbread, N. 1972. *The evolution of the nursery-infant school*. London: Routledge.

White, G. 1987. Labour market reform in Chinese industry. In *Management reforms in China*, M. Warner (ed.), 113–26. London: Frances Pinter.

— 1993. *Riding the tiger: the politics of economic reform in post-Mao China*. London: Macmillan.

White, M. 1987. The virtue of Japanese mothers: cultural definitions of women's lives. *Daedalus* **116**, 149–63.

Whyte, M. K. 1984. Sexual inequality under socialism: the Chinese case in perspective. In *Class and social stratification in post-revolution China*, J. L. Watson (ed.), 198–238. Cambridge: Cambridge University Press.

Whyte, M. K. & W. L. Parish 1984. *Urban life in contemporary China*. Chicago: University of Chicago Press.

Whyte, W. H. 1960. *The organisation man*. London: Penguin.

Wilson, E. 1977. *Women and the welfare state*. London: Tavistock.

Witherspoon, S. 1988. Interim report: a woman's work. In *British social attitudes: the 5th report*, R. Jowell, S. Witherspoon, L. Brook (eds), 173–200. Aldershot, England: Gower.

Wolf, M. 1987. *Revolution postponed: women in contemporary China*. London: Methuen.

Wu, X. & Zhang Y. 1987. *Daqiuzhuang zhi fu zhi lu [Daqiuzhuang's road to wealth]*. Beijing: Zhongguo Nongye Keji Chubanshe [Chinese Agricultural Science and Technology Press].

Yang, M. M. 1989. Between state and society: the construction of corporateness in a Chinese socialist factory. *Australian Journal of Chinese Affairs* **22**, 31–60.

Yoshino, K. 1992. *Cultural nationalism in contemporary Japan: a sociological enquiry*. London: Routledge.

Zhang Ping 1984. *Riben de hunyin yu jiating [Japanese family and marriage]*. Beijing: Zhongguo funü chubanshe [Chinese Women's Press].

Zimmeck, M. 1986. Jobs for the girls: the expansion of clerical work for women, 1850–1914. In *Unequal opportunities: women's employment in England, 1800–1918*, A. V. John (ed.), 153–77. Oxford: Basil Blackwell.

Index

Date Due